DUAL CITIZENSHIP IN EUROPE

Dual Citizenship in Europe
From Nationhood to Societal Integration

Edited by

THOMAS FAIST
Bielefeld University, Germany

ASHGATE

Published by
Ashgate Publishing Limited
Gower House
Croft Road
Aldershot
Hampshire GU11 3HR
England

Ashgate Publishing Company
Suite 420
101 Cherry Street
Burlington, VT 05401-4405
USA

Ashgate website: http://www.ashgate.com

British Library Cataloguing in Publication Data
Dual citizenship in Europe : from nationhood to societal
    integration
    1. Dual nationality - Europe
    I. Faist, Thomas, 1959-
    323.6'3

Library of Congress Cataloging-in-Publication Data
Dual citizenship in Europe : from nationhood to societal integration / edited by
Thomas Faist.
        p. cm.
    Includes bibliographical references and index.
    ISBN: 978-0-7546-4914-4 1. Citizenship--Europe. 2. Dual
nationality--Europe. I. Faist, Thomas.

    JN40.D83 2006
    323.6'3--dc22

2006031446

ISBN: 978-0-7546-4914-4

Printed and bound in Great Britain by MPG Books Ltd, Bodmin, Cornwall.

Contents

List of Figures

Notes on Contributors

Thomas Faist is Professor of Transstate Relations and Sociology of Development at the Faculty of Sociology, Bielefeld University, Germany. Formerly, he directed the programme in International Studies in Political Management (ISPM) at the University of Applied Sciences Bremen. Thomas Faist received his PhD degree from the New School for Social Research in New York. His research focuses on international migration, ethnic relations, social policy and transnationalization. He is currently the director of international research projects on 'Transnational Knowledge Transfer and Development' and 'Democratic Legitimacy of Immigration Control Policy'. His publications include *The Volume and Dynamics of International Migration and Transnational Social Spaces* (Oxford University Press, 2000), *Transnational Social Spaces* (Ashgate, 2004), and *Citizenship: Discourse, Theory and Transnational Prospects*, co-authored with Peter Kivisto (Blackwell, 2007).

Jürgen Gerdes is a Research Fellow at Bielefeld University in Germany. He is currently working in the research project 'Democratic Legitimacy of Immigration Control Policy'. He received his MA in politics and sociology at Bremen University, Germany. He previously worked on an international research project on dual citizenship, supported by the Volkswagen Foundation, which compared the politics of dual citizenship in several immigration and emigration countries. His research focuses on the relationship between democracy, human rights and immigration. He is the author of reviews and articles on questions of multiculturalism, minority rights, tolerance, cultural recognition and dual citizenship including 'Dual Citizenship as a Path-Dependent Process', *International Migration Review* 38:3, 913-44, co-authored with Thomas Faist and Beate Rieple in 2004.

Agata Górny is Assistant Professor at the Faculty of Economic Sciences, Warsaw University, Poland. She has been a fellow at the Centre of Migration Research in Warsaw since 1995. She was awarded a PhD in social sciences in 2002 from the School of Slavonic and East European Studies, University College London. Her PhD thesis was devoted to the role of social, economic and political networks in settlement migration from Ukraine to Poland. She has published several articles in Poland and elsewhere on citizenship, on the mechanisms of illegal migration, adaptation of immigrants and the application of research techniques in migration studies. She is a co-editor (with Paolo Ruspini) of the book *Migration in the New Europe: East-West Revisited* (Palgrave, 2004). In 2003, she was awarded a scholarship by the Foundation for Polish Science.

Aleksandra Grzymała-Kazłowska is a Researcher at the Centre of Migration Research in Warsaw, Poland. She graduated from the Faculty of Psychology, Warsaw University, in 2000. In the same year she completed a programme in Inter-Faculty Individual Studies in the Humanities at Warsaw University and received an MA in social and cultural anthropology from the Catholic University of Leuven, Belgium. In 2002 she was a Marie Curie Research Fellow at the Sussex Centre for Migration Research (England). In 2005 she earned her PhD in sociology from Warsaw University, with a thesis on the representations of immigrants in public discourse and in opinion polls in Poland. Grzymała-Kazłowska is a co-author (with Marek Okólski) of the chapter 'Amorphous Population Movements into Poland and Ensuing Policy Challenges' in the forthcoming textbook *Immigration Worldwide* by U. Segal, N. Mayadas, and D. Elliott (eds). She has published reviews and articles in *The Journal of Ethnic and Migration Studies* and is a consulting editor for *The Journal of Immigrant and Refugee Studies*. Her main academic interests are modern sociological theory, dimensions of immigrant adaptation, immigrant communities, cultural representations of immigrants and attitudes towards foreigners, changes in ethnicity and ethnic identity, and institutions for cultural diversity regulation and ethnic conflict solutions.

Betty de Hart is a Senior Researcher at the Centre for Migration Law at the University of Nijmegen, the Netherlands. She received her doctorate (2003) in the field of sociology of law, with research focused on mixed couples in nationality law and immigration law. Her current research concerns debates and practices in dual nationality in the Netherlands, the United States and Germany. Her publications include: 'The Morality of Maria Toet: Gender, Citizenship, and the Construction of the Nation-State', *Journal of Ethnic and Migration Studies* (2005); *Migration and the Regulation of Social Integration*, special issue of IMIS-Beiträge, co-edited with Anita Böcker and Ines Michalowski (2004); 'Political Debates on Dual Nationality in the Netherlands (1990-2003)', in A. Böcker, B. de Hart, and I. Michalowski (eds) (2004); and 'Not without My Daughter: On Parental Abduction, Orientalism and Maternal Melodrama', *European Journal of Women's Studies* (2001).

Zeynep Kadırbeyoğlu holds an MA in economics from Boğaziçi University Istanbul (Turkey), an MPhil in social and political sciences from the University of Cambridge (United Kingdom), and is currently a PhD candidate in political science at McGill University (Montreal, Canada). Her research interests include transnational networks, citizenship, decentralization and democratization. Her recent work focused on the changing conceptions of citizenship in Turkey. Her publications include 'The Transnational Dimension of the Bergama Campaign against Eurogold' in T. Faist and E. Özveren (eds) (2004), 'Assessing the Efficacy of Transnational Advocacy Networks' in F. Adaman and M. Arsel (eds) (2005), and 'Changing Conceptions of Citizenship in Turkey' in R. Bauböck, B. Perchinig, and W. Sievers (eds) (forthcoming). Her previous works have been published in *New Perspectives on Turkey*.

Piotr Koryś is an economist and historian and is Assistant Professor in the Chair of Economic History of the Faculty of Economic Sciences at Warsaw University, Poland. He earned his doctoral degree in economics in 2004 from Warsaw University. His dissertation dealt with the economic ideology of the Polish nationalist party in the 1920s. His research focuses on international migration and citizenship problems as well as on the history of nationalism and modernization in twentieth-century Poland. He has published articles in Polish economic and sociological journals, including *The Polish Sociological Review* and together with Marek Okólski in 2005 an article about 'Świat w podróży. Globalny kontekst współczesnych polskich migracji' (World in Journey. The Global Context of Contemporary Polish Migration) in *Przegląd Polonijny* 3, 7-26. Koryś has been a fellow at the Centre of Migration Research in Warsaw since 1997. He was a recipient of the Bosch Junior Fellowship (IWM, Vienna) and a scholarship from the Foundation for Polish Science.

Beate Rieple has been working since 2005 at the Stiftung Wissenschaft und Politik in Berlin. She studied political science and economics at the University of Bremen, Germany, where she received her Master's degree. From 2002 Rieple was a research fellow in the project 'Multiple Citizenship in a Globalizing World – Germany in Comparative Perspective' at the University of Applied Sciences Bremen, sponsored by the Volkswagen Foundation. She has published on dual citizenship and the economics of transnational social spaces, including 'Dual Citizenship as a Path-Dependent Process', *International Migration Review* 38:3, 913-44, co-authored with Thomas Faist and Jürgen Gerdes in 2004. During her studies Rieple conducted research abroad with the Fondation du Roi Abdul-Aziz Al Saoud pour les Etudes Islamiques et les Sciences Humaines in Casablanca, Morocco (1996), and at the Institut de Recherches et d'Etudes sur le Monde Arabe et Musulman in Aix-en-Provence, France (1995).

Mikael Spång is Assistant Professor of Political Science at the School of International Migration and Ethnic Relations, Malmö University, Sweden. He holds a PhD from Lund University, Sweden, where he wrote a dissertation entitled 'Justice and Society: Problems of Reformist Politics' in the Department of Political Science. His research interests include citizenship and migration policy as well as more general questions of political theory, especially theories of democracy and justice. One of his newest publications is the chapter 'Sweden: Europeanization of Policy, but not of Politics?' edited by T. Faist, A. Ette and M. Baumann (Palgrave, 2006) He is teaching in the areas of human rights and democracy at Malmö University, and has recently published a book in Swedish on the latter. Currently, he is studying the democratic legitimacy of policy-making in the field of immigration policy in Sweden as well as the impact of Europeanization on Swedish immigration policy.

Agnieszka Weinar received her MA from the American Studies Center in 2000, and her MA in Inter-Faculty Individual Studies in the Humanities in 2001, both at Warsaw University, Poland. She specializes in ethnic studies, with expertise in

Native American Studies and Italian immigration in the US. In 2001, she became a PhD researcher at the Institute for Social Studies, and joined the Centre of Migration Research in Warsaw. Weinar has been awarded several scholarships, the most recent of which include: European University Institute/Robert Schuman Centre for Advanced Studies in Florence, Visiting Research Student (2001); University of Michigan, ICPSR Summer Program (2002); University of California, Berkeley, Junior Visiting Fulbright Scholar (2003/04). She has published in Polish and international journals and monographs in the field of migration studies, including, with Piotr Koryś, the country study of Poland in the volume *Immigration as Labour Market Strategy – European and North American Perspectives*, edited by J. Niessen and Y. Schibel. Her latest publication will be her forthcoming book (Warsaw: Scholar, 2006) with the title *Europeizacja polskiej polityki wobec cudzoziemców w debatach parlamentarnych 1990-2003* (Europeanization of Polish Migration Policy, 1990-2003). Her current work focuses on migration policy regimes, discourse on immigration in liberal democracies, immigration theory, immigrant narratives and theories of citizenship.

Preface

Dual Citizenship is of central theoretical and contemporary political concern. In an age of terrorism and securitized immigration, it is doubly so. Although there has been some work on dual citizenship, scholars have largely neglected it in favour of studies of national citizenship, in a single country or comparatively. And while there are partial exceptions, none of the existing studies has engaged in a systematic international comparison of the politics of dual citizenship. This volume was written to fill that gap. All of the case studies follow the same analytical framework, encompassing both an institutional and a discursive analysis of the politics of dual citizenship.

The core intellectual tension explored in this volume lies in the simultaneous trend towards the expansion of individual rights, on the one hand, and the continued prerogatives of states over full membership in the political community, on the other hand. One of the main tendencies over the past decades has been a growing emphasis on individual rights vis-à-vis state prerogatives in liberal democracies, many of which are immigration countries. One of the results of this tendency has been the increasing tolerance of dual citizenship. The range of cases analyzed – Germany, the Netherlands, Sweden, Poland and Turkey – helps to describe and to explain the politics of dual citizenship in selected immigration and emigration countries, and across a continuum from liberal states to more restrictive ones, in which dual citizenship is not accepted as a rule.

This volume is the result of intensive cooperation among researchers from Germany, Sweden, the Netherlands, Poland and Germany. The Volkswagen Foundation supported the research for this book from 2002 until 2005 through its research programme on 'Global Structures and Their Regulation'. Alfred Schmidt at the Volkswagen Foundation gave valuable advice. The University of Applied Sciences Bremen in Germany and Malmö University in Sweden provided institutional support for the organization of the meetings. I am especially grateful to Edith Klein at the University of Toronto who generously improved the readability of the contributions to this book. Peter Kivisto at Augustana College supported the project and commented on earlier versions. In addition, Jürgen Gerdes provided valuable ideas throughout the course of this work. Michael Wittig took care of formatting the text. I would also like to extend my thanks to the German Academic Exchange Service (DAAD) and the Institute of European Studies at the Munk Centre for International Studies of the University of Toronto, which generously afforded me time to arrange for the publication of the book during my tenure as DAAD Visiting Professor in the academic year 2004-2005.

April 2006 Bielefeld   Thomas Faist

List of Abbreviations

AIA   Administration and Internal Affairs Committee – Komisja Administracji i Spraw Wewnętrznych (*ASW*) (Poland)

ANAP   Anavatan Partisi – Motherland Party (Turkey)

BVerfGE   Bundesverfassungsgericht – Federal Constitutional Court (Germany)

BVerwGE   Bundesverwaltungsgericht – Federal Administrative Court (Germany)

CDA   Christen Democratisch Appel – Christian Democratic Party (The Netherlands)

CDU   Christlich Demokratische Union – Christian Democratic Union (Germany)

CHP   Cumhuriyet Halk Partisi – People's Republican Party (Turkey)

CSU   Christlich-Soziale Union – Christian Social Union (Germany)

D66   Democraten 66 – Democrats 66 (The Netherlands)

DsA   Departementsserien – State Commission Publication (Sweden)

DYP   Doğru Yol Partisi – True Path Party (Turkey)

EU   European Union

GDR   German Democratic Republic – Deutsche Demokratische Republik

IND   Immigratie en Naturalisatiedienst – Immigration and Naturalization Service (The Netherlands)

IOT   Inspraak Orgaan Turken – Advice Organ Turks

LPA   Committee on Liaison with Poles Abroad – Komisja Łączności z Polakami za Granicą (*LPG*)

MHP   Milliyetçi Hareket Partisi – Nationalist Action Party (Turkey)

MP   Member of Parliament

NGO   Non-Governmental Organization

NJCM   Nederlands Juristen Comité voor de Mensenrechten – Dutch Legal Committee for Human Rights

NSC   National Security Council (Turkey)

PDS   Partei des Demokratischen Sozialismus – Party of Democratic Socialism
            (Germany)

PKK   Partiya Karkerên Kurdistan – Kurdistan Workers Party (Turkey)

PR   Parliament Records

PvdA   Partij van de Arbeid Labour Party – Social Democratic Party (The
            Netherlands)

RP   Refah Partisi – Welfare Party (Turkey)

SFS   Svensk författningssamling – Swedish Legal Documents

SGP   Staatkundig Gereformeerde Partij – National Reformed Party (The
            Netherlands)

SHP   Sosyal Demokrat Halkçı Parti – Social Democratic People's Party
            (Turkey)

SOU   Statens offentliga utredningar – State Commission Publication
            (Sweden)

SPD   Sozialdemokratische Partei Deutschlands – Social Democratic Party
            (Germany)

TBMM   Türkiye Büyük Millet Meclisi – Grand National Assembly of the
            Republic of Turkey

TCCSGB   Türkiye Cumhuriyeti Çalışma ve Sosyal Güvenlik Bakanlığı – Ministry
            of Labour and Social Security

TGD   Türkische Gemeinde in Deutschland – Turkish Immigrants Union

VVD   Volkspartij voor Vrijheid en Democratie – People's Party for Freedom
            and Democracy (The Netherlands)

WRR   Wetenschappelijke Raad voor het Regeringsbeleid – Scientific Council
            for Government Policy (The Netherlands)

Chapter 1

The Fixed and Porous Boundaries of Dual Citizenship

Thomas Faist[1]

Introduction

In the year 2000 the German government changed its citizenship law to allow children born in Germany of alien parents to be granted German citizenship automatically if at least one parent had legally resided in Germany for eight years and possessed a permanent residence status. Under the old system, German-born children of migrants maintained their parents' citizenship and thus were officially classified as foreigners, according to the 1913 *Reichs- und Staatsangehörigkeitsgesetz*. Another change was made, following the steps already taken in the early 1990s after German reunification, to ease naturalization for first-generation immigrants, by shortening the waiting time for a claim to citizenship from fifteen to eight years. At the same time, however, a more far-reaching proposal for reform of dual citizenship,[2] put forth by the governing party coalition of Social Democrats and Greens, did not survive debate. Dual citizenship is still not allowed as a rule, although the range of exceptions has been growing. Those naturalizing as Germans are generally still required to renounce their original citizenship, and those now enjoying birthright citizenship by virtue of non-citizen parental residence in Germany are required to choose between their German and alternative nationalities under what has been labelled the 'option model'.

Viewed from the prevailing perspectives on citizenship, this policy outcome, in which the *jus sanguinis* element was complemented by a far-reaching *jus soli*, is puzzling. According to the 'tradition of nationhood' thesis (Brubaker 1992), citizenship laws and policies are shaped by particular and deeply rooted understandings of nationhood. In contrast to France's inclusive model based on

---

1 I would like to thank Per Gustafson and Mikael Spång for helpful comments. The usual disclaimer also applies: all remaining errors are mine.

2 The use of 'dual' implies that triple and more plural citizenship is becoming increasingly significant as a result of the conjunction of modes for acquiring citizenship, deriving from marriage, naturalization, and reacquisition of former citizenships. Therefore, some authors use terms such as 'plural' or 'multiple' citizenship rather than dual citizenship partly because individuals may, and increasingly probably do, carry multiple national memberships.

its republican national tradition and 'civic' concept of nationhood, this argument goes, Germany's exclusive model, based on ethno-cultural tradition and an 'ethnic' concept of nationhood, has had the effect of excluding millions of former guest-workers. Civic-republican concepts define membership as a question of subjective will, whereas ethno-cultural or ethno-national concepts are rooted in criteria such as descent and language. Each state's membership politics are viewed as continuing along familiar trajectories, laid down during critical periods of state formation. On the matter of dual citizenship, we would conclude that a republican understanding of nation leads to more inclusive measures for immigrant integration, while a more ethnically and culturally defined concept of nation tends to be much more exclusive vis-à-vis immigrants but at the same time tolerant of its own citizens residing abroad and holding more than one citizenship. Thus a civic-republican understanding of citizenship is alleged to be linked to liberal naturalization policies in general and tolerance of or indifference to dual citizenship in particular; whereas an ethno-cultural or, worse, ethno-national understanding of nationhood is linked to poor prospects for dual citizenship for immigrants. Yet, the shift in Germany meant a move to *jus soli* and eased as-of-right naturalization without a corresponding shift on the issue of dual citizenship. Moreover, dual citizenship for Germans living abroad remained out of reach. Interestingly, the debates in the German parliament on this matter in the late 1990s could not be described as ethno-cultural or even ethno-national in substance and content. Thus, a fundamental question arises: Is it useful to juxtapose a civic or republican against an ethnic concept of nationhood? Does the recent German experience suggest that, to paraphrase Nathan Glazer's cogent book title, we are all republican now?[3] The implication is that republican arguments could be used both in favour of and against dual citizenship. Moreover, we would need to change the dominant conceptual apparatus to capture the explanation of citizenship policies and laws, and examine the types of belief systems that drive policy debates on (dual) citizenship.

Citizenship is an essentially contested and fluid concept of social order. Public and academic debates over citizenship go to the very heart of the understanding of social cohesion and political integration. Modern, democratic states and societies are integrated in large part through the constitution of citizenship. In recent decades dual citizenship has been a focus of debate as nation-states have faced the challenges of the political integration of immigrants, emigrants, and national minorities. States have increasingly come to tolerate various forms of dual citizenship.

---

3   Here, the argument is that the *jus soli* element, eased as-of-right naturalization, and the increased toleration of dual citizenship would have been consistent with a further blurring of the boundaries of citizenship. Of course, *jus soli* per se would not signal a more liberal or tolerant access to citizenship. Combined with restrictive immigration policies, *jus soli* could be an instrument of exclusion. Conversely, the birthright principle of *jus sanguinis* without *jus soli* could be fairly liberal in case of easy access to as-of-right naturalization. For example, Sweden is characterized by comparatively liberal naturalization rules. Therefore, we also need to look at the arguments justifying the various policy options.

Dual citizenship in the formal sense of citizenship means that citizens combine memberships in and of several states. Thus political membership overlaps two or more national polities and eludes the neat trinity of state territory, state authority, and the people. Moreover, there is no congruence of political and social membership. What makes dual citizenship such an interesting research site is that we are dealing neither with exclusive citizenship in tightly bounded political communities nor with denationalized citizenship, but rather with a sort of multi-nationalized citizenship. In short, dual citizenship is an instance of 'internal globalization': it is an example of how nation-state regulations implicitly or explicitly respond to ties of citizens across states. Dual citizenship is distinct from citizenship in a single nation-state on the one hand and from emerging forms of citizenship beyond the nation-state in supranational governance structures such as the European Union (EU) on the other hand. Dual citizenship is a simultaneous rather than successive model of citizenship by which one may retain only one citizenship at a time. Recognition of dual citizenship may contribute to the further blurring of the boundaries between immigrants and citizens across borders. We have seen such an impact from the liberalization of naturalization rules, the complementation of *jus sanguinis* by *jus soli*, and the expansion of *denizenship* between some categories of immigrants – permanent residents – and natives within one country. In the latter instance the implication is that, increasingly, aliens acquire rights that have formerly been the prerogatives of citizens.[4]

Here, the overarching proposition is that fundamental beliefs about societal integration that is, the role of individuals, civil society, and the state in political communities, have structured the debates and the legislation on dual citizenship. Societal integration refers to both the overall integration of the polity and the social integration of immigrants into a polity. Political actors' views on societal integration inevitably reflect contested notions of citizenship. This proposition opens up space for exploring membership beyond an exclusive allegiance to one state and leads us to consider the nature of societal integration beyond tightly bounded national communities.

Although the road to increasing tolerance of dual citizenship has been uneven, there is nevertheless a clear direction favouring it, even in those liberal democratic states that do not as a rule recognize dual citizenship. This is astonishing when one considers that only a few decades ago citizenship in a nation-state and political loyalty to that state were considered inseparable. The proponents of dual citizenship have welcomed it as a means to equalize individual rights between natives and newcomers.

---

4   The often noted tendency towards an expansion of *denizenship*, i.e. significant civil and social rights for permanent resident immigrants, should not be taken to be a linear development. After all, certain categories of migrants cannot turn their residence into permanency, such as contract-workers (Faist 1997), and persons belonging to some categories may fail to do so, such as asylum seekers whose claims may be rejected. Moreover, the legal granting of rights is not coterminous with their institutionalization – for example, social rights in the welfare state made available by actual social services – and their potential 'erosion' in actual market processes (Morris 2002), characterized by manifold mechanisms of social closure along the lines of ethnicity, race, religion, gender, and class.

Critics have worried that membership overlapping nation-states threatens societal solidarity and reciprocity among citizens and in civil society, and may even threaten state security.

The goal of this volume is to explore the changing boundaries of citizenship by looking at public debates on dual citizenship legislation concerning immigrants.[5] The boundaries and attendant rights of citizenship define, in part, the limits of day-to-day political conflict in liberal democracies because they are deeply entrenched, constitutionally and in legislation. The chapters in this volume trace the changing boundaries of citizenship in selected European immigration and emigration countries through the empirical analysis of the ideas and beliefs of those involved in political decision-making processes and an examination of how porous or fixed citizenship boundaries might be. The case studies explore the negotiated character and boundaries of political membership within distinct political cultures and institutional settings that have shaped debates and policies on citizenship. The analyses serve to explore the similarities and differences in the politics of dual citizenship with a view to identifying the dominant terms of public debate within and across selected immigration and emigration states, institutionally set within causal processes along path-dependant lines. The contributions cover a wide spectrum of cases of immigration countries ranging from the fairly restrictive German case to the more tolerant Dutch case, characterized by many exceptions to the rule, to the Swedish case, in which dual citizenship is explicitly accepted. Two emigration countries, Turkey and Poland, are also covered in this volume. In these two cases dual citizenship for their emigrants is tolerated.

Concepts and Propositions

In the public debates in these various countries, the respective belief systems and the framing of ideas and arguments have served as a catalytic function in the decisions on dual citizenship. This observation rests on the basic assumption that political reality is perceived through the prism of distinctive belief systems. These 'ideas', reflected by those active in the political process, shape the policy concepts, the frameworks of discussion – and even the 'interests' – actors bring to bear in the claims- and policy-making processes. Institutions can thus be seen as congealed or thickened beliefs and norms. Political actors within relevant institutions not only articulate interests and preferences but also exchange arguments, which are an integral part of public debates and political decision-making (*cf.* Habermas 1981). In turn, policies and institutions do not simply affect and guide the behaviour of citizens but also constitute the 'identity' of actors. This is why policies guiding citizenship acquisition are fundamentally important. The analyses assembled here suggest how

---

5   This focus largely excludes the problematic of state succession and thus national minorities and the consequences of colonialism and thus indigenous peoples. On state succession and national minorities, see Barrington 1995 and Shevchuck 1996; on indigenous people and dual citizenship, see Carens 2000, chapter 7.

the discursive elements shaped the political and public debates on dual citizenship and how these debates have been shaped by and in turn funnelled back into the institutional realm, that is, into public policies and *de facto* rules. In tracing the belief systems on (dual) citizenship within distinctive institutional contexts, the analyses in this volume thus shed light on the political culture of the changing boundaries of political membership.

The debates on dual citizenship have occurred within seminal institutional developments. These are captured by two framing hypotheses. The first thesis is that one of the main tendencies over the past decades has been the growing emphasis on individual rights vis-à-vis state prerogatives in liberal democracies, many of which are immigration countries. This has been an outgrowth of the marked expansion of citizenship and its greater inclusiveness over the course of the last two hundred years. Among others, property and gender qualifications have been abolished, so that today virtually all adult citizens in liberal democracies enjoy this status. This dynamic of individual rights expansion, with an added impetus provided by the 'rights revolution' since the 1960s, has been driving the growing tolerance of dual citizenship. From this perspective, the analyses in this volume constitute an exploration of the prospects for and the limits of democratizing the non-democratic element of democracy, state sovereignty in its relationship to individual rights.

Accordingly, dual citizenship debates have been characterized by the blurring of old boundaries, such as a declining tendency to treat men and women in bi-national marriages differently (an erosion of legal gender inequality), and the blurring of the distinction between aliens and citizens, captured by the term *denizenship*. The latter tendency, in particular, has been essential in advancing the debates on immigrant dual citizenship. After all, the blurring of the boundaries between aliens and citizens in terms of individual rights – although not entirely in terms of civil rights (e.g. deportation) – have only two logical lines of extension: granting basic political rights to *denizens* (for example the right to vote on the national level), or further liberalizing naturalization procedures. One of the instruments for the latter option has been dual citizenship (Hammar 1990).

Countries of emigration, too, have tolerated or even encouraged dual citizenship, although for different reasons. The second framing thesis proposed here is thus that the governments of many emigration countries have seized upon dual citizenship as an instrument to forge and maintain transnational links with emigrants living abroad. This transnationalism is state-led and exclusionist, that is, differentialist. First, emigration countries tend to pursue a strategy of 'selective tolerance' (Górny, Grzymała-Kazłowska, Koryś and Weinar, this volume, chapter 6). Differentialist transnationalism tends to be ethno-national in that it usually targets citizens and emigrants living abroad but does not apply to immigrants from other countries living in these 'emigration states'. Second, differentialist transnationalism tends to be state-centric since dual citizenship is seen primarily as a means for governments and state institutions to forge ties with citizens abroad, that is, a tool to control border-crossing social formations, such as diasporas, expatriate communities, emigrant organizations, religious communities, or kinship networks (*cf.* Faist 2000, chapter 7).

In these cases the acceptance of dual citizenship does not serve to acknowledge the multiple ties of citizens in a globalizing world. Rather, in tolerating dual citizenship emigration countries are attempting to further their own economic interests, such as continued flows of remittances and investments by emigrants in the country of origin, or political aims, such as using emigrants as loyal lobby groups or controlling their activities, which might be directed against the regime of the sending country. Nonetheless, in an asymmetric power system of states, this transnational dimension of dual citizenship has been possible only as a result of the growing tolerance of dual citizenship in immigration countries and thus the dynamics of individual rights in liberal democracies.

The processes suggested by the first two framing hypotheses can be seen as path-dependant.[6] Dual citizenship emerged in connection with international migration and the different rules in force in nation-states for naturalization, such as *jus soli* and *jus sanguinis*. Nowadays, many nation-states tolerate and even accept the notion that the acquisition of citizenship is not contingent upon renunciation of one's original citizenship, and that citizenship is not lost upon acquiring the citizenship of another state. Once states accept certain elements which are the logical preconditions leading to a higher degree of toleration of dual citizenship – such as exempting persons threatened by statelessness from the renunciation requirement, tolerating dual citizenship for children arising from bi-national marriages, or the principle of reciprocity between EU member states – they do not normally revoke these rules. Yet, this path-dependence does not imply that the process has, so far, been linear. Indeed, there are significant differences in the ways in which countries have responded. On a *de jure* level some countries such as Sweden have accepted dual citizenship as a legal category and abolished the renunciation requirement. Others do not as a rule recognize dual citizenship but have substantial exemptions, as in the Netherlands, while others, such as the Federal Republic of Germany, do not provide for dual citizenship but over the years have introduced a growing number of exemptions. Even more complex is the situation in major emigration countries, which have also

---

6   The political-economic notion of path-dependence has a sociological counterpart, cumulative causation. Both concepts can be described by using the metaphor of a 'funnel' in which, once an actor such as a state has taken certain decisions, it eliminates, by that very act, other possible courses of action. For example, a twenty-year-old college student has a wide range of possible career options at her fingertips that are not available to a forty-year-old professor who has heavily invested in that career path. Thus the concept of cumulative causation is similar to the notion of path-dependence which is based upon the stable equilibrium concept in economics. Yet, unlike path-dependence, which searches for the choices and consequences of processes, locked into a certain pattern, cumulative causation focuses on the very context and mechanisms that makes spiraling effects possible. Thus the concept of cumulative causation is a specific form of analyzing presumed causalities (Maruyama 1962, 175). In short, path-dependence seems to be more concerned about the choices of actors and their consequences while cumulative causation emphasizes processes that enable spiraling processes (positive feedback loops) or return to the original state of affairs (negative feedback loops). Here, the focus is on choices and results, not so much on the endogenous dynamics and spiraling effects.

experienced substantial immigration, such as Turkey, or are on their way to becoming major receivers in the context of EU integration, such as Poland.

The contributors to this volume attempt to shed light on these cases and to go beyond the two well-known perspectives in citizenship research; the first based on nationhood, and the second on immigrant integration. Although we do not yet have a detailed understanding in the social sciences as to which strategies, conditions, and perceptions drive belief systems shaping citizenship, these two paradigms enable us to make the connection between 'ideas' and citizenship policies. Rather than rejecting them, the approach here builds upon and transforms them. The nationhood approach is a perspective 'from above', which deduces the main citizenship policies from ideal-typical understandings of the political community, usually thought to be congruent with a nationally-bounded society. The immigrant integration approach is a perspective 'from below', which looks at the policies employed to absorb newcomers into the political community. While both of these approaches shed light on tolerance of dual citizenship, the two literatures have been myopic. The nationhood literature has been mainly concerned with concepts of political identity, collective membership, and statehood. Research on immigrant integration has mostly focused on parity of individual migrants with the majority society (*cf.* Alba and Nee 2003), a perspective that lends itself to questions about equal rights and their institutionalization.

Yet, the traditions of both the nationhood and immigrant integration paradigms ignore the diversity in immigration and emigration countries not only in terms of social relations such as gender and class. They have not taken into account the diversity of assumptions about what societal integration means on the level of the state, civil society, and the individual. Clearly, there are different versions of the understanding of integration cross-nationally but also within national communities, reflected in distinct belief systems, which correspond to fundamental ideological fault lines in national societies. To account for this complexity we suggest that a more comprehensive perspective is needed, one that places the issues at hand in the context of political-cultural understandings of societal integration, and that examines the different belief systems political actors hold about the role of the individual in society, the nature of civil society, and the role of the state.

It is important to note that we started our research, in 2002, with the paradigms of 'nationhood' and 'immigrant integration' to describe the belief systems relating to dual citizenship. In fact, we began with clear propositions about the influence of the understandings of nationhood and immigrant integration models on the stance towards dual citizenship. We hypothesized that civic-republican concepts of nationhood are more amenable to dual citizenship for immigrants than ethnic concepts, and that ethnic concepts tend to favour dual citizenship for emigrants. Moreover, we proposed that multicultural models of immigrant integration are more likely to allow tolerance of dual citizenship than assimilationist ones. The re-conceptualization of these approaches into the societal integration perspective just described has resulted from the empirical research process itself. It was only during the course of conducting the research that we started to look for more comprehensive concepts to capture the discursive dimension of dual citizenship – linking nationhood and immigrant integration to even deeper belief systems on societal integration.

The remainder of this introduction is organized in five sections: The first deals with the definition of citizenship as a normative concept, both in its legal dimension and its perennially contested political dimension. While the cases analyzed deal with changes in the legal realm, the debates reflect the political understanding of citizenship. The second part sketches in broad strokes the development of national legislation and international norms on dual citizenship. The third section offers a triadic typology of perspectives to understand citizenship, presenting the outlines of the national, the postnational, and the transnational view, each of which helps to analyze certain segments of the growth of tolerance towards dual citizenship but also the resistance against toleration or even acceptance. The fourth part explains the case selection for comparative analysis of national variations in a configurative manner, namely Germany, the Netherlands, Sweden, Turkey, and Poland. Because Germany has commonly been referred to as a typical instance of an ethno-cultural or even ethno-national understanding of nationhood, that country serves as the linchpin case for the immigration countries. The fifth and final section outlines the realms of inquiry in the country case studies, broadly divided into institutional and discursive structures. The analysis of the belief systems guiding the thinking on societal integration must be embedded within the institutional structures. The elements of the institutional structures include the political party systems, the role of the judiciary, and the interaction of various institutions along the division of branches, namely parliaments, governments, and the courts. With respect to the discursive structure, the emphasis is on building upon the tradition of nationhood and a stylized immigrant integration approach. A novel approach based on an analysis of the belief system 'societal integration' is presented.

Citizenship as a Normative Concept: Legal and Political

Throughout this book, citizenship is used as a normative concept in two ways: as a legal construct and as a political concept. Both are intricately related but constitute distinct dimensions.[7] Citizenship as a political concept is an 'essentially contested

---

7   In some countries, the distinction between citizenship as a legal concept and citizenship as a political concept is expressed in different terms: nationality refers to the legal side and citizenship to the political. The distinction between nationality and citizenship is a west-central European one, with the meaning of the terms roughly similar in various languages: *nationality, nationalité, nacionalidad, Staatsangehörigkeit* on the one hand, and *citizenship, citoyenneté, citudania* and *Staatsbürgerschaft* on the other hand. It should be noted that the distinction between nationality and citizenship is not to be found in 'classical' immigration countries, such as Canada, the United States of America, and Australia (all citizenship), and is also absent in some European countries, such as Turkey (*yurttaslik* or *vatandaslik*) and Poland (*obywatelstwo*). Also, certain academic disciplines such as law use the terms differently: one prominent usage connects the term nationality to the international law forum and the term

Figure 1.1   Dimensions of Citizenship and Dual Citizenship

Dimension of Citizenship	Dual Citizenship as Contested Ground
Democratic Self-Governance	Feedback between the governing and the governed; 'one person, one vote'; Congruence between the resident population and the demos.
Rights and Duties	Legal equality; substantive citizenship, i.e. full participation in economic, political, and cultural life in the place of residence.
Affiliation with Political Community	Solidarity and reciprocity required for peaceful coexistence and welfare state redistribution.

concept': 'There is no notion more central in politics than citizenship, [yet] none more variable in history or contested in theory' (Shklar 1991, 1). The central question then is how does the legal construct of citizenship as a formal status fit with the broader notions of citizenship implicit in the political dimension, i.e. democratic self-determination, full citizens' rights, membership in a political community, and citizens' participation in the polity and its citizenship practices?

Citizenship as a legal concept means full membership in a state and the corresponding tie to state law and subjection to state power. The inter-state function of citizenship is to clearly define a people within a relatively clearly delineated territory and to protect the citizens of a state against the outside, at times hostile, world. The intrastate function of citizenship is to define the rights and duties of members. According to the principle of *domaine réservé* – exclusive competence – each state decides within the limits of sovereign self-determination on the criteria required for access to its citizenship. One general condition for membership is that nationals have some kind of close ties to the respective state, the so-called 'genuine link' (Rittstieg 1990, 1402).

Citizenship viewed as a contested political concept, in contrast, concerns the relationship between citizens, the state, and democracy: 'Without a state, there can be no citizenship; without citizenship, there can be no democracy' (Linz and Stepan 1996, 28). In essence, citizenship builds on collective self-determination, i.e. democracy, and essentially comprises three mutually qualifying dimensions: first, the legally guaranteed status of equal political freedom and democratic self-determination; second, equal rights and obligations; and third, membership in a political community (*cf.* Cohen 1999). These dimensions are paralleled by state functions and are suggestive of substantive questions concerning citizenship (Figure 1.1).

Issues of dual citizenship thus have constitutional importance. This may seem an odd formulation at first, since there is no explicit constitutional right to dual

citizenship to domestic legal forums. Moreover, nationality – unlike the usage here – also has the meaning of membership in a national community of shared history and culture that need not to be established as an independent state (e.g. *narodowosc* in Polish and *uyrukluk* in Turkish).

citizenship. But in fact the issue has great bearing on principles entrenched in many constitutions of states and in international conventions. For example, there is, first, the principle of democratic legitimation regarding the acceptance of rule and the process of rule-making. Second, we find the principle of the rule of law regarding the right to national citizenship and rights associated with this kind of citizenship, such as social policies to ensure a minimum standard of living. Third, there are requirements of state-citizen relations underlying constitutions, which cannot be created by the state. These include reciprocity, solidarity, and trust among citizens.

Democracy

In the first dimension citizenship means above all the principle of unity of both those governing and those being governed, whatever forms the democratic procedures of each state may take in detail. Ideally, citizens endowed with equal political liberty obey the laws in the creation of which they have participated and to whose validity they thus consent (Walzer 1989). Without democratic procedures guiding citizens' political self-determination, citizenship would mean little more than members of political communities being subjects of a sovereign. Dual citizenship raises the question whether dual citizens are still part of the feedback system between the governing and the governed, or whether – as the critics charge – they can withdraw at any time from decisions they helped to bring about in choosing the exit option and relocating to another country. Empirically, we observe that national citizenship has developed over the past few centuries in regions such as Europe in territorially enclosed, relatively coherent in the social aspect, and inter-generationally viable political communities with effective state authorities (*cf.* Rokkan and Urwin 1983). Dual citizenship, in the eyes of the critics, may thus erode state sovereignty. Moreover, multiple loyalties are often seen as damaging to the public spirit. According to the sceptics, the ties of citizens reaching into multiple states seem to challenge the supposed congruence of the demos, state territory, and state authority and, in particular, violate basic principles such as 'one person, one vote'. By contrast, proponents of dual citizenship do not perceive any substantive threat because dual citizens do not have multiple votes in one polity but only one in each polity of which they are full members. The issue becomes more complicated when borders themselves move, rather than people across borders. The first case refers to national minorities, the second to immigrants. The case of national minorities holding citizenship of the country of residence in addition to a (former) home country may raise matters of sovereignty. For example, the country of residence may fear intervention by the patron state, as in the case of the Hungarian community in Romania (Kovács forthcoming). Dual citizenship is of further importance because of the norm of congruence between the permanently resident population and those who determine government, the demos. Thinking on citizenship has traditionally assumed some kind of congruence between the people (*demos*), state territory, and state authority (*cf.* Jellinek 1964, 406-27). Those in favour of tolerating dual citizenship point to the requirement of congruence between the people and the resident population. Ideally, citizens are the basic law givers in a democratic society and the beneficiaries of a law should see themselves as its authors (*cf.* Rousseau 1966). Over the long run, incongruence between the permanent resident population on the one hand and the demos on the other hand would not be compatible with the democratic principle of congruence. Inclusion into the political community therefore is a prerequisite for participation in political and even social life.

Rights and Duties

The second dimension of citizenship refers to the constitutions of modern states which enshrine human and fundamental rights of liberty as a legal status. In general, citizens' rights fall into various realms, for example, civil or negative rights to liberty, political rights to participation such as the right to vote and to associate, and social rights (the latter including the right to social benefits in case of sickness, unemployment, old age, and the right to education, *cf.* Marshall 1964). It is highly contested whether, to which degree, and for which category of citizens cultural or even group-differentiated rights should be a constitutive part of citizenship. Critics charge that cultural rights could form the basis for new divisions among citizens contradicting the notion of equal democratic citizenship (*cf.* Offe 1998). The duties corresponding to citizens' entitlements are the duty to serve in the armed forces in order to protect state sovereignty against exterior threats, while the duty to pay taxes, to acknowledge the rights and liberties of other citizens, and to accept democratically legitimated decisions of majorities structure the internal sphere. This dimension has been strongly emphasized in approaches guided by a rights discourse, often fused with social democratic (Marshall 1964) or multicultural tendencies (Kymlicka 1995).

Public debates have pondered the relationship between immigrant integration and citizenship. Should immigrants show some proof, for example, that they have incorporated before being allowed to naturalize and thus have access to full rights? Or does full citizenship represent rather a beginning of the integration process, a sort of necessary prerequisite for full incorporation? The proponents of dual citizenship propose that legal equality should be a prerequisite for 'substantive citizenship', i.e. full participation in economic, political, and cultural life in the place of residence (*cf.* Hammar 1989). In this view state authorities need to create favourable conditions for the political integration of newcomers and to provide the individual rights necessary for successful incorporation. The claim hinges on the observation that those states tolerating dual citizenship have, ceteris paribus, proportionally more immigrants who have naturalized. In political debates, dual citizenship is also justified as a mechanism to enhance the political participation of immigrants, or to motivate political representatives to take into account immigrants' interests, along with other tools such as political rights for resident non-citizens such as *denizens* (e.g. Jones-Correa 1998).

Collective Affiliation

In a third dimension, citizenship rests on an affinity of citizens with certain political communities, the partial identification with and thus loyalty to a self-governing collective, often a nation or a multi-nation (*cf.* Weber 1972, 242-4). In modern national states, citizens identify with a self-governing collective which claims to establish a balance between the individual and common interests on the one hand and rights and responsibilities within the political community on the other. To what extent citizenship is bound to nation-states, or whether it can also be tied to sub-state (e.g. regional, local, city) and supranational (e.g. EU) entities, is disputed. Affiliation with a collective, whether a nation or another entity, expressed as a set of relatively continuous, social, and symbolic ties of citizens otherwise anonymous to each other, is linked to the status dimension of citizenship because of reciprocal obligations of members in a political community, akin to a social treaty (Dahrendorf 1992, 116). The expansion of citizenship is not simply a process of expanding or contracting individual rights, but of changing the relation between individual rights and a collective dimension. This is why the development of citizenship is not congruent with the neo-liberal approach foregrounding individual (property) rights, but rather, in T. H. Marshall's insightful formulation, constitutes a status, based on a collective understanding, to counter market forces; in short, a status mechanism for ameliorating class inequalities.

The notion of collective identity has become important in referring to the cultural side of citizenship. In citizenship theory, there have been two variants. The first approach looks at individual and group rights of minorities as a source for political inclusion in multicultural societies (Kymlicka and Norman 2000). The second has been associated with the question of how far citizenship and attendant national identities can be extended beyond their traditional association with an exclusive national community to several communities or even to global or cosmopolitan communities (e.g. Bosniak 2002). Here the question of loyalty or allegiance arises persistently: as a rule, those opposed to dual citizenship regard loyalty as an indivisible asset and refer to the 'national interest', while those tolerating dual citizenship tend to think of loyalty as a divisible good. In another formulation, the concept of 'relational nationality' assumes that loyalties are potentially multiple, variable, and interactive (*cf.* Knop 2000), within and beyond state borders. Seen in this way state-citizen relations are connected to civil society and its resources. Solidarity and reciprocity are deemed a requirement for peaceful coexistence and welfare state redistribution. In this third dimension in particular, the potential incongruence between a single polity and social relations is quite obvious.

In sum, citizenship as a legal status and citizenship as a political concept are intricately related. The underlying argument here is that changing state-citizen relations and also state-*denizen* ties have implications for the growing tolerance of dual citizenship. In international law, for example, citizenship has come to be viewed increasingly as a human right, as in the case of stateless persons (*cf.* Motomura 1998). And on the national level, rights of non-citizens, in particular *denizens* have expanded and impacted upon the institutions, practices, and discourses on citizenship. One result has been that in countries such as the Netherlands and Sweden dual citizenship was discussed as an alternative to extending local voting rights for permanent residents from the local to the national level.

In this volume the empirical analysis takes as its starting point the politics of dual citizenship as a legal status, and the case studies are concerned with legislation on dual citizenship. Yet, the concept of citizenship as a set of political norms is highly relevant because the criteria used to analyze the politics and ideas of dual citizenship as legal status are derived from the four dimensions of citizenship as a political concept. Indeed, the political actors themselves use ideas of citizenship as a political concept to argue for or against concrete rules to tolerate or prohibit dual citizenship.

Citizenship Rules and Dual Citizenship

In accordance with the principle of *domaine réservé*, every state has the sovereign right to determine the criteria for acquiring the citizenship of that state. The only conditions for international recognition of citizenship are that (1) it is related in a certain way to the legal system of the state in question, (2) a so-called genuine link exists between the state citizen and the respective state, and (3) the self-determination of other states is likewise respected. From the point of view of international law, further restrictions may arise only out of international agreements.

Until a few decades ago, it was common international consensus that dual citizenship should be avoided as far as possible, as reflected both in the citizenship laws of individual states and in bilateral and international conventions and agreements. All shared the premise that multiple allegiances were undesirable and should be eradicated where possible. There was 'a widely held opinion that dual citizenship (was) an undesirable phenomenon detrimental to both the friendly relations between nations and the well-being of the individuals concerned' (Bar-Yaacov 1961, 4). Witness the Hague Convention of 1930 and the European Convention on the 'Reduction of Cases of Dual Nationality and Military Obligations in Cases of Dual Nationality' of 1963 – although these agreements were not as binding as international human rights regimes. One brief statement summarizes the dominant international perspective throughout most of the twentieth century: 'All persons are entitled to possess one nationality, but one nationality only' (League of Nations 1930).[8] States regarded dual citizenship as a potential catalyst for treason, espionage, and other subversive activities. From the mid-nineteenth century until long after World War Two, states

---

8   Article 1 of the Hague Convention provides: 'It is for each State to determine under its own law who are its nationals. This law shall be recognized by other States in so far as it is consistent with international conventions, international custom, and the principles of law generally recognized with regard to nationality.' Article 2 continues: 'Any question as to whether a person possesses the nationality of a particular State shall be determined in accordance with the law of that State.'

adhered to two iron laws. The first was that losing one's original citizenship was the price for adopting another. Most states expatriated citizens automatically when their subjects became naturalized in another state, but also if there was significant evidence of political or social loyalty to another state, such as entry into military service, for instance, or the assumption of a political office or even participation in political elections abroad. In some cases, immigration countries made naturalization conditional on the relinquishment of the previous citizenship. The second iron law by which many states attempted to overcome the problem of dual citizenship ensuing from birth on their territory was that such individuals had, on reaching maturity, to choose one of the two citizenships, or were otherwise expatriated.

Dual citizenship could never be completely avoided, however, because people have always moved across state borders and settled down, sometimes for longer periods than originally intended. A cause for dual citizenship thus usually arises, for example, whenever a person is born within the territory of a country where the law of territoriality (*jus soli*) holds, but whose parents are citizens of a country that observes the blood principle (*jus sanguinis*). On this point, developments in relation to gender equality under the citizenship law were the main legal mechanism for the expansion of dual citizenship. In 1957, the New York Protocol revised the status of women, who had hitherto legally been entirely dependant on their husbands and automatically acquired their husbands' citizenship upon marriage. The right to retain their own citizenship, independent of their husbands, has been taken up in the citizenship laws of a growing number of countries, while at the same time naturalization has been facilitated for the better protection of the family. Since then, the principle of gender equality has increasingly been applied to *jus sanguinis* as well, so that now it is frequently the case that the child can be given the citizenship of either parent.

Furthermore, in recent years there has been an increasing tendency in European immigration countries to make the naturalization of immigrants less conditional on the relinquishment of their previous citizenship, as reflected in the change of national citizenship laws, relaxation of administrative practices, and the more generous interpretation of international agreements. The stipulations on the loss or relinquishment of one's citizenship show similar tendencies. Some states, for instance France in 1973, Portugal in 1981, and Italy in 1992, which in the past required a person to relinquish her citizenship if she became naturalized in another state, have changed their citizenship laws in this respect in various ways. Nowadays, the retention of the original citizenship is possible to a much greater degree. For their part, numerous emigration countries – for instance Mexico, Turkey, Tunisia, El Salvador, Columbia, the Dominican Republic – have modified their citizenship laws, either enabling their nationals to become naturalized elsewhere while retaining their original citizenship, or facilitating the re-acquisition of their original citizenship, or mitigating the consequences of losing one's citizenship. This is noteworthy because we would expect the highest levels of dual citizenship in cases where both immigration and emigration countries tolerate it. Furthermore, in those states that still uphold the principle of avoiding dual citizenship, there are various exemption clauses. The most widespread exemption is one that occurs in the event the other state will not permit persons to relinquish their citizenship or makes it conditional on unreasonable demands.

There has been a notable evolution towards a right to citizenship as a legal status, which is normally extended only to certain categories of individuals such as stateless persons (*cf.* Weis 1976), although no court – as of yet – has upheld such a right. Nonetheless, this development brings to the fore the tension between the principles of universal human rights, on the one hand, and the principle of democratic self-determination, which requires some sort of closure, on the other hand. This tension constitutes, in the words of Seyla Benhabib (2004), the 'paradox of democratic legitimacy', and qualifies the first framing hypothesis, individual rights vs. state sovereignty. State sovereignty is circumscribed by peoples' self-determination in democracies. Interestingly, this tension between human rights and democratic self-determination comes to the fore when we consider the significant difference between admission to the territory of a nation-state and admission to full membership. We see that admission rules have become more restrictive in OECD countries over the past decades for unwanted categories such as asylum seekers, and have generally been eased for the more welcome highly skilled professionals in certain sectors. When it comes to access to full membership, however, the tension is not as starkly visible, in part because immigrants who have achieved permanent residence tend to enjoy a relatively high degree of civil and social rights, i.e. rights associated with *denizenship*; whereas it is political and cultural rights that are at stake when naturalization is discussed. The importance of dual citizenship lies in part in its function as an alternative to extending significant political rights to *denizens*. What is noteworthy here is that the paradox, however defined, is much more muted in the case of membership than in the case of admission.

Perspectives on Citizenship: National, Postnational, and Transnational

While terms such as 'transnational citizenship' (Bauböck 1994b) and 'postnational membership' (Soysal 1994) have animated discussions on citizenship and immigration, dual citizenship – oddly enough – has rarely been theorized systematically along these lines. Political theory has been mostly bound to the model of national communities. And if it was theorized beyond normative and nation-bound considerations, dual citizenship has either been seen through the lens of comparative national models (Aleinikoff and Klusmeyer 2001), or as a transitory stage towards more postnational forms of membership in political communities (*cf.* Bosniak 2002). Within these frameworks dual citizenship is still conceptualized in terms exclusively relating to national political communities, or at most as some sort of citizenship beyond borders. It is essential, however, to disaggregate the obfuscated notion of postnational citizenship, which apparently refers to two developments that are analytically distinct. One line of postnational thinking refers to an alleged decline in state sovereignty (Jacobson 1995), another one to the rise of transnational personhood and subjecthood and thus of transnational individual political actors. In order to avoid confusion, the first line of thinking is called here postnational in the true sense of the word, the second transnational. It is thus useful to extend the national perspective and include a transnational perspective which casts dual citizenship as overlapping and simultaneous membership of citizens across states.

Rather than speaking of national, transnational, postnational, or even global citizenship as if these were actual phenomena existing 'out there' and capable of being observed, we use these associated concepts as lenses through which to view the development of political conflicts surrounding dual citizenship. In the national, and more traditional, perspective the question of dual citizenship is predominantly defined as a problem pertaining to individual states and immigrant integration, while from the postnational and the transnational perspective, dual citizenship is characterized as also including transborder forms of state-citizen relations. From a postnational point of view citizenship is related to rights and democratic norms beyond the national state, which originate in international conventions. From a transnational point of view dual citizenship is discussed in relation to the sometimes cross-border life-worlds of citizens and the attempts by governments to regulate these social formations. Each of these somewhat stylized notions place a different emphasis on aspects such as membership, legal status, the rights and duties of citizens, and the bedrock of modern political order – democracy.

The National Perspective: Dual Citizenship as a Mechanism of Immigrant Integration

In an anomalous way, citizens living abroad belong to territorially and inter-generationally bounded political communities. It is no coincidence that many countries are usually more tolerant of the multiple memberships of their own citizens living abroad than they are for immigrant newcomers on their territory. From the national perspective there may also be plausible reasons for tolerating or even accepting dual citizenship for immigrants. The most persuasive is that dual citizenship increases the propensity among immigrants to naturalize in the country of settlement. In other words, dual citizenship may actually encourage immigrants to naturalize, and naturalization is likely to facilitate – as well as reflect – the integration of newcomers (*cf.* Schuck 1998, 164). Empirical surveys suggest that immigrants prefer maintaining their old citizenship when naturalizing in another country (e.g. Chavez 1997, 131; Groenendijk 1999).

The Transnational Perspective: Overlapping Social and Political Ties

In an age of globalization, the locus of eventual integration is an open question: Whether immigrants and minorities eventually integrate within immigration countries, or whether other realms of integration such as diaspora communities should also be considered, can be determined only by exacting empirical analysis (*cf.* Faist and Özveren 2004). The national perspective on dual citizenship does not take into account the importance of transnational ties of citizens and the resources inherent in relationships of reciprocity and solidarity. Examples abound: Chinese entrepreneurs have long been known to rely on *guanxi* – friendship-communal – networks to integrate economically in a great variety of countries all over the globe (Ong 1997). Similarly, in the political sphere, Irish-Americans, Polish-Americans, and Jewish-Americans have supported national projects in their ancestral homelands, support that often crosses into fourth and fifth generations following settlement. What is even more obvious in a transnational perspective is the engagement of emigration country governments to control their expatriates abroad, or at least to maintain ties when these persons naturalize in a country of immigration.

A transnational perspective captures a range of possibilities. First, it could be that immigrants or emigrants and their associations engage in transnational political behaviour, and try to impact on dual citizenship legislation or engage in transnational citizenship practices. Second, governments of countries of origin are interested in encouraging emigrants or expatriates to retain a link with the home country; similarly, governments of immigration countries acknowledge border-crossing ties of their expatriates living abroad. Third, immigration countries may place importance on the ties immigrants sustain with their countries of origin.

Little is known about the activities of emigrants and immigrants on the matter of dual citizenship, or about their transnational political behaviour. For example, it is not clear to what extent migrant transnational ties and dual citizenship are congruent. It may be safe to assume that migrant transnationalism is fostered by dual citizenship. In earlier work I have suggested that dual citizenship could be conceived of as the political foundation of the transnational experience, enabling transnational migrants and their children to lead multiple lives across borders (Faist 2000, chapter 7). But two caveats are in order. First, it is plausible to assume that not all dual citizens are transnationals. Consider, for example, immigrants who desire to transfer their fundamental loyalty to the country of naturalization. They may be hindered in doing so because their country of origin does not release them from citizenship. Then there are those who retain a second citizenship in a purely passive sense, for example, children of dual citizens living abroad. Second, not all transnationals are dual citizens. Not all transnationals even have legal status in the country of settlement – for example, undocumented migrants.

In contrast, somewhat more is known about state actors, especially those in emigration countries. In what would be a case of state-led transnationalism, emigration countries may accommodate the wishes of emigrants or try to maintain links for economic reasons, such as a continued flow of remittances or investments by emigrants. Political motives may also play a major role, such as building or maintaining a lobby group abroad, or otherwise attempting to exert control over emigrants. In some cases the tolerance of dual citizenship for emigrants applies only to emigration country citizens but not to immigrants or national minorities within these countries: thus we can speak of differentialist transnationalism, which is not only state-led but also has ethno-national characteristics. Authorities in immigration countries may in some cases guard against unwanted migration by their own national minorities living abroad. In the German-Polish case, for example, dual passports of German minorities in Poland's Silesia serve as insurance to exit and thus actual return to Germany.

Third, a transnational perspective offers a way of seeing dual citizenship as an extension of multicultural policy. In immigration countries naturalization policy could qualify as a multicultural cum transnational policy where it has been modified in order to accommodate immigrant individual and collective identities, including the maintaining of links with their country of origin (Gustafson 2005). This might be called multicultural transnationalism, a framework that implies equal treatment of one's own citizens abroad as well as immigrants at home.

All of this suggests that relatively dense and continuous interstitial ties of citizens are not located beyond states but in fact cross state borders. A transnational perspective also implies that dual citizenship is not a separate form of membership in political communities such as national citizenship in sovereign states or supranational citizenship in multi-level governance systems. Rather, dual citizenship is essentially a form of political membership complementing national membership within states interested in maintaining and/or tolerating citizens' transnational social and symbolic ties for instrumental purposes.

The Postnational Perspective: Dual Citizenship as a Transitory Phenomenon

The postnational perspective comes in at least two variants: postnational membership and supranational citizenship. Postnational membership focuses on the impact of interstate norms upon the rights of persons in states. Supranational citizenship raises questions about the rights of citizens in multi-level governance systems such as the European Union (EU). Overall, some authors in the postnational vein even go so far as to suggest that the nation-state has lost its ability to 'cage' (Mann 1993, 61), that is, to frame and govern, to control its borders, to regulate its economy, and to maintain a unified national citizenship. Yet most authors using the term seem to refer not to the dissolution of the nation-state system but to a development in which national forms of membership have simply lost their assumed predominance.

Postnational Membership   The key idea is that two of the three main components of citizenship – in the postnational membership concept, simply rights and duties and collective identity – have gradually decoupled over the past decades. Thus, for example, human rights, once tightly connected to citizenship, have come to apply equally to non-citizen residents. This means that settled non-citizens also have access to significant human, civil, and social rights. Therefore, citizenship as a 'right to have rights' (Arendt 1949, 166) is no longer the fundamental basis for membership in political communities. Instead, the discourses of interstate norms, such as those found in the various charters on fundamental rights under the auspices of the United Nations (UN) and the European Union (EU), are presumed to contribute to postnational membership (Soysal 1994). This perspective, however, does not take account of the democratically legitimated part of citizenship status and the importance of affective ties to and within states, i.e. the first dimension of citizenship discussed earlier. It is thus no coincidence that analysts speak of postnational *membership* instead of *citizenship*. The principle of democratic legitimation of membership in political communities, of utmost importance for any democratic regime, gets lost. Instead, the focus is on courts upholding international norms, that is, 'rights across borders' (Jacobson 1995). The very basis of equal political liberty is neglected by the postnational membership concept.

Supranational Citizenship   This concept refers primarily to citizenship in the political multi-level system constituted by the European Union (EU). At first sight, supranational citizenship appears to be the logical next step in the centuries-old evolution of citizenship in what are today termed liberal democracies. It is a current process much like the one by which sovereign states have gradually centralized and assimilated local and regional forms of citizenship over the past centuries. During the last several decades, this process has developed under propitious political-economic conditions, such as continued prosperity and the absence of war, and under the umbrella of a sort of proto-federal system, the EU. The formidable obstacles on the road to substantive EU citizenship include the acceptance of democratic majority decisions, and the resources necessary for the integration of political communities, such as trust and solidarity. European Union citizenship, as it has developed since the Treaty of Maastricht (1991), is not coterminous with dual citizenship, overlapping several sovereign states. Rather, Union citizenship is nested on several governance levels – regional, state, and supranational. Only citizens of a member state are citizens of the Union. Although only a few entitlements such as participation in elections to the European Parliament are tied to Union citizenship, there are the rudimentary signs of a European consciousness, necessary to the evolution of a collective political identity on the EU level (Faist 2001). Yet, in such a supranational perspective dual citizenship is ultimately of secondary importance only.

Nonetheless, the postnational perspective is analytically useful when separated from a simple claim of declining state sovereignty over membership. After all, there is no other kind of institution that has interposed itself between citizen and state, granting formal membership. In a more nuanced way the growth of tolerance of dual citizenship reflects a reality that the claims of states over individual citizens are less absolute than they once were. Citizens, for their part, are less rigidly tied to particular states both psychologically in terms of their felt affiliations and legally in terms of the weight placed on individual rights in determining citizenship.

In sum, to capture the truly seminal development of contested dual citizenship we need to expand our conceptual horizon and go beyond nationally-bounded political systems to include a postnational and a transnational perspective. This is one way to counter 'methodological nationalism' (Herminio Martin in 1974 quoted by Smith 1979, 191) in comparative political studies which has unduly privileged the idea that national systems could be conceived of as tightly bounded political containers. To take the charge against 'methodological nationalism' seriously means to look at how citizenship within nation-states has accounted for border-crossing ties of citizens and permanent residents and to study the intersection of ties within nationally-bounded citizenship, a case of 'internal globalization' (Faist 1995). National, transnational, and postnational perspectives are all necessary to give a satisfactory account of the development and consequences of dual citizenship in the context of immigrant policies and political incorporation. Each perspective is useful for explaining different parts of the puzzle: the postnational perspective on the extension of personhood rights vis-à-vis states highlights the gradual extension of citizenship as a human right in international law; the transnational perspective is a reflection of citizens', *denizens'*, and aliens' cross-border life-worlds and the attempts of states to control them; and the national perspective on political incorporation is helpful in accounting for variations in the tolerance of dual citizenship across national states. From all three perspectives the evidence seems to point in the same direction: in legal cases and legislation, the rights of citizens and persons have gained in importance vis-à-vis considerations of state sovereignty. Equally important, a view sensitive to methodological nationalism brings in not only perspectives beyond the nation-state but also those from below. For example, these perspectives would highlight the case of indigenous peoples who may not only be viewed as 'margizens', that is, deprived of certain rights *de facto* and *de jure* but, in multinational states such as Canada, also bearers of multicultural rights, such as partial political self-government. This would make indigenous peoples ideal cases for the analysis of dual citizenship within one state (Carens 2000, chapter 8).

A Framework for Empirical Analysis (1): The Comparative Perspective

The country-specific analyses are thus set within an overall framework which considers both inter- and supranational developments of norm-making, and takes into account the evolution of a transnational subject as well as the efforts of states to rein in such evolutions. Dual citizenship is part of a trend of porous boundaries of national citizenship in liberal democracies (Weil 2001, 34) and in emigration countries. Nonetheless, there are significant variations in the trend towards tolerance of dual citizenship: the case studies on Germany, the Netherlands, Sweden, Turkey, and Poland serve to explore these variations (on the USA, the UK, and France, see Kivisto and Faist 2006, chapter 5). The comparative framework comes close to what can be called 'disciplined' configurative inquiry (Verba 1967). Here, configurations are sets of factors belonging to the institutional context, such as the party system and the legal system, and to the discursive realm, such as the understanding of nationhood and immigrant integration, and including, above all, concepts of societal integration.

There are two ways of classifying the stance taken on dual citizenship. The first is to look at states' *de jure* tolerance of vs. restriction on dual citizenship. The second is to analyze the *de facto* behaviour of states. As mentioned above, dual citizenship arises when children are born in countries where the *jus soli* principle holds, while the countries of their parents' origin apply the *jus sanguinis* principle. *De facto* tolerance may also be present when states are indifferent to dual citizenship for various reasons. For example, the 'oath of allegiance' notwithstanding, the United States does not require written evidence that immigrants have actually renounced a previous citizenship (*cf.* Bloemraad 2004). Other countries, such as the United Kingdom, do not bother to regulate dual citizenship (Hansen 2002). Here, the analysis focuses on the *de jure* dimension. The comparative analysis of the immigration countries includes Germany, the Netherlands, and Sweden. These three countries have varying policies on the acceptance of dual citizenship and can be classified accordingly on a continuous scale ranging from *restrictive* to *tolerant* and, finally, *open*. The most restrictive cases are characterized by the following criteria:

1. Assignment by birth: only one citizenship possible;
2. Obligation to choose one citizenship on reaching maturity;
3. Renunciation requirement (in some cases also proof required) upon naturalization in another country; and
4. Forced expatriation upon naturalization in another country.

The more strictly the acquisition of a citizenship is governed by principles (1) to (4), the more restrictive the regime – and conversely, the more lenient the procedure, or the more exemptions there are from these requirements, the more open the regime in question is to dual citizenship. The most important form of *de jure* tolerance in this respect is the abolishment of the renunciation requirement in the naturalization process, and the option principle in birthright citizenship. By selecting for analysis those cases falling along a broad spectrum ranging from tolerance at one end to intolerance at the other avoids the problem of 'selecting on the dependant variable', i.e. choosing cases where a phenomenon of interest has occurred while ignoring the instances where it has not taken place. Instead, the cases selected for this empirical analysis cover the whole range of *de jure* tolerance.

The thrust of the comparison with the German linchpin case is, first, on the Netherlands and Sweden, because both these countries are immigration countries. Second, Poland and Turkey are included to allow a better understanding of their respective initiatives in regard to the large number of citizens living abroad and their reactions to changes in legislation, especially in Germany. In order to allow for systematic comparison along these two lines, the analyses of all countries studied – Germany (Gerdes, Rieple and Faist), Sweden (Spång), the Netherlands (de Hart), Poland (Górny, Grzymała-Kazłowska, Koryś and Weinar), and Turkey (Kadirbeyoğlu) – largely replicate the conceptual and empirical approach sketched here (see Figures 1.2 and 1.3).

In all immigration countries the boundaries of dual citizenship have been changing since the early 1980s and 1990s. In Germany, the legislation that eased access for the children of immigrants in introducing *jus soli*, was also, *de jure*, still very restrictive concerning dual citizenship. Of the three immigration countries, Germany is the most restrictive *de jure* concerning dual citizenship, the Netherlands

Figure 1.2   Access to Citizenship in Germany, Sweden and The Netherlands (after 2000)

	Germany	Sweden	The Netherlands
As-of-right naturalization	After 8 years of residence. *Conditions attached:* • no welfare dependence; • language test: evidence of sufficient knowledge of German.	As-of-right after 5 years of residence. *Conditions attached:* • 5 years for citizens from non-Nordic countries; • 2 years for citizens from Nordic countries.	As-of-right after 5 years of lawful residence. *Conditions attached:* • ability to conduct a simple conversation in Dutch was deemed sufficient (until recently); • criterion of 'being incorporated' did not play any role in practice; • since 2003: language proficiency and citizenship courses required.
Second and subsequent generations	• *Jus sanguinis*; *jus soli*, provided that one parent has lived for eight years in Germany or holds a permanent residence permit for at least three years (since 2000); • also: educated in Germany for 8 years for second generation (since 1991).	• *Jus sanguinis*, coupled with socialization principle for those born or raised in Sweden.	• *Jus sanguinis* and limited form of *jus soli*: option right (since 1984); • foreign children born in the Netherlands have an 'option right': they can acquire Dutch citizenship by unilateral declaration between the ages of 18 and 25.
Dual citizenship	• Accepted for ethnic Germans; • and in specific circumstances, such as economic loss involved or when country of origin does not allow expatriation; • 'optional principle': if the child obtains the parents' nationalities, it must give up either the non-German or German citizenship before reaching the age of 23.	• Dual citizenship explicitly allowed since 2001; • no requirement to renounce former citizenship; • before 2001, the rules were as restrictive as in Germany.	• Dual citizenship allowed as a rule (1991-1997); • since then a wide range of exceptions; • further restrictions (2003); • now easier for Dutch emigrants to retain Dutch citizenship and hold dual citizenship.

more tolerant, and Sweden – since 2001 – definitely the most liberal. Although the recent extension of the *jus soli* clause in Germany's citizenship legislation is somewhat more generous compared to countries like France but also Sweden and the Netherlands, the principle of avoiding dual citizenship is *de jure* adhered to strictly. The individuals in question must, by the end of their twenty-third year, opt for one or the other citizenship, or else be deprived of their German citizenship. As previously, in the case of naturalization – apart from the special case of late repatriates of

Figure 1.3   Access to Citizenship in Turkey and Poland (after 2000)

	Turkey	Poland
As-of-right naturalization	After 5 years of residence. *Conditions attached:* • individual should be an adult; • intention to settle in Turkey; • speaking enough Turkish; • good moral conduct; • causing no serious danger to public health; • having a profession that could provide for her and dependents' livelihood. *Exceptions:* • individuals married to Turkish citizens can naturalize after 3 years of marriage if they fulfil the criteria; • those who lose their citizenship due to marriage automatically become citizens.	1. After 5 years of residence (on the basis of permanent residence permit). *Conditions attached:* • no additional formal conditions attached, but the law-makers use the form 'the citizenship can be granted'; • there are some subjective criteria used like financial situation, criminal record and attachments to Poland. *Comment:* • for stateless persons the above has, in fact, a form of as-of-right procedure; • for others, the procedure is rather discretional. For stateless persons it is municipal authority that decides; • for others it is the president of Poland. It is important because the president does not have an obligation to explain his decisions. 2. Being married to a Polish citizen for 3.5 years.
Second and subsequent generations	• *Jus sanguinis* (those who have a Turkish mother or father are Turkish citizens whether they are born within Turkey or outside); • complemented by *jus soli* (those who cannot get the citizenship of their parents become Turkish citizens if they are born in Turkey).	• *Jus sanguinis, jus soli* only in the exceptional case of foundlings; • child of at least 1 Polish citizen has the right to Polish citizenship; • in the case of one Polish and one foreign parent, parents can choose foreign citizenship for their child (within 3 months from its birth), then the child at the age of 16-18.5 can still decide for Polish citizenship by submitting an appropriate state of will to the local authority.
Dual Citizenship	• Dual citizenship allowed, provided the council of ministers agrees; • persons who are disloyal to the state can be deprived of Turkish citizenship (1981); • disloyalty clause abolished because of incompatibility with human rights (1992); • introduction of 'pink card' as a response to countries which do not allow dual citizenship as a rule (1995).	• A Polish citizen cannot be a national of another state (laws of 1920 and 1962); • wide margin of interpretation: a. general prohibition of dual citizenship; or b. only Polish citizenship counts on Polish territory; • bills to liberalize existing law (1999-2000) but not passed in parliament; Poles returning from territories of the former USSR may keep former citizenship in Poland; proposal for special status of expatriates (Polish Charter).

German origin (so-called ethnic Germans or *Spätaussiedler*) – the relinquishment of the other citizenship is generally required. Nevertheless, several exceptions apply for immigrants, for example, when there are overriding constitutional grounds, or if there are no provisions for the relinquishment of the citizenship of the other country in question, or if it is refused or obstructed. Moreover, German citizens abroad have been allowed to keep German citizenship upon naturalizing in another country if they can show family ties to Germany. The Netherlands has been, overall, somewhat more tolerant. Briefly during the early 1990s, dual citizenship was tolerated without exception on naturalization, but relinquishment of the prior citizenship is now once again generally mandatory since 1997. By comparison with Germany, however, there are much more extensive exemption clauses in other countries. In Sweden, for example, legislative reform has been completed and dual citizenship is now accepted in general. Sweden previously belonged to the restrictive category and demanded the relinquishment of the previous citizenship.

Much of the research on citizenship has so far focused almost exclusively on immigration countries. To include major emigration countries not only has the benefit of providing insight into the interactive nature of citizenship acquisition – citizenship is the prerogative of each sovereign state – but also has value in two other ways. First, the political systems in many of the major emigration countries may be somewhat different from liberal democracies in Western Europe. In Turkey, for example, veto powers such as that enjoyed by the military have played a significant role in government in the late twentieth century. It is therefore of interest to ask about the stratification of rights towards membership; e.g. are emigrants treated the same way as immigrants? Second, although one may describe the international system of states as anarchic and thus not bound by tight formal rules of exchange regarding citizenship, it is also an asymmetrical power structure, in which some immigration countries may have significant indirect leverage over the dual citizenship practice of emigration countries, e.g. in not demanding the renunciation of the previous citizenship if the sending state does not allow for it.

In order to incorporate the views of major countries with emigration flows, Turkey and Poland are examined more closely.[9] These emigration countries are among the most important source countries for Germany. Turkey can be positioned at the more liberal end of the *de jure* tolerance spectrum, because it accepts dual citizenship and has made legal provisions for such cases. In the early 1980s, the Turkish government passed a law that guaranteed Turkish-born emigrants who have acquired the citizenship of the state in which they reside equality with Turkish citizens on a number of issues such as pensions and property questions. Since the mid-1990s Turkish citizens who naturalize in Germany can hold a 'pink card', which allows for rights equivalent to those held by full Turkish citizens, except the right to vote in Turkish elections. Poland is of particular relevance to Germany because it has not allowed dual citizenship in principle *de jure* but has interpreted it in a

---

9   It is clear that Turkey and Poland are not simply emigration countries but have experienced sizeable immigration flows over the past decade (*cf.* SOPEMI reports throughout the 1990s). For the purpose of this analysis they are still called emigration countries because they have been characterized by relatively large emigration flows. Nonetheless, the issue of tolerance of dual citizenship concerning immigrants in these countries is also considered.

tolerant manner for both Polish migrants abroad and the German national minority in Poland, thus allowing a selectively *de facto* tolerance of dual citizenship held by emigrants and privileged minorities. And Germany accepts dual citizenship in the case of ethnic Germans from Poland.

One caveat must be considered from the outset. The focus on *de jure* regulations might obscure significant *de facto* trends. It should not be forgotten that even in the relatively more restrictive cases, such as Germany, the reality of the law may have been more tolerant than the letter. For example, there are crude estimates that between a quarter and a third of all those naturalized in Germany in the 1970s and 1980s – apart from ethnic Germans – retained their former citizenship and thus were dual citizens. In 2000, more than 40 per cent of all naturalizations in Germany occurred with maintenance of the original citizenship (*cf.* Netzwerk Migration in Europa 2001:1, 2). For its part, Poland has rejected dual citizenship among its emigrants *de jure* but has consented to it *de facto*. The obvious question resulting from such observations is whether *de facto* tolerance of dual citizenship among selected categories of immigrants and emigrants is one of the endogenous factors contributing to eventual *de jure* tolerance of dual citizenship.

A Framework for Empirical Analysis (2): Institutional and Discursive Dimensions

All five case studies follow an analytical scheme consisting of the elements discussed earlier in this section, namely the importance of the belief system for societal integration, the two framing hypotheses on individual rights vs. state sovereignty, and the concept of differentialist transnationalism. Institutionally, the expectation is that growing tolerance is not primarily a product of changing relations between nation-states in a global system but the consequence of an increase in the codification of individual rights in international law, above all relating to statelessness, gender equity, and democratic congruence in the case of *denizenship* rights. While state-state relations have not been unimportant, they serve mostly as propitious enabling factors, such as supranationalization of the EU with a spread of the principle of reciprocity, and the absence of major wars between liberal democracies. The primary factors have thus been endogenous to liberal democracies. Nonetheless, in an asymmetrical world system of states, emigration countries have picked up on this trend and have also been leaning towards increased tolerance of dual citizenship. The analysis of institutional aspects – political and legal settings – is critical to understanding the political debates on dual citizenship and the way political actors have advanced arguments, embedded in broader belief systems. The legal opportunities have enabled and restricted dual citizenship within the frame of the constitution and the laws of the respective sovereign states and international law. The relevant political opportunities consist of continuous – but not necessarily formal or permanent – dimensions of the political environment that provide incentives for people to influence citizenship legislation.

Institutional Structures: Global and National

The discourses in political debates on dual citizenship are firmly embedded in distinct institutional structures, both on the global and the national level. Today, we can discern an increased tolerance of dual citizenship in comparison to the beginning of the twentieth century (Renshon 2001, 45). During this time dual citizenship presented an anomaly, a status disfavoured to the point that dual citizenship was considered immoral or even a form of 'self-evident absurdity' (Teddy Roosevelt 1915, 15 quoted by Spiro 1997). In a nutshell, the proliferation of dual citizenship is today not only a question of decision-making on the policy level, but is a widespread practice exhibiting a progressive trend. Even states that are quite restrictive in their *de jure* legislation for dual citizenship react, by and large, when confronted by *de facto* realities, in a manner that is much more tolerant of dual citizenship than might be expected. The main question that arises here is: what conditions and developments in the national and international context explain the rising tolerance of dual citizenship, starting in the 1950s and continuing unabated today? In the context of the analytical framework used in this volume, the increasing tolerance of dual citizenship is seen as a specific instance, the so-called 'rights revolution' in a path-dependant manner.

Existing explanations for the growing tolerance of dual citizenship on a global scale have identified the relationships between sovereign nation-states as the main driving factor but have not analyzed the implications for state-citizen ties. There are two main lines of thought. The first portrays nation-states, especially those with liberal-democratic regimes, as cooperating on ever increasing levels. The second view depicts the system of states as so anarchic that trends towards dual citizenship cannot be adequately regulated. The two arguments respectively can be attributed to two schools of thought in the field of international relations. The institutional cooperation argument is part of the 'liberal' school, while the argument focusing on anarchy belongs to the '(neo-)realist' school.

The institutional cooperation framework understands cooperation as the outcome of many incremental steps to overcome the security dilemma (the tendency for states to arm themselves because of mutual mistrust, which can lead in turn to further armament and to an arms race), which is sometimes captured in a rationalist way as a series of mutually reassuring games involving small steps. The basic idea is that the environment of states would be structurally insecure in an anarchic world. Therefore, state institutions have great incentives to look for avenues of cooperation to counter the ever-present danger of inter-state war and violent conflict. Ultimately, the argument is that liberal democracies are very unlikely to go to war with each other. This thought harkens back to Immanuel Kant's 'Eternal Peace' (1970), in which he suggests that democracies are political systems in which not the state itself but factions interested in peace – such as the bourgeoisie – are among the main pressure groups in foreign policy making. It could be argued that, as more and more countries become democratic and as democracies do not fight wars against each other, states become less concerned about the loyalty of citizens (*cf.* Spiro 1997), and this tendency that may be noted, for example, in the conversion of former conscript armies into professional armies. Overall, as warfare states have turned into welfare states in the liberal-democratic world, citizenship has become disentangled from the duty to serve in the armed forces. In turn, loyalty to the state is no longer directly connected to military purposes. In such a world it is less likely for liberal-democratic states to see dual citizenship as a threat to the national interest and national security, hence there is less resistance to the idea of dual citizenship. Increased state-state cooperation in emergent political systems such as the European Union (EU) is central in two respects. First, inter-state cooperation constitutes a background condition for intra-state changes in state-citizen ties in that dual citizenship can be most efficiently administered in a system of states with high levels of cooperation. Second, liberal democratic states are likely to be at the vanguard of changes in citizenship law, while most emigration states adapt their legislation to the precedents set in immigration countries.

One of the problems with this argument, however, is the optimistic and linear assumption of a growing tolerance. While it is certainly true that tolerance has increased worldwide, the argument does not address the extensive national variations. In particular, we do not learn how this macro-political context is translated into politics and laws on the nation-state level. Therefore, the argument may not be wrong but simply partial. In other words, increased international cooperation among liberal democratic states is a necessary but not a sufficient condition for increasing tolerance. Moreover, and somewhat oddly, liberalism in international relations theory is less concerned with one of the central tenets of liberal thought in political theory, namely the importance of individual rights vis-à-vis state authority. Despite its focus on domestic political actors and thus also non-state actors, it is still state-centred and therefore does not encompass the state-citizen view necessary to account for changing levels of tolerance.

According to the conceptually opposite perspective, the neo-realist interpretation of international relations, anarchy is the defining feature of the international system of states, and international politics is a struggle for state survival. Sovereign nation-states are considered unitary actors, who espouse 'differences of capability, not of function' (Waltz 1979, 15). In this academic worldview states are rational actors with a rather clear hierarchy of interests. In international law the consequence is obvious: States dominate the attribution of citizenship unilaterally and other states may not impinge on decisions to grant citizenship. In other words, citizenship is the sole prerogative of states. For example, dual citizenship arises when children are born in countries where the *jus soli* principle holds, while the countries of their parents' origin apply the *jus sanguinis* principle. In this case, the country in which children are born can hardly deny the parents' state the decision to grant citizenship to their offspring (Koslowski 2001). Yet, there are two main problems with this neo-realist interpretation. First, the confluence of the two main principles of attributing dual citizenship through birth, *jus soli* and *jus sanguinis*, accounts only partly for the rise of dual citizenship over recent decades. Moreover, it also overlooks the fact that states have agreed on international conventions enabling the transmission of the citizenship of both parents to children: an element of inter-state cooperation. Without some degree of legal gender equity, dual citizenship would also not have arisen to the extent it actually has. Second, as neo-realists readily concede, the power structure in the system of nation-states is asymmetrical. In particular, immigration states may exert pressure on emigration states to stop practices aimed at increasing the number of dual citizens in case immigration states do not foresee dual citizenship as a rule – as is the case with Germany and Turkey (see Kadirbeyoğlu, this volume, chapter 5). This contrasts with cases in which governments that do not *de jure* tolerate dual citizenship nevertheless agree on a bi-national level to grant exceptions to significant minorities, as the German and Polish governments do for ethnic Germans originating or residing in Poland (Górny, Grzymała-Kazłowska, Koryś and Weinar, this volume, chapter 6). Moreover, to an even greater extent than the liberal school of thought, the neo-realist approach does not take into account citizens' and citizenship practices as one of the driving forces of increasingly porous boundaries of citizenship.

Both the liberal and the neo-realist view can help us understand the necessary conditions for the growing tolerance of dual citizenship. But only an analysis specifying the mechanisms that have driven tolerance along path-dependant development can constitute a comprehensive account. Path-dependence here means that once citizenship laws and integration policies funnelling dual citizenship are enacted on the international and national level, the chance that this trend will continue on the national level is very high.

With respect to the debates and the legislation in the five cases on the national level, five broad sets of factors need to be considered. These factors set the stage for a more elaborate analysis of belief systems. First and foremost is the close relationship between *denizenship* and dual citizenship: The question is whether the extension of voting rights for permanent resident aliens emerged as an issue in debates, and whether dual citizenship was considered as an alternative to this strong push towards porous boundaries of citizenship. A second set of institutional factors looks at how *de facto* tolerance of dual citizenship may have led to more explicit forms of recognition, as in the Swedish case. A third set of factors concerns the major institutions in political systems, such as political parties and courts, which may have acted as the main filters and accumulators of ideas and proposals in debates. The primary proposition regarding differences and similarities between the countries is that the structure of the party system and the legal institutions has influenced whether legislation on dual citizenship becomes a matter of public debate and how legislation proceeds. For example, the more polarized the respective party system is along ideological lines and the less consensus-oriented the political style of confrontation, the higher are the chances that political issues around nation, culture, and citizenship will tend to be conflict-ridden. Thus the analyses explore the strategies of the relevant political actors during the legislative process and the politics of coalitions and alliances between the political actors concerned. Empirically, the explorations in the case studies focus on public debates, parliamentary debates, and public exchanges in the mass media. The fourth set of factors concerns other actors, in particular legal institutions. The structure of legal institutions may make a difference as to which actors define the issues and in which way. For example, the dominance of the legal profession and the role of the Federal Constitutional Court in Germany give legal experts and the judiciary a much greater role in framing and making the decisions than in a country such as Sweden, in which there is no constitutional court and in which legal experts are only one of several groups present in expert committees. Immigrant groups, with few exceptions, have had little impact on policy debates and outcomes. The fifth set of factors to be considered is state representatives, such as governments of emigration countries, and less prominently, of immigration countries, which have developed control strategies vis-à-vis their extra-territorial citizenry.

Discursive Structures

It is insufficient simply to inquire who benefits and who loses from a particular policy. In order to understand any policy debate and its outcome it is necessary to comprehend the belief systems of major political actors who contest and defend the legislative status quo. Fundamentally, there is no such thing as an 'objective' debate. The competition among belief systems in general, and between symbols and arguments based on conceptual representation more specifically, forms a crucial basis for policy decisions (Stone 1997). Even more than the institutional structure, the discursive side needs clarification because the impact of ideas on policy processes is less obvious in a traditional analytical framework.[10] Policy choices can be understood only in their broader ideological context because beliefs frame the political issues and concepts. The discursive realm concerns the belief systems and the attendant argumentative contributions to debates and decision-making. The analysis of the cases in this volume looks at the arguments advanced by relevant political actors in the respective national legislative processes relating to dual citizenship, and categorizes these arguments in the light of more general belief systems on citizenship.

Broader belief systems provide political actors functioning within them a sense of coherence, consistency, and continuity of perceiving, thinking about, and making judgments on issues. Dual citizenship legislation opens up fundamental questions about the collective identity of a 'nation', the political community, and reaches deeply into 'collective representations' (*cf.* Durkheim 1964). Such belief systems represent central presumptions about the nature of individuals, groups, and the organization of the social and political world. Belief systems consist of some primary conceptual elements which structure to a certain extent the imaginations, confessions, assumptions, programmes, policy proposals, and sometimes also the emotions of political actors. By belief system we understand existing and familiar ideas such as worldviews (*Weltanschauung*), ideologies, and systems of values and norms, which have intellectually derivable normative implications for how society should be organized (*cf.* North 1981). In a nutshell, the term 'belief system', as

---

10 Max Weber's famous dictum in his *Sociology of Religion* reads: 'Not ideas, but material and ideal interests, directly govern men's conduct. Yet very frequently the "world images" that have been created by "ideas" have, like switchmen, determined the tracks along which action has been pushed by the dynamic of interest' (Weber 1946, 280).

used here, closely corresponds to what has been aptly called an 'ordered system of symbols' (Geertz 1973, 196).[11]

The analysis looks at the clusters of arguments encountered and examines how they fit into the existing belief systems of the respective parties and organizations (*cf.* Converse 1964) in relation to various aspects of citizenship: the role of the individual in democracy, the constitution of civil society, and the role and functions of the state. The belief systems and the vocabulary used are decisive factors in facilitating or restricting the perception of certain problems, in determining how actors describe these problems and what possible solutions are assumed to exist (Pocock 1973, 25). The assumption is that the more arguments relating to dual citizenship are able to pick up the threads of existing belief systems, the more convincing they appear. The first stage of the empirical analysis of the five cases therefore examines those belief systems that relate to the underlying notion of the respective political community, in particular those relating to nationhood, i.e. ethno-cultural vs. republican concepts of nationhood, and immigrant integration, i.e. multiculturalism vs. assimilation. Because of the limits of both the tradition of nationhood and the immigrant integration perspective, the analysis drills down to even more fundamental belief systems concerning the roles of individual, civil society, and the state.

The analysis dissects belief systems on the level of arguments, which constitute important components of belief systems. Here, arguments are understood as transactions between political actors in which statements, declarations, practical proposals, objectives, evaluations, norms, or judgments regarding dual citizenship are justified. In addition to bargaining between strategically oriented actors, certain forms of arguing such as deliberation – which draws on negotiable grounds or arguments – play an important role in political decision-making processes. In liberal democratic systems, the separate roles of government and opposition, the parliamentary procedures, and the principle of open politics rule out the possibility of policies being implemented without plausible justifications. The selection of certain options must ultimately be so well presented and founded that they are justifiable to the public (van den Daele and Neidhardt 1996). Argumentative debates are one of the fundamental requirements for negotiations between political actors. Last but not least, apart from their symbolic value, arguments also constitute part of the struggle for political power in debates over political interpretations that serve to win votes. Into these negotiations, made possible by the exchange of arguments, flow strategic calculations with a view to establishing a balance of interests through compromise (*cf.* Cohen 1989).

Arguments, in contrast to non-argumentative speech acts – for example simple announcements, confessions, promises, threats, offences – imply that speakers must

---

11 There are other definitions of belief system or ideology; for example, ideologies as economizing devices by which individuals understand, and express ideas about, politics (Downs 1957) and ideologies as complex, dogmatic belief systems by which individuals interpret, rationalize, and justify behaviour and institutions (Sartori 1965). These definitions are not opposed to the one used. Instead, they emphasize different aspects of a common core: belief systems are collections of guiding ideas.

give reasons for an articulated statement, interpretation, or proposal. The formal structure of any argument can be characterized as a threefold relation: an actor (1) makes an assertive claim and (2) gives some relevant reasons (3) which are aimed to justify the claim in order to reach consent without force (*cf.* Toulmin 2003; Habermas 1981, 38). The main distinction drawn here is between pragmatic vs. principled arguments, a distinction that makes it possible to determine whether concepts of integration and citizenship are consensual or conflictual. If consensual, we expect a predominance of pragmatic arguments; if conflictual, we hypothesize that the debates are characterized by principled arguments. Pragmatic arguments relate to the choice of adequate means, instruments, strategies, and methods to achieve ends or to uphold values, which are considered desirable and uncontroversial. Principled arguments relate to those ends and goals that are taken for granted in pragmatic arguments, hence making the debate about ends explicit. Principled arguments can be differentiated into two dimensions. The first encompasses those arguments that are moral in the sense of the Kantian 'Categorical Imperative': persons should not be treated only as means for other ends, but always as ends in themselves as well.[12] If statements and justifications are related to the integrity and identity of persons and their basic rights, then they are moral arguments (*cf.* Dworkin 1978). The second dimension of principled arguments is expressive. Expressive arguments refer to a shared end among members of a given political community, for example, ideas about social justice in a particular welfare state. It is only to be expected that individuals develop their sense of identity and solidarity within concrete groups.[13]

In sum, arguments and belief systems are intricately related. It is not sufficient to examine only the claims made and the evidence brought forward to sustain these claims in the form of arguments. We must also look at the premises and preconditions that make these claims and arguments meaningful. Belief systems constitute 'warrants' which back arguments (*cf.* Toulmin 2003).

From Nationhood and Immigrant Integration to Societal Integration

We began our empirical research with two conceptual approaches: the tradition of nationhood and the immigrant integration approach. Both sets of literatures are concerned with the inclusion and exclusion of newcomers and deal with the changing boundaries between those 'in' and those 'out'. Both approaches entail clear positions as to which kind of dominant belief system is most conducive to the tolerance of dual citizenship. First, the tradition of nationhood approach distinguishes a civic-republican from an ethno-national concept, and suggests that the individual choice-

---

12 Also, instrumental arguments do not imply that persons are treated as means. For example, the Swedish debate on dual citizenship was characterized by a high degree of pragmatic argumentation. This was based on a high degree of consensus on political-moral goals such as equal political rights.

13 For a more fine-grained distinction between types of arguments, see Gerdes, Rieple and Faist, this volume, chapter 2.

oriented republican idea is more responsive to dual citizenship of immigrants than the ethnic concept. Second, the immigrant integration approach, in essence, identifies two fundamental modes of the incorporation of newcomers, multiculturalism and assimilationism. The proposition to be derived is that the cases characterized by a multicultural approach – and thus a predominance of cultural pluralist policies – are more amenable to dual citizenship than assimilationist ones.

Traditions of Nationhood

Following Brubaker (1992), many studies have claimed a close relationship between the understanding of nationhood and citizenship. Brubaker's central claim is that modern states are membership organizations based on distinct nations. Citizenship serves as a central marker of nation-state membership and a means of regulating inclusion and exclusion of (non-)members. The respective policies are shaped by particular and deeply rooted understandings of nationhood. Since 'judgments of what is in the interest of the state are mediated by self-understandings, by cultural idioms, by ways of thinking and talking about nationhood', national traditions dictate the course of immigration and citizenship policymaking. Drawing on his case studies of France and Germany, Brubaker distinguishes state-centred civic models, which encourage assimilation, from ethno-cultural differentialist forms, which engender 'an interest in exclusion' (Brubaker 1992, 15). France's alleged success in assimilating successive waves of immigrants is attributed to its republican national tradition, while Germany's exclusion of millions of former guest-workers is deemed a consequence of its differentialist ethno-cultural tradition. Each state's membership politics thus continues along familiar trajectories, laid down during formative periods of state formation in the eighteenth and nineteenth centuries. Concerning dual citizenship, we would conclude that a republican understanding of nation will lead to more inclusive measures of immigrant integration while a more ethnically and culturally defined concept of nation will tend to be much more exclusive regarding immigrants and more inclusive towards emigrants, a proposition that is not necessarily applicable to national minorities (*cf.* Bauböck forthcoming). In other words, according to this view, a republican understanding of citizenship is more amenable or at the very least indifferent to liberal naturalization policies in general and dual citizenship for immigrants in particular; whereas an ethno-cultural or ethno-national understanding of nationhood is not conducive to dual citizenship for immigrants, and favours this status only for its emigrants.

The studies in this volume use these dichotomous categories to describe and capture policy orientations of both immigration and emigration countries. For example, Turkey and Poland, in varying ways, tolerate dual citizenship for emigrants living abroad but have no provisions allowing for dual citizenship of immigrants or national minorities within their borders. This is clearly an ethno-nationalist orientation because tolerance extends only to co-ethnics, i.e. persons born in Turkey or Poland (Kadırbeyoğlu this volume, chapter

5; Górny, Grzymała-Kazłowska, Koryś and Weinar this volume, chapter 6). Similar tendencies can be observed in the Netherlands since the late 1990s where policy proposals aim at alleviating the retention of Dutch citizenship for Dutch citizens living abroad while for immigrants the renunciation requirement is to be strengthened (de Hart this volume, chapter 3). Germany, however, usually categorized as ethno-cultural, does not allow dual citizenship for German citizens living abroad.

The republican vs. ethno-cultural dichotomy is too narrow or even misleading with respect to the case of immigrants for at least two reasons. First, while the typology seems to speak to two ideal-typical cases – France and Germany – it does not capture the variations of citizenship elsewhere in Europe, which cannot be mapped along the dichotomy of a republican *Staatsnation* versus an ethno-national *Kulturnation*. Indeed, in mapping in a comparative fashion the diverse paths to citizenship formation, rules, and practices we find that there is substantial diversity among the polities (Cesarani and Fulbrook 1996; Janowski 1998). The examples of the Netherlands and Sweden are particularly instructive in this regard. The Netherlands has only recently espoused a sense of explicit Dutch nationhood in public debates on immigration, using elements from both strands. In the past, expectations towards social conformity have been more important (de Hart this volume, chapter 3). Sweden can best be characterized as having a socio-political understanding of nationhood, based on inclusion into the social-democratic welfare state (Spång this volume, chapter 4). This form of nationhood falls neither into the civic nor the ethnic category. Second, it is quite debatable whether strong ethno-cultural elements are a decisive element in modern expressions of nationhood in liberal democracies of Western Europe. Here, the German case is crucial. Arguments in this vein also face difficulties accounting for change. With regard to Germany, the introduction of *jus soli* is a radical departure from an allegedly ethnic understanding of nationhood, and marks a decisive move towards a more civic-republican conception of membership. It is impossible to explain changes in conceptions of nationhood by reference to their enduring character.

Immigrant Integration

While the approaches discussed above link citizenship to nationhood, there are others that link access to citizenship to the model of immigrant integration pursued by nation-states. Although the tradition of nationhood approach is closely associated with the immigrant integration approach (*cf.* Miller and Castles 2003, 43-7), the two are distinct. The former focuses analytically on the macro-level context of the 'nation'; the latter emphasizes the integration of the 'individual' immigrant into the national political community. At least two models of immigrant integration can be distinguished: multiculturalist and assimilationist.[14] Multicultural policies are based

---

14 Castles and Miller distinguish five models: imperial, folk or ethnic model, republican, multicultural, transnational (Castles and Miller 2003, 44-5). However, this fine-grained and valuable distinction does not fundamentally challenge our expectations regarding the ceteris

on the assumption that the ability to uphold one's own cultural traditions, language, and religion is crucial to personal identity and self-confidence and therefore a precondition for successful economic, social, cultural, and political integration. Multicultural policies include various forms of public support for immigrant organizations and their cultural practices, the provision of immigrant language instruction in schools, and rights concerning their religious freedom and practices. Assimilationist policies, by contrast, aim towards the melting of immigrants into the majority core or other groups of an immigrant society. According to this view, in order to foster the integration of immigrants into the mainstream, no special provisions for immigrants should be made available in the political or cultural realm. The expectation would be the following, ceteris paribus: The more actively an immigration state pursues the integration of immigrants into a political community along political-cultural pluralist lines, through, for example, multicultural policies favouring equality of immigrants as individuals or groups or even special policies, the better the chances for the political tolerance of dual citizenship. By contrast, the more that state policies are geared towards assimilation, i.e. aimed at melting immigrants into the 'majority core' or distinct established groups in immigration societies, the fewer opportunities there are for actors to push dual citizenship onto the political agenda. In other words, immigration states with a more multicultural outlook are more accommodating of dual citizenship than those with a strict assimilationist model. We would expect that states espousing strong multicultural tendencies are more tolerant of dual citizenship than assimilationist ones because the former could interpret multiple citizenship as a central prerequisite for accommodating potential transnational ties of new citizens while the latter would see it as a matter of 'divided loyalties' and attachment. Again, as in the case of the nationhood dichotomy, this hunch is partly born out by the fact that, at least at first sight, 'multicultural' Sweden has been more accommodating to dual citizenship than the more 'assimilationist' Germany. Yet the distinction between multiculturalist and assimilationist models presupposes a one-to-one connection between multiculturalism and civic concepts of nationhood on the one hand, and assimilationism and the ethnic tradition of nationhood on the other hand. A quick glance at the French experience indicates that a civic-assimilationist combination is possible. France can be found in the camp of those countries that tolerate dual citizenship rather reluctantly (*cf.* de la Pradelle 2002). Moreover, multiculturalism of a more exclusionary kind goes along with a more ethno-cultural model, as is evidenced by the German experience during the 1960s. Indeed, along similar lines, efforts have been undertaken to combine the two typologies to allow for mixed combinations among the integration regimes (Koopmans and Statham 2000): e.g. republican-assimilationist (civic republicanism, e.g. France), republican-multicultural (civic pluralism, e.g. Australia), ethnic-assimilationist (ethnic assimilationism, e.g. Austria), and ethnic-multicultural (ethnic

---

paribus outcomes: The more multiculturalist models – imperial, multicultural and transnational – are more likely to tolerate dual citizenship than the assimilationist model – the folk or ethnic model.

segregationism, e.g. Switzerland). This approach brings in the dimension of 'cultural rights' in the broader sense. For example, it captures the fact that naturalization in civic republicanist France may be more tolerant than in any of the two ethnic models but that, at the same time, acquisition of citizenship is tied to assimilation to a unitary national political culture.

Overall, the tradition of nationhood and immigrant integration frameworks have both displayed characteristic strengths and weaknesses, leading to the development of a more comprehensive approach aimed at capturing the impact of ideas and beliefs on the process of dual citizenship politics. It is certainly one of the strengths of the nationhood concept that it deals with the integration of society as a whole. Yet, it unduly prioritizes only the third dimension of citizenship, namely affiliation to a political community, and is silent on the role of the individual and civil society, and citizenship practices. The immigrant integration approach speaks to citizenship and integration in very precise terms and rests upon solid sociological foundations, dating back to the pioneering work of the Chicago School of Sociology. However, the focus is mainly on the integration of individual immigrants (at least in classical assimilation theory: Gordon 1964). Groups and civil society, not to mention aggregate and abstract concepts such as the state, are not included in this framework (*cf.* Shibutani and Kwan 1965). Even in newer versions of assimilation theory, political integration definitely takes a secondary role vis-à-vis cognitive integration (e.g. language acquisition) and structural integration (e.g. insertion into labour markets). These two silences can be addressed by looking comprehensively at integration and the respective belief systems.[15]

Societal Integration

Citizenship is a functional prerequisite for political integration and reflects the state of societal integration. A comprehensive approach to citizenship's importance for political and social integration therefore has to include arguments and beliefs concerning all three elements of integration: persons, civil society, and the state. An integration approach addresses (1) the individual rights of aliens, *denizens*, and citizens; (2) the foundations of trust and reciprocity as resources necessary for citizenship but which cannot be provided by individuals on their own nor by the state, and (3) the functions of the democratic state, such as security, legitimation, and welfare. Two dimensions of integration need to be distinguished: systems integration and social integration (Lockwood 1964; *cf.* Münch 2001). First, systems integration

---

15 Only implicitly, nevertheless, could one derive an equal rights position regarding citizenship – the second dimension of citizenship. Assimilation theory, for example, touches upon the issue of *de facto* parity between immigrants and natives. And multicultural theorists claim that there is no one-size-fits-all approach on a *de jure* level because allegedly universal policies may actually disadvantage minority groups and their members. Therefore, it is not too far fetched to speak of a selective affinity between the immigrant integration approach towards parity and the citizenship concept on equal rights.

refers to the interdependence of parts of a state or a society, that is, the interdependence of parts forming a whole. Systems integration depends on functionally differentiated societies, with specified systems like economy, law, science, education, the media, arts and literature, religion, or – of utmost importance here – polity. Functionally differentiated sub-systems, such as the economy, the polity, and the rule of law, are characterized by generalized media – in these cases money, power, and law (*cf.* Parsons and Smelser 1956). Democratically legitimated power is the main medium of liberal polities and serves as a means of systemic integration (*cf.* Luhmann 1988). The opposite of this state of affairs is described as disintegration, anomie, or decoupling of social systems. Indeed, fierce adherents to a national unity approach based on a civic-republican perspective have described overlapping ties in dual citizenship as a sign of disintegration (Huntington 2004, chapter 8). Second, social integration refers to the extent and intensity of the interlinkages among the constituent parts of a social unit, be it a family or a state. Where boundaries are concerned, social integration relates to the entry of actors into a system. Overall, social integration's normative thrust reinforces the notion of the parity of life chances of immigrants with the majority, and thus logically, equal rights and equal opportunities for participation.

A societal integration approach foregrounds the basic and always contested questions about the role and functions of individual persons, civil society, and the state. With respect to the function and role of the individual, there could be various interpretations which constitute ideals. For example, a position privileging equal rights for all residents (rights) could be opposed to an approach emphasizing the contributions of individuals to the overall political community (duties). Such notions could also be country specific. On the civil society level, one position could focus on resources that cannot be created by the state, such as trust and reciprocity among citizens. Ultimately, such resources are the basis of social solidarity (*cf.* Miller 1979). Such a view corresponds to a belief that political communities are at heart socially and culturally defined. An opposing belief system could highlight instead the formative role of political institutions and the enabling function of states for individual human rights and civil society associations. As for the state, one could imagine positions that privilege the law and order function of states, and thus concentrate on these areas as the foundations for effective legitimacy of democratic rule. An opposing stance would emphasize a procedural understanding of democracy, which looks at the state as creating the preconditions for societal integration.

The meta-concept of societal integration is also conducive, in principle, to a relational approach, which emphasizes the boundaries between different social groups, or, more precisely, the perceptions of boundaries (*cf.* Barth 1969). In this context one may usefully speak of two basic kinds of boundaries, fixed vs. porous (Bauböck 1994a; Zolberg and Long 1999). Boundaries that are porous allow for flexible incorporation. Citizenship with porous boundaries implies a high degree of tolerance of dual citizenship, and rather short waiting periods for naturalization (see Figure 1.3). Fixed boundaries refer to citizenship policies that emphasize rather restrictive rules, both in terms of naturalization – long time periods, strict qualifications – and for dual citizenship. Construction of the boundaries between

Figure 1.4   Societal Integration: Legal-Political Aspects

Boundaries	Fixed	Porous

Institutional	Restrictive access to citizenship:
	1. naturalization:
	    a. long waiting periods;
	    b. strict qualification requirements
	    (language, crime record,
	    local community acceptance);
	2. birthright citizenship:
	    • *jus sanguinis* without *jus soli*;
	3. dual citizenship:
	    • renunciation requirement.
		Liberal access to citizenship:
		1. naturalization:
		    a. shorter periods;
		    b. tolerable qualification requirements;
		2. birthright citizenship:
		    • *jus sanguinis* complemented by
		    jus soli;
		3. dual citizenship:
		    • further decoupling of rights and
		    citizenship.

Discursive		
Individual	• Naturalization is the end result of the integration process; • one-sided adaptation of immigrants to society of settlement (one-way street).	• Naturalization as one of the prerequisites for successful integration, enabling aspect of citizenship dominant; • integration more open ended.
Civil society	• Native groups allowed to protect their cultural integrity and their prerogatives; • various communitarian variants; avoidance of 'parallel societies'.	• Group pluralism desirable; • no unduly high entry thresholds for non-state groups into public life.
State	• State has above all function of security and redistribution; • in return, undivided loyalty of citizens to state is required.	• State (partially) has interventionist function to ensure parity of immigrants and natives.

immigrants and the second generation on the one hand and natives on the other hand is, in each case, a path-dependant process that hinges on the resources available in the legal, political, and other institutional domains of the respective societies as well as on the characteristics and the resources the immigrants themselves have available. Fixed boundaries are characterized by native-immigrant distinctions with great differences in religion and language, strong power asymmetries between immigrants and majorities, and differences in social status. By contrast, porous boundaries allow for the crossing by individuals or even the shifting of boundaries altogether. Proponents of porous boundaries generally emphasize the second dimension of citizenship, i.e. rights and duties. The proponents of fixed boundaries, on the other hand, usually emphasize the third dimension, affiliation with an inter-generationally and territorially clearly delineated political community which forms the basis for reciprocity and solidarity. They also raise more fundamental questions with respect to systems integration. The integration-boundaries approach can be applied to two realms in each dimension, that is, institutional and discursive (see Figure 1.4). In the institutional realm, rules of access to citizenship are more restrictive with fixed boundaries, and more liberal with porous boundaries. In the discursive realm it is meaningful to distinguish persons, civil society, and the state. As to persons, especially prospective citizens, the difference boils down to whether naturalization is the final result of a successful socio-economic and cultural integration process, as in the fixed model, or an enabling resource to guide further integration of immigrants into society, as in the porous boundaries model. In the realm of civil society, the fixed boundaries model would prioritize a homogeneous national political culture, into which immigrants are to be integrated, whereas a higher degree of group pluralism would be tolerable according to the porous boundaries model. And, finally, in the realm of the state the porous boundaries model demands a higher degree of public intervention to ensure equal rights for newcomers and established citizens than does the fixed boundaries model.

The Confluence of Institutional and Discursive Structures: Political Discourses

Although there has been an unmistakable trend towards liberalizing access to citizenship in general and increasing tolerance of dual citizenship in particular in all the countries analyzed in this volume, there are important elements of opposition. First and foremost, in immigration countries the use of citizenship as meta-politics has played a role in populist mobilization against dual citizenship and is thus a more general example of immigrant integration politics. Populist politics is characterized by (1) symbolic politics and (2) rallying against political elites. Although politics always carries both symbolic and substantial aspects (Edelman 1971), symbolic politics can be defined as the shift of a problem from substantive policies to argumentative strategies and symbolic performances. Symbolic politics prioritizes political presentation over political solutions via substantive policies (Sarcinelli 2005). Therefore, symbolic politics is not directly concerned with the problems to be solved, but rather often consists of simplistic arguments and vague allusions to means-end relationships in the proposed policies. Rallying against political elites is a staple of populist politics. Major political parties, in order to contain the influence of competing populist parties, sometimes respond by picking up their main issues. Populist politics is also meta-politics (Faist 1994; *cf.* Lasswell 1948). In meta-politics, dual citizenship is linked, for example, either to ethnic or assimilationist elements or to unrelated policy issues such as increased immigration, threats to welfare state systems, and criminality. The relationship between institutional and discursive factors framing the political decisions process is especially relevant. One of the decisive questions is how and which institutional structures can be interpreted as incentives for political actors to use symbolic politics, for example, as a part of a political strategy gaining more public support, votes, and power. Of course, the weight of these factors and the nature of the variables could differ from country to country in significant ways.

In the emigration countries, by contrast, the issues that can be expected to serve as the focus of public debate might include, for instance, the right to vote for non-resident citizens, their contribution to economic development through the transfer of economic and human capital, and finally their rights in their country of origin, such as inheritance and property rights. In general, the issues around (dual) citizenship lend themselves particularly well to symbolic politics because they are intimately related to core questions of nationhood and cultural sovereignty. Charges of dual loyalty and parallel societies formed by immigrants and emigrants abound. It is noteworthy that dual citizenship has become a central concern in debates in Germany and the Netherlands, while it has been notably absent in Sweden. These differences are in need of explanation.

References

Alba, R. and Nee, V. (2003), *Remaking the American Mainstream. Assimilation and Contemporary Immigration* (Cambridge, MA: Harvard University Press).

Albert, M., Jacobsen, D. and Lapid, Y. (eds) (2001), *Identities, Borders, Orders* (Minneapolis: University of Minnesota Press).

Aleinikoff, T. A. and Klusmeyer, D. (eds) (2000), *From Migrants to Citizens: Membership in a Changing World* (Washington, D.C.: Carnegie Endowment for International Peace).

Aleinikoff, T. A. and Klusmeyer, D. (2001), 'Plural Nationality: Facing the Future in a Migratory World', in Aleinikoff, T.A. and Klusmeyer, D. (eds), 63-88.

Aleinikoff, T. A. and Klusmeyer, D. (eds) (2001), *Citizenship Today: Global Perspectives and Practices* (Washington, D.C.: Carnegie Endowment for International Peace).

Apter, D. (ed.) (1964), *Ideology and Discontent* (New York: Free Press).

Arendt, H. (1981 [1949]), "Es gibt nur ein einziges Menschenrecht", in Höffe, O., Kandelbach, G. and Plumpe, G. (eds), 152-67.

Ball, T., Farr, J. and Hanson, R. L. (eds) (1989), *Political Innovation and Conceptual Change* (Cambridge: Cambridge University Press).

Bar-Yaacov, N. (1961), *Dual Nationality* (New York: Praeger).

Barrington, L. (1995), 'The Domestic and International Consequences of Citizenship in the Soviet Successor States', *Euro-Asia Studies* 47:5, 731-56.

Barth, F. (1969), *Ethnic Groups and Boundaries* (Boston, MA: Little Brown).

Bauböck, R. (1994a), *The Integration of Immigrants* (Strasbourg: Council of Europe).

Bauböck, R. (1994b), *Transnational Citizenship: Membership and Rights in International Migration* (Aldershot: Edward Elgar).

Bauböck, R. (forthcoming), 'The Trade-Off between Transnational Citizenship and Political Autonomy', in Faist, T. (ed.).

Benhabib, S. (2004), *The Rights of Others: Aliens, Residents, and Citizens* (Cambridge: Cambridge University Press).

Bloemraad, I. (2004), 'Who Claims Dual Citizenship? The Limits of Postnationalism, the Possibilities of Transnationalism, and the Persistence of Traditionalism', *International Migration Review* 38:2, 389-426.

Bosniak, L. (2002), 'Multiple Nationality and the Postnational Transformation of Citizenship', *Virginia Journal of International Law* 42:4, 979-1004.

Brubaker, R. W. (ed.) (1989), *Immigration and the Politics of Citizenship in Europe and North America* (Lanham, MD: University Press of America).

Brubaker, R. W. (1992), *Citizenship and Nationhood in France and Germany* (Cambridge, MA: Harvard University Press).

Carens, J. (2000), *Culture, Citizenship, and Community: A Contextual Exploration of Justice as Evenhandedness* (Oxford: Oxford University Press).

Castles, S. and Miller, M. J. (2003), *The Age of Migration: Population Movements in the Modern World* (London: Macmillan).

Cesarani, D. and Fulbrook, M. (eds) (1996), *Citizenship, Nationality and Migration in Europe* (Cambridge, MA: Harvard University Press).

Chan, J. M. M. (1991), 'The Right to a Citizenship as a Human Right: The Current Trend towards Recognition', *Human Rights Law Journal* 12:1-2, 1-14.

Chavez, P. L. (1997), 'Creating a United States-Mexico Political Double Helix: The Mexican Government's Proposed Dual Nationality Amendment', *Stanford Journal of International Law* 33, 119-51.

Cohen, J. (1989), 'Deliberation and Democratic Legitimacy', in Hamlin, A. and Petit, P. (eds), 67-98.

Cohen, J. (1999), 'Changing Paradigms of Citizenship and the Exclusiveness of the Demos', *International Sociology* 14:3, 245-68.

Conrad, C. and Kocka, J. (eds) (2001), *Staatsbürgerschaft in Europa. Historische Erfahrungen und aktuelle Debatten* (Hamburg: Körber Stiftung).

Converse, P. E. (1964), 'The Nature of Belief Systems in Mass Publics', in Apter, D. (ed.), 206-61.

Dahrendorf, R. (1992), 'Citizenship and the Modern Social Conflict', in Holme, R. and Elliot, M. (eds), 112-25.

de la Pradelle (2002), 'Dual Nationality and the French Citizenship Tradition', in Hansen, R. and Weil, P. (eds), 191-214.

Deutscher Bundestag (ed.) (1999), *Stellungnahmen der Sachverständigen zur öffentlichen Anhörung des Innenausschusses*, Ausschußdrucksache 14/14 from 1999-04-14 (Berlin: Deutscher Bundestag).

Downs, A. (1957), *An Economic Theory of Democracy* (New York: Harper & Row).

Durkheim, É. (1964 [1893]), *The Division of Labor in Society*, translated by George Simpson (New York: Macmillan).

Dworkin, R. (1978), *Taking Rights Seriously* (Harvard: Harvard University Press).

Edelman, M. (1971), *The Symbolic Uses of Politics* (Urbana: University of Illinois Press).

Faist, T. (1994), 'How to Define a Foreigner? The Symbolic Politics of Immigration in German Partisan Discourse, 1978-1993', *West European Politics* 17:2, 50-71.

Faist, T. (1995), 'A Preliminary Analysis of Political-Institutional Aspects of International Migration: Internationalization, Transnationalization, and Internal Globalization', *Working Paper Series* No. 10/1995 (Bremen: Centre for Social Policy Research, University of Bremen).

Faist, T. (1997), 'Migration in Contemporary Europe: European Integration, Economic Liberalization, and Protection', in Klausen, J. and Tilly, L. (eds), 223-48.

Faist, T. (2000), *The Volume and Dynamics of International Migration and Transnational Social Spaces* (Oxford: Oxford University Press).

Faist, T. (2001), 'Social Citizenship in the European Union: Nested Membership', *Journal of Common Market Studies* 39:1, 37-58.

Faist, T. (2004), 'Dual Citizenship as Overlapping Membership', in Joly, D. (ed.), 210-32.

Faist, T. (ed.) (forthcoming), *Dual Citizenship: Rights, Democracy and Identity in a Globalizing World* (Houndsmills, UK: Palgrave Macmillan).

Faist, T. and Özveren, E. (eds) (2004), *Transnational Social Spaces: Actors, Networks and Organizations* (Aldershot, UK: Ashgate).

Freeman, G. P. and Ögelman, N. (1998), 'Homeland Citizenship Policies and the Status of Third Country Citizens in the European Union', *Journal of Ethnic and Migration Studies* 24:4, 769-88.

Geertz, C. (1973), *The Interpretation of Cultures* (New York: Basic Books).

Gerth, H. and Wright Mills, C. (eds) (1946), *From Max Weber* (New York: Basic Books).

Gordon, M. (1964), *Assimilation in American Life* (New York: Oxford University Press).

Groenendijk, K. (1999), 'Stellungnahme zu den Gesetzentwürfen zur Reform des Staatsangehörigkeitsrecht', in Deutscher Bundestag (ed.), 71-83.

Gustafson, P. (2005), 'International Migration and National Belonging in the Swedish Debate on Dual Citizenship', *Acta Sociologica* 48:1, 5-19.

Habermas, J. (1981), *Theorie des kommunikativen Handelns* 2 vols. (Frankfurt am Main: Suhrkamp).

Hamlin, A. and Petit, P. (eds) (1989), *The Good Polity: Normative Analysis of the State* (Oxford: Oxford University Press).

Hammar, T. (1989), 'State, Nation, and Dual Citizenship', in Brubaker, R.W. (ed.), 81-95.

Hammar, T. (1990), *Democracy and the Nation-State: Aliens, Denizens and Citizens in a World of International Migration* (Aldershot: Gower).

Hansen, R. (2002), 'The Dog that didn't Bark: Dual Nationality in the United Kingdom', in Hansen, R. and Weil, P. (eds), 179-90.

Hansen, R. and Weil, P. (eds) (2002), *Dual Nationality, Social Rights and Federal Citizenship in the U.S. and Europe* (New York/Oxford: Berghahn Books).

Höffe, O., Kandelbach, G. and Plumpe, G. (eds) (1981 [1949]), *Praktische Philosophie/Ethik* 2 (Frankfurt: Fischer).

Holme, R. and Elliot, M. (eds) (1992), *1688-1988: Time for a New Constitution* (Basingstoke: Macmillan).

Huntington, S.P. (2004), *Who Are We? The Challenges to America's National Identity* (New York: Simon & Schuster).

Jacobson, D. (1995), *Rights across Borders: Immigration and the Decline of Citizenship* (Baltimore: Johns Hopkins University Press).

Janowski, T. (1998), *Citizenship and Civil Society: A Framework of Rights and Obligations in Liberal, Traditional and Social Democratic Regimes* (Cambridge: Cambridge University Press).

Jellinek, G. (1964 [1905]), *System der subjektiven öffentlichen Rechte*, Reprint of the 2nd Edition of 1919 (Aalen: Scientia Verlag).

Joly, D. (ed.) (2004), *International Migration in the New Millenium: Global Movement and Settlement* (Aldershot, UK: Ashgate).

Jones-Correa, M. (1998), *Between Two Nations. The Political Predicament of Latinos in New York City* (Ithaca: Cornell University Press).

Kant, I. (1970 [1781]), 'Perpetual Peace. A Philosophical Sketch', in Reiss, H. (ed.), 93-130

Kivisto, P. and Faist, T. (2006), *The Future of Citizenship* (Oxford: Blackwell).

Klausen, J. and Tilly, L. (eds) (1997), *European Integration in Social and Historical Perspective. 1850 to the Present* (Boulder, CO: Rowman & Littlefield).

Knop, K. (2001), 'Relational Citizenship: On Gender and Citizenship in International Law', in Aleinikoff, T. A. and Klusmeyer, D. (eds), 89-124.

Koopmans, R. and Statham, P. (eds) (2000), *Challenging Immigration and Ethnic Relations Politics: Comparative European Perspectives* (Oxford: Oxford University Press).

Koslowski, R. (2001), 'Demographic Boundary Maintenance in World Politics: Of International Norms on Dual Citizenship', in Albert, M., Jacobsen, D. and Lapid, Y. (eds), 203-23.

Kovács, M.M. (forthcoming), 'The Politics of Dual Citizenship in Hungary', in Faist, T. (ed.).

Kymlicka, W. (1995), *Multicultural Citizenship: A Liberal Theory of Minority Rights* (Oxford: Clarendon Press).

Kymlicka, W. and Norman, W. (2000), *Citizenship in Diverse Societies* (Oxford: Oxford University Press).

Lasswell, H. (1948), *Power and Personality* (New York: Harper & Row).

League of Nations (1930), 'Convention on Certain Questions Relating to the Conflict of Nationality Laws' (1930-04-12), *Treaty Series: Treaties and International Engagements Registered with the Secretariat of the League of Nations*, 179:4137, 1937-8.

Linz, J. J. and Stepan, A. (1996), *Problems of Democratic Transition and Consolidation: Southern Europe, South America, and Post-Communist Europe* (Baltimore: Johns Hopkins University Press).

Lockwood, D. (1964), 'Social Integration and System Integration', in Zollschan, G. K. and Hirsch, W. (eds), 244-57.

Luhmann, N. (1988), *Die Wirtschaft der Gesellschaft* (Frankfurt am Main: Suhrkamp).

Mann, M. (1993), *The Sources of Social Power, vol. 2: The Rise of Classes and Nation-States, 1760-1914* (Cambridge: Cambridge University Press).

Marshall, T. H. (1964), *Class, Citizenship, and Social Development, Essays by T.H. Marshall* (New York: Doubleday & Company).

Martin, D. A. and Hailbronner, K. (eds), *Rights and Duties of Dual Citizens: Evolution and Prospects* (The Hague: Kluwer Law International).

Miller, D. (1979), *Social Justice* (Oxford: Oxford University Press).

Miller, M. J. and Castles, S. (2003), *The Age of Migration: International Population Movements in the Modern World* (Houndsmills, Basingstoke: Palgrave Macmillan).

Morris, L. (2002), *Managing Migration: Civic Stratification and Migrants' Rights* (London: Routledge).

Motomura, H. (1998), 'Alienage Classifications in a Nation of Immigrants: Three Models of "Permanent Residence"', in Pickus, N. J. (ed.), 199-222.

Münch, R. (2001), 'Integration: Social', in Smelser, N. (ed.), 11, 7591-96.

Netzwerk Migration in Europa e.V. (ed.) (2001), *Migration und Bevölkerung* [Newsletter], 2001:1, 2.

North, D. C. (1981), *Structure and Change in Economic History* (New York: W.W. Norton)

Offe, C. (1998), '"Homogeneity" and Constitutional Democracy: Coping with Identity through Group Rights', *The Journal of Political Philosophy* 6:2, 113-41.

Ong, A. (1997), *Underground Empires: The Cultural Politics of Modern Chinese Transnationalism* (New York: Routledge).

Parsons, T. and Smelser, N. J. (1956), *Economy and Society* (New York: Free Press).

Pickus, N. J. (ed.) (1998), *Immigration and Citizenship in the 21ˢᵗ Century* (Lanham, MD: Rowman & Littlefield).

Pocock, J. G. A. (1973), *Politics, Language and Time* (New York: Atheneum).

Reiss, H. (ed.) (1970), *Kant's Political Writings* (Cambridge: Cambridge University Press).

Renshon, S. A. (2001), *Dual Citizenship and American Identity* (Washington, D.C.: Center for Immigration Studies).

Rittstieg, H. (1990), 'Doppelte Staatsangehörigkeit im Völkerrecht', *Neue Juristische Wochenschrift* 43, 1401-5.

Rokkan and Urwin (1983), *Economy, Territory, Identity: Politics of West European Peripheries* (London: Sage).

Rousseau, J.-J. (1966 [1762]), *Du contrat social: ou Principes du droit politique* (Paris: Garnier).

Sarcinelli, U. (2005), *Politische Kommunikation in Deutschland. Zur Politikvermittlung im demokratischen System* (Wiesbaden: VS Verlag für Sozialwissenschaften).

Sartori, G. (1965), *Democratic Theory* (New York: Praeger).

Schuck, P. H. (1998), *Citizens, Strangers, and In-Betweens: Essays on Immigration and Citizenship* (Boulder, CO: Westview Press).

Shevchuck, Y. I. (1996), 'Dual Citizenship in Old and New States', *European Journal of Sociology* 37:1, 47-73.

Shibutani, T. and Kwan, K. M. (1965), *Ethnic Stratification* (New York: Macmillan).

Shklar, J. (1991), *American Citizenship* (Cambridge, MA: Harvard University Press).

Smelser, N. (ed.) (2001), *International Encyclopedia of the Social and Behavioral Sciences 11* (Amsterdam: Elsevier).

Smith, A. (1979), *Nationalism in the 20th Century* (New York: New York University Press).

Soysal, Y. N. (1994), *The Limits of Citizenship* (Chicago: University of Chicago Press).

Spiro, P. J. (1997), 'Dual Nationality and the Meaning of Citizenship', *Emory Law Review* 46, 1411-85.

Spiro, P. J. (2003), 'Political Rights and Dual Citizenship', in Martin, D. A. and Hailbronner, K. (eds), 134-52.

Stone, D. (1997), *Policy Paradox: The Art of Political Decision Making* (New York: W.W. Norton).

Tilly, C. (1995), 'Citizenship, Identity and Social History', *International Review of Social History* 40: 3, 1-17.

Toulmin, S. (2003 [1958]), *The Uses of Argument*, updated ed. (Cambridge: Cambridge University Press).

van den Daele, W. and Neidhardt, F. (1994), 'Regierung durch Diskussion – Über Versuche, mit Argumenten Politik zu machen', in van den Daele, W. and Neidhardt, F. (eds).

van den Daele, W. and Neidhardt, F. (eds) (1994), *Kommunikation und Entscheidung. Politische Funktionen öffentlicher Meinungsbildung und diskursiver Verfahren. WZB-Jahrbuch 1996* (Berlin: Edition Sigma).

Verba, S. (1967), 'Some Dilemmas of Comparative Research', *World Politics* 20:1, 111-28.

Waltz, K. (1979), *Theory of International Politics* (New York: McGraw-Hill).

Walzer, M. (1989), 'Citizenship', in Ball, T., Farr, J. and Hanson, R. L. (eds), 211-19.

Weber, M. (1946), 'The Social Psychology of World Religions', in Gerth, H. and Wright Mills, C. (eds), 276-301.

Weber, M. (1972 [1922]), *Wirtschaft und Gesellschaft*, 5th Edition (Tübingen: J.C.B. Mohr).

Weil, P. (2001), 'Zugang zur Staatsbürgerschaft', in Conrad, C. and Kocka, J. (eds), 92-111.

Weis, P. (1976 [1959]), *Nationality and Statelessness in International Law*, 2nd ed. (Amsterdam: Sijthoff & Noordhoff).

Zolberg, A. R. and Long, L. W. (1999), 'Why Islam is like Spanish: Cultural Incorporation in Europe and the United States', *Politics & Society* 27:1, 5-38.

Zollschan, G. K. and Hirsch, W. (eds) (1964), *Explorations in Social Change* (Boston: Houghton Mifflin).

Chapter 2

'We are All "Republican" Now': The Politics of Dual Citizenship in Germany

Jürgen Gerdes, Thomas Faist and Beate Rieple

Abstract

This chapter gives an overview of the political debate and the policy process leading up to the unusual outcome of the recent German Citizenship Law Reform in 1999 in comparative perspective, a reform that provided a very liberal *jus soli* introduction and at the same time a restrictive attitude towards dual citizenship. The somewhat contradictory outcome is essentially the result of a compromise between two opposing political camps holding quite different interpretations of the relationship between state and citizen, the function of citizenship law, and the integration of both immigrants and overall society. It is argued that the delay of citizenship law reform in Germany, at least during the last fifteen years, cannot be explained by means of an ethnic concept of nation, as many scholars have contended. Rather it is characterized by a persisting ideological conflict structure, which has been reinforced by institutional patterns of the political and legal system. The opposing views regarding the significance of citizenship are embedded within republicanism, stressing citizenship as activity on the one hand and citizenship as a right on the other hand.

Introduction

The global trend in recent years has been an increase in the number of dual citizens worldwide. More and more immigration states have revised their citizenship laws explicitly tolerating dual citizenship in several instances of naturalization, *jus soli* supplementation, and citizenship acquisition of domestic born foreign children at maturity on simple declaration (*cf.* Hailbronner 1992; Aleinikoff and Klusmeyer 2001; Faist, Gerdes and Rieple 2004). Accepting dual citizenship was intended as one of several measures to ease the conditions of citizenship acquisition for increasing numbers of permanent immigrants and their descendants. Germany, in contrast, does not follow this global trend, choosing instead, in its recent citizenship law reform of 1999, to uphold the principle of avoiding dual citizenship.

Notwithstanding this principle, all political parties in Germany had agreed for years on the need to reform the old German citizenship law of 1913 in order to raise the comparatively extremely low naturalization rates. From the beginning of the 1980s until 1998, when it became clear that many of the former so-called 'guest-workers' (*Gastarbeiter*) recruited in the 1960s would remain permanently in Germany, all political parties, from some federal states (*Bundesländer*) and from the Second Chamber of parliament (*Bundesrat*), put forth numerous initiatives, proposals, and draft legislation for citizenship law reform. None of these various initiatives, however, achieved a majority. Two main issues have consistently been a stumbling block: the introduction of an *jus soli* amendment and the possibility of increased toleration of dual citizenship. Only partial reforms with regard to citizenship acquisition were passed in 1990 and 1993: the introduction of as-of-right naturalization for young foreigners after eight years of legal residence and for immigrants of the first generation after fifteen years of legal residence under certain conditions. These changes were the outcome of a compromise between the Christian Democrats (*CDU/CSU*) in government and the Social Democrats (*SPD*) in opposition, achieved within a broader agreement in order to reach a two-thirds majority for a constitutional amendment necessary for a reform of the asylum article in the German constitution in 1992.

After 16 years in opposition the SPD came back into political power as the majority party after winning the elections in September 1998. But they still needed a coalition partner which they found in the Greens. This government coalition immediately envisaged a new and fundamental German citizenship law reform as one of its most important reform projects. Initially, it was proposed, first, to introduce the *jus soli* principle for foreign children born in Germany if one of the parents was German-born or had entered the territory before the age of fourteen and actually possessed a residence permit. Second, renunciation of previous citizenship would no longer be required in all cases of as-of-right naturalizations. The CDU/CSU, who had to cope with their severe defeat in the federal elections and who faced serious problems regarding irregularities with party financing at that time, quickly picked up the issue as its first great theme in opposition and organized a petition campaign immediately prior to the first state elections in Hessen after the federal elections. The heated campaign concentrated on the general introduction of dual citizenship 'as a rule', as the CDU/CSU framed the issue. After losing the elections in Hessen and thus the majority in the *Bundesrat*, the SPD and the Greens had to collaborate with the Free Democrats (*FDP*) to achieve a compromise solution which became law and took effect at the beginning of 2000.

The German citizenship law reform of 1999 is puzzling because it contains two very contradictory general dimensions. On the one hand, one of the most far-reaching *jus soli* supplements in citizenship law on the European continent has been introduced: children of foreign parents now acquire German citizenship automatically by birth, if one of the parents has resided in Germany for at least eight years prior while having held for at least the previous three years an unlimited residence permit. This is clearly an *jus soli* for the second generation from the very beginning, which does not even exist in France, where the second generation acquires French citizenship only at maturity. On the other hand, the new law adheres to the principle of avoiding dual citizenship to an extent well beyond other European states, because it is applied also to the new *jus soli* acquisition at birth. Those who acquire dual citizenship at birth by *jus soli* are obliged to opt for one citizenship only until the age of twenty-three. If they make no such decision, they lose German citizenship, except in cases where the other state refuses or delays renunciation of citizenship or requires unacceptable conditions, for instance making it conditional on military service.[1]

How can this outcome be explained? Is the German adherence to the principle of avoiding dual citizenship an aspect of a restrictive German tradition in citizenship law, based on an older ethnic national self-understanding?

It is a widely shared assumption in political science that the legal conditions and terms of inclusion and exclusion of newcomers within a given nation-state are strongly related to the prevailing self-understanding of political community. The concept of nation in particular, but sometimes also ideas on the legitimate and desirable extent of cultural pluralism, are considered decisive and influential factors in establishing the terms of law regarding immigrant residents and, more importantly, the legal conditions for acquisition of citizenship. According to the most comprehensive and oft-cited historical analysis:

> [c]itizenship in a nation-state is inevitably bound up with nationhood and national identity, membership of the state with membership of the nation. Proposals to redefine the legal

---

1 Further elements of reform are: In cases of as-of-right naturalization the required period of legal and habitual residence was shortened from fifteen years to eight years. As before, *preconditions of naturalization* are: no dependence on social assistance, unless the applicant is not responsible for such dependence, and 'sufficient' knowledge of German language. The following preconditions have been added: no reasons for deportation; acceptance of the principles of the German constitution; 'no factual indication warranting the assumption that the applicant supports or has supported' efforts against the liberal democratic basic order, public security, or impeding public administration and authorities. Regarding *dual citizenship*, renunciation of original citizenship is required. Compared to the previous citizenship law the exception clauses regarding allowance of dual citizenship were extended. As before, dual citizenship is permitted if the emigration state makes renunciation of previous citizenship impossible or conditional on unreasonable demands. Ethnic Germans and their descendants automatically become Germans by the new law without the precondition of renouncing original citizenship; according to the previous citizenship law they have the right to immediate naturalization without obligation to renounce citizenship. Accepted refugees are now no longer required individually to give proof that renunciation of previous citizenship is impossible. Additionally, citizens of European Union member states are allowed to retain their previous citizenship in cases of bilateral reciprocity. Also new is the exception made when renunciation of former citizenship would result in serious economical or proprietary disadvantages. Regarding rules of *loss of citizenship* two changes should be mentioned. First, as previously, German citizenship is lost when a person acquires another citizenship, but according to the new law this provision is also valid if one actually resides on German territory. Second, a person can be exempted from automatic loss of German citizenship when acquiring another citizenship if she 'can make demonstrative credible continuous ties to Germany'.

criteria of citizenship raise large and ideologically charged questions of nationhood and national belonging ... The politics of citizenship today is first and foremost a politics of nationhood. (Brubaker 1992, 182; see also Castles and Miller 1993, 35ff., 223ff.)

The dominant general assumption is more specific, namely that a republican understanding of nation will lead to more inclusive measures of immigrant integration while a more ethnically and culturally defined concept of nation will tend to be much more exclusive. Conversely, according to this logic, an ethnic concept of nation is presumed to be more conducive to dual citizenship for ancestral citizens emigrating and acquiring citizenship in another country.

Germany's comparatively exclusive citizenship law and the delays in reforms have often been explained by the persistence of a predominantly ethnic understanding of nation, transmitted down through German history to the post-Second World War Federal Republic. Contrary to this assumption, our thesis is that although an ethnic understanding of nation might well explain the old German citizenship law of 1913 and possibly some of the prevailing political views in the early Federal Republic of Germany, it is seriously misleading when considering the recent German debates and conflicts on the issue. A closer look at the political and public debates and positions of the political actors involved in citizenship law reform reveals that specific features of the legal and political system and the way they constrain political action and encourage political conflicts have to be taken more seriously. Moreover, an ideological cleavage line other than that of republican vs. ethnic nation is much more relevant in explaining the outcome of citizenship law reform in Germany. This can aptly be called the 'integration' belief system. Political discourse was dominated by diametrically opposed and conflicting versions of this belief system and the policies that should be based upon this belief system. A particular feature of the German discourse was a very broad understanding of integration, and it is used both with respect to aspects of social integration of immigrants as well as to modes of overall societal integration. Thus, our thesis is that the politics of citizenship in Germany (with regard to both dual citizenship and the outcome of the citizenship law debate) is essentially framed and to be explained by two conflicting views of integration. On the one hand, the proponents of *jus soli* and tolerance of dual citizenship see naturalization as a necessary element of immigrant integration and conceive of it primarily as a matter of equal individual rights. On the other hand, the opponents of *jus soli* and dual citizenship take integration as a precondition for naturalization. In their view citizenship has to be evaluated first and foremost from what can be called a state-communitarian standpoint. The two contradictory dimensions of the new citizenship law reflect a political compromise of these two conflicting political camps and their very different belief systems on immigrant and societal integration.

Our findings are based on a comprehensive analysis of two central debates on citizenship law reform: one that took place in 1993/94 in the German parliament and another that took place in 1999 among the general public and parliament. To understand the fundamental strategic and symbolic cleavage line between the main political camps it is, first, appropriate to outline some general features of the German institutional opportunity structure within which the individual arguments for and against dual citizenship have been framed and exchanged. Second, with regard to the discursive opportunity structure for political parties in Germany, we shall place the dominant arguments on dual citizenship within three belief systems in order to examine their suitability for tying the different arguments together and therefore for explaining the positions of the political actors: 'nationhood', 'assimilation or multiculturalism' and 'integration'. Finally, it turns out that tying arguments to the 'integration' belief system, meaning here immigrant integration and societal integration simultaneously, is comparatively more useful for making sense of the different positions of the competing political camps than linking them with the concepts of nationhood or assimilation vs. multiculturalism. Within the 'integration' belief system different opinions on citizenship law reform are connected to a far deeper division over general aspects of politics and society. The question of state sovereignty and the relationship between state and citizen, rather than the conception of 'nation', was more highly contested. However, the extent of differences of the opposing understandings is essentially determined by existing political institutions.

The Institutional Opportunity Structure

Institutional and political settings in Germany constitute certain enabling and constraining patterns for political action. Within the institutional opportunity structure some important legal as well as political features must be taken into account. The German Basic Law, for instance, broke with the tradition of legal positivism of the Weimar Republic, according to which legitimate law was what had been politically decided in a procedurally correct way. By contrast, the Basic Law builds on the idea of a pre-political order of values in the name of human dignity which stands before and independently of contingent political majorities.[2] On this basis the constitutional court was founded as the pivotal 'guardian of the constitution' (Hüter der Verfassung) and has been provided with a comparatively wide range of competences (von Beyme 1999, 404). Political actors make efforts to ensure that their policy proposals are compatible with the constitution and its interpretation by the constitutional court, in order not to risk the proverbial 'walk to Karlsruhe' by their political opponents. This is a constant threat in German political debates and policy-making.[3]

In general, there are two constitutional dimensions which can explain the delay on citizenship reform in Germany. First, the resumption of the old German citizenship law of 1913 was aimed at upholding the possibility of reunification of Germany after the Second World War. Thus, the reluctance to embark on fundamental reforms before reunification could partly be explained by the overriding political objective not to endanger the possibility of unification. The old German citizenship law served

---

2 The basic principles of human rights and democracy as enshrined in the constitution can never be suspended or even altered by the respective ruling political actors (*cf.* Article 79, Paragraph 3 in connection with Article 1 and 20 of the German Basic Law).

3 All translations of official German documents are the authors'.

deliberately as an instrument to undermine the legitimacy of the existence of the German Democratic Republic (*GDR*) and its own citizenship law that claimed to represent all Germans. If former West Germany had enacted a new citizenship law including the people of the GDR, it would have been in violation of international law, because no state is allowed to declare citizens of another state as its own (Bös 2000, 101). Thus, an ethnic understanding of the Federal Republic of Germany, which had been severely discredited by the racist aberration of the Nazis, cannot explain the re-establishment of the old law of 1913 and the subsequent delay of reform. It was only a contingent factual linkage between the maintenance of a restrictive citizenship law affecting new immigrants and the unresolved national question (Joppke 2000, 153; Green 2001, 25f.). The German Basic Law as such contains no ethnic definition of citizenship but leaves its definition to the political process. Second, a more republican cast to the delay of reform is reflected in the discussion and interpretation of the article disallowing deprivation of citizenship (Article 16 of the Basic Law).[4] This article has been invoked repeatedly by legal experts and politicians for the purpose of ruling out the possibility of general tolerance of dual citizenship. Article 16 of the Basic Law constitutes strong institutional protection against the deprivation of citizenship and has been embodied as a reaction to expatriation practices of the Nazi Regime. Thus it could be considered to be a protection of the human right to citizenship as the basis for individual rights. In comparison with legislation in other liberal democratic states, the German citizenship law prohibits deprivation of citizenship under any but the most restrictive conditions. In the light of this, it has been argued that the rules of acquisition of citizenship would have to be equally restrictive, thus effectively ruling out general acceptance of dual citizenship.

The constitutional court passed two important judgements with respect to the citizenship law, which subsequently influenced the political debates. First, the constitutional court stated in its landmark decision of 1974 that dual citizenship is in principle an 'evil' to be avoided at all costs in the name of the states and individuals concerned. The court also explicitly acknowledged that dual citizenship is not prohibited by international law. It furthermore argued that dual citizenship is to a certain degree unavoidable because of states' sovereign right to define the conditions of acquisition of their citizenship on their own account. Since then it has become commonly understood that avoiding dual citizenship is an important principle which could be overruled only by higher-ranking constitutional values.[5] Second, in 1990

---

4   Article 16, Paragraph 1 of the German constitution reads: 'German citizenship may not be deprived. The loss of citizenship may happen only because of a law and against the will of the person affected only if she would not become stateless thereby'.

5   The case of German re-settlers (Article 116, Paragraph 1 of the German Basic Law) and of persons who were deprived of citizenship under the Nazi Regime (Article 116, Paragraph 2) and gender equality (Article 3, Paragraph 2) are examples of such higher-ranking principles. In its decision of 1974 the constitutional court ruled that the then valid Article 4 of the German citizenship law was unconstitutional because of gender equality. The former Article 4 provided in cases of bi-national marriages that the legitimate child of a German father acquired German citizenship by *jus sanguinis* in any case, but that the legitimate child

the German constitutional court overruled the establishment of local voting rights for resident non-citizens, a proposal made by the German *Bundesländer* Hamburg and Schleswig-Holstein. Nevertheless, the court explicitly accepted the underlying claim of the need to reduce the gap between those who are subject to the law and those who are entitled to full democratic participation, arguing that this principle corresponds exactly to the ideas of freedom and democracy. While under valid constitutional law the court considered alien voting rights unconstitutional, at the same time it was left to the legislators to facilitate naturalization by reforms of citizenship law.[6] In view of the fact that there are in principle two ways to provide political inclusion of immigrants in nation-states, namely facilitating naturalization (including tolerance of dual citizenship), or granting political rights on the basis of a consolidated and secured residence status (Hammar 1990), the decision of the constitutional court definitively obstructed the latter alternative. Thus, easing naturalization by altering German citizenship law was the only political option.

The combination of Germany's party system and its federal structure plays a decisive role in shaping the German policy process, which in citizenship law reform is characterized by a persistent conflict between two main camps. The German party system is essentially structured by a relative power balance of two mostly competing catch-all parties. Both the Christian Democrats and Social Democrats with some smaller parties as their prospective coalition partners compete in elections for the decisive share of votes necessary to reach a majority. There is a similar constellation on the regional level, where the smaller coalition partners of the CDU and SPD may change, but grand coalitions are a rare exception. In recent decades the Social Democrats countered a structural preponderance of the Christian Democrats by a greater range of options regarding prospective coalition partners: whereas the CDU is dependant on cooperation with the Free Democrats, the Social Democrats are in principle prepared to form a coalition not only with the Free Democrats, but also with the Green Party and, in the newly-formed *Bundesländer* of the former GDR, occasionally also with the regionally strong Party of Democratic Socialism (PDS). The federal system reinforces the competition and conflict structure in two respects. First, in many cases, passing a law requires not only a simple majority in the federal parliament (*Bundestag*) but also in the Second Chamber (*Bundesrat*), where the state governments are represented roughly in proportion to respective population size. Moreover, because of a relatively even chronological spread of elections to the *Bundesländerparlamente*, which are regularly regarded as predictors of the actual voting proportions on the federal level, there is a high probability of enduring

---

of a German mother could do so only if the child becomes stateless. The court decided that the acquisition of citizenship by *jus sanguinis* has to be passed on by both parents on the same conditions regardless of the emergence of dual citizenship. It was left to legislators to allow dual citizenship at all or to take some other measures to avoid it in these cases (BVerfGE 37, 217; *cf.* von Mangoldt 1993, 971; Goes 1997, 46f.).

6   BVerfGE 83, 37. For a more detailed description of this political and legal dispute on alien voting rights in Germany, see Joppke 1999, 194ff.

election campaigns, especially in cases of slim majorities and possible changes of governments. A strong incentive exists for political parties to undertake intense efforts to accentuate differences with their opponents and thus to use symbolic and populist politics in order to gain public support and political influence.

Within this institutional context the two opposing political camps on citizenship law reform have been formed and reinforced. The Social Democrats, Greens, PDS, and Free Democrats made several proposals regarding an *jus soli* amendment and toleration of dual citizenship. But the Christian Democrats refused to agree to any of these proposals. Within the two CDU/CSU-FDP coalition periods from 1990 until 1998 several negotiations on the issue failed to lead to an agreement on substantive reform. It is worth noting that the conflict ran not only between the two coalition partners but also among the Christian Democratic parties. There were also some Christian Democrats who favoured some versions of an 'option model'[7] – which was finally enacted in 1999 by Social Democrats and Greens. Nevertheless, the Christian Democrats, during the final debates, presented themselves as a homogeneous block and vehemently rejected even the 'option model', which was meant as a compromise between the diverse political forces. When the new government parties in 1998 presented their first new and comprehensive reform plan allowing for dual citizenship in all cases of as-of-right-naturalizations, the Christian Democrats took this as an opportunity to mobilize the general public by organizing a nation-wide petition campaign against 'dual citizenship as a rule'. This significantly contributed to their victory in the elections in Hessen in February 1999, when the government coalition lost their majority in the *Bundesrat*.[8] The use of a petition campaign against dual citizenship shortly after their major defeat in national elections and as a central element of mobilization within the context of a regional election is a strong indication that the issue was essentially used to regain public political support. In framing dual citizenship in the public

---

7   This designation refers to an important feature of the enacted citizenship law reform, i.e. to the obligation of persons who acquire dual citizenship by *jus soli* to decide at maturity on one citizenship only. Such a proposal had also been made by the Free Democrats already in 1997. However, the term 'option model' is somewhat misleading; a term such as 'mandatory-option-model' would have been more appropriate.

8   Initially, there was an internal party conflict over whether such a petition campaign would be politically and morally useful. Many CDU politicians advocated a more comprehensive concept of integration of immigrants. By careful and clever mediation between the different forces and positions within the CDU/CSU, the chairman of the nation-wide CDU at that time, Wolfgang Schäuble, managed an agreement within both sister parties on such a petition campaign according to the slogan: 'Dual citizenship: No, Integration: Yes'. A working group within the CDU under leadership of its vice-chairman in parliament, Jürgen Rüttgers, was appointed to work out a concept of a more ambitious social integration of immigrants. The resulting paper was titled 'Integration and Tolerance'. Aside from demands for some measures of social integration (e.g. language training courses, more funds for schools with a high proportion of immigrant children) the paper also called for some multicultural policy proposals – though without using the term (e.g. promotion of bilingual education, religious instructions for Muslim children) (German Parliament, Printed matter 14/534, 1999-03-16).

debate predominantly as a serious threat to public safety[9] the Christian Democrats obviously tried to exploit the issue in the manner of populism and symbolic politics.[10] Since 1982 the Christian Democrats brought issues of immigration and integration of immigrants repeatedly to the public agenda, often before elections, apparently as a primary instrument to influence public opinion for their benefit (cf. Meier-Braun 2002). Those attempts to use resentments against immigrants are aimed symbolically at reframing the main political problems of unemployment, organized criminality, and social insurance schemes into the policy area of immigration control. The structural incentive of such politics seems to be that problems caused by globalization processes could be symbolically brought back in under the control of the nation-state. In this sense, politics in the area of immigration and integration could serve as a 'meta-issue' and could be related to a host of political problems of a very different kind (cf. Faist 1994). The petition campaign against dual citizenship initiated by the Christian Democrats was at least partly intended to collect support from xenophobically oriented people and to re-mobilize non-voters who were disappointed with political performances. Such instrumental use of immigration issues for electoral purposes, however, is a feature which can be observed in other European countries as well (cf. Thränhardt 1993).[11]

Moreover, the Christian Democrats consistently intermingled questions of immigration and integration during the debate. They repeatedly tried to suggest in public debate that allowing dual citizenship would be an incentive to further immigration, and thus neglected to mention that other preconditions of naturalization would have been upheld regardless. Even when the government coalition offered a compromise by expanding the preconditions of as-of-right naturalizations substantially by abstaining from the initial plan of general

---

9 At the peak of the public debate the chairman of the Bavarian CSU, Edmund Stoiber, in an interview with a weekly magazine, provocatively remarked that dual citizenship would endanger 'security in Germany more seriously than the terrorism from the "Red Army Faction" in the 1970s and 1980s', because German authorities could no longer deport foreign offenders if they also held German citizenship (Focus, 1999-01-04).

10 Although politics and policies always contain both symbolic and substantive aspects (Edelman 1971) symbolic politics can be defined as prioritizing political presentation over political solutions via substantive policies (Sarcinelli 1989). Symbolic politics is not directly concerned with the problems to be solved and often consists of simplistic arguments and vague allusions to relations between means and ends in the proposed policies.

11 Also in the case of this campaign the Christian Democrats certainly were able to attract people with cultural prejudices and racist orientations. However, it is doubtful whether the predominant xenophobic orientations are still based on ethnic and cultural grounds. It might also be conceivable that relevant groups rather exhibit a sort of 'welfare chauvinism' which relates to the distribution of membership in inclusion and exclusion mechanisms between relatively closed nation-states as such. Under internal conditions of increasing social and economic inequality the deprived parts of the population are simply in favour of immigration restrictions hoping to secure the leavings of their citizenship-based claims vis-à-vis immigrants and non-citizens. Such a view would also correspond with the empirical evidence that xenophobia is clearly not confined to ethnic nations.

tolerance of dual citizenship, the Christian Democrats refused to agree. Instead, they accused the government parties of trying to continue the 'politics of dual citizenship'. However, the fact that both the FDP and the CDU nevertheless accepted that dual citizens may hold political office indicates that the problems of dual citizenship were clearly exaggerated for electoral purposes.[12]

The Discursive Opportunity Structure

The discursive opportunity structure was evaluated on the basis of a comprehensive content and argument analysis of the citizenship reform debates in parliament and the expert hearings which took place in 1993/94 and 1999 and of the public debate in 1998/99.[13] In order to evaluate the underlying ideological cleavage structure in the German debate, the articulated arguments[14] for and against some aspects of reform, especially those relating to dual citizenship, have been classified in an ideal-typical way in four different forms. In the analysis of the German case the basic distinction between pragmatic and principled arguments (see Faist, this volume, chapter 1) is further subdivided in order to capture the multi-faceted public and political debates. The following categorization helps to distinguish principled arguments of different types (expressive and moral arguments) and adds another dimension – legal arguments.[15] First, pragmatic or instrumental arguments are related to the choice of adequate means, instruments, strategies, and methods to achieve ends or to uphold values that are considered desirable and uncontroversial. Second,

---

12 Only a few months later in Rhineland-Palatinate the FDP, which had strongly resisted further exceptions of the renunciation obligation, appointed a German-Chilean dual citizen as minister of the interior (*Frankfurter Rundschau*, 1999-09-23). The Christian Democrats had meanwhile appointed a dual citizen, McAllister, as chair of the parliamentary party in Lower Saxony. The new minister-president of the *Bundesländer*-government, Christian Democrat Christian Wulff, was one of the most vigorous opponents of dual citizenship in the 1999 debate.

13 The public debate was analyzed on the basis of newspapers. These are listed in the '*References/Documents*'.

14 In contrast to non-argumentative speech acts – for example, simple announcements, confessions, promises, threats, offences – the giving of reasons for an articulated statement, interpretation, or proposal is the necessary and sufficient element of an argument. The formal structure of any argument can be characterized as a threefold relation: an actor (a) makes an assertive claim and (b) gives some relevant reasons (c) which are aimed to justify the claim in order to reach consent without force (*cf.* Toulmin 1958; Habermas 1981, 38; Kopperschmidt 1989, 91).

15 This classification is a slightly altered, supplemented, and renamed conceptualization of an element from Habermas's discourse ethics, where after a basic distinction between empirical and normative arguments he further differentiates within the normative dimension between pragmatic, ethical and moral questions, arguments and discourses related to spheres of effectiveness, goodness, and justice. See his 'Faktizität und Geltung' 1992, 197ff., 217ff. See also his application of the same dimensions as standards of rational individual action (Habermas 1991).

expressive arguments are those made in proposals and interpretations calling for fundamental values, norms, and traditions to be adhered to and protected as the bases of community and for ideals of common life to be pursued in the future. From the perspective of the people of a nation-state arguments of this kind inevitably concern the shared self-understanding and identity of political community (nationhood, elements of social cohesion, level of solidarity, etc.) and its (good) citizens (traits and habits, virtues, required duties). Third, moral arguments rely on the basic premise of modern morality that conflicts should be resolved by impartial consideration of the legitimate claims of all persons concerned and that individual persons should regard each other and be treated by the state as being of equal worth. That means that individual persons have some sort of legitimate interests which cannot be reduced to their social roles and functions and collective affiliations.[16] Because individual persons are considered as the basic units of morality, the protection of the physical and psychological integrity of persons is the core of modern morality. Fourth, legal arguments refer to existing laws. They can be related to three distinct spheres of law: international law, constitutional law, or single law. Such arguments essentially contain considerations and interpretations of the compatibility of policies and new legislation with international and constitutional law and their possible consequences for other realms of law.

For this analysis the different arguments have been situated within the broader belief systems (see Faist, this volume, chapter 1) of the political parties in Germany. In order to make sense of the dominant and persistent ideological cleavage structure within the German citizenship law reform debate we situated the most frequently articulated arguments for and against certain aspects of citizenship law reform and dual citizenship within three different belief systems: nationhood, multiculturalism, and integration. The first two categories have often been used to explain certain elements of citizenship laws in different countries. However, as it turned out, the third belief system, integration, is far more important for an understanding of the different positions of the contending political parties.[17]

Nation

The adoption of the old *Reichs- und Staatsangehörigkeitsgesetz* of 1913 at the formation of the West German state and the protracted restrictive conditions of naturalization for migrant workers who immigrated since the late 1950s has often

---

16 The basic intuition of moral arguments can be aptly grasped through the sometimes so-called second formula of the Kantian 'Categorical Imperative', according to which persons should not be treated only as means for other ends, but always as ends in themselves as well. If statements and justifications are related to the integrity and identity of persons and their basic rights these are moral arguments or, as Dworkin puts it, 'arguments of principle' in contrast to teleological arguments about the prospective benefits of the overall group, community, or state (*cf.* Dworkin 1978).

17 The following account of arguments and the classification in three different belief systems is based on an argumentation analysis of the documents listed in the '*References/Documents*'.

been explained by the continuity of an ethno-cultural understanding of nation (*cf.* Oberndörfer 1991; Brubaker 1992; Heckmann 1992, 211ff.; Hoffmann 1992, 61ff.). The scholarly canonization of the ideal-typical distinction between republican and ethnic concepts of nation is due to an exaggerated juxtaposition of traditional French and German nation concepts. This polarity has been unfolded within the conflict over the legitimate 'belonging' of Alsace-Lorraine (*cf.* Gosewinkel 2001). The 'French concept' of nationhood, which became the ideologically dominant model of the modern political nation and is based on territory, assimilation, and consent, stood in strong contrast to the 'German concept'. The latter emphasized the particularistic characteristics of an ethnic community of common origin and descent, and a national character based in language and tradition. The German ethno-cultural understanding of nation has its historical roots in 'late-nation' status and its cultural basis in the romantic philosophy of Fichte and Herder. According to these philosophers each people has its own particular soul, mind, and character. This credo has been considered as the ideological basis of 'German exceptionalism' until World War Two (Brubaker 1992). Essentially two criteria are relevant for the distinction of the two concepts of nation. On the level of the individual, republican membership is a question of subjective will and of individual readiness for affiliation and loyalty to state and nation. On the level of the political community, inclusion of all permanent residents who are subjected to valid laws into the nation and thus into citizenship is seen as a crucial precondition for public-mindedness. By contrast, an ethnic understanding of nation emphasizes the objective belonging to the cultural and linguistic community and political membership is acquired predominantly by descent. Thus, inclusion into the nation is seen as pre-political and is traced to common descent, cultural traditions, or lineage. Political participation and opportunities are seen and interpreted as an issue of inter-generational continuity. Thus, access to citizenship in ethnic nations is often differentiated according to ethnic origin and assumed cultural proximity, whereas it is open under the same conditions and equally for all kinds of immigrants in republican nations (*cf.* Alter 1985, 19ff.; Lepsius 1990; Brubaker 1992; Castles and Miller 1993, 35ff., 224ff.).

Since World War Two, however, the German concept of nation has undergone drastic changes. First, because the specific form of German nationalism has been identified as one of several factors contributing to the catastrophe of Nazi rule and the Holocaust, a strong denationalization process took place after the war – which saw decreasing levels of national identification and national pride on the part of German citizens. Second, the West German politics of western integration and the country's strong pro-European orientation as a consequence of occupation by the western allies and in the context of the Cold War significantly transformed national self-understanding in the Federal Republic of Germany (*cf.* Winkler 1991). Third, economic prosperity and the growth of the welfare state during the 'economic miracle' came increasingly to provide an alternative basis of collective pride and identity. Fourth, in the aftermath of the student revolts in 1968 a fundamental change took place in German political culture, namely a significant public sensitivity regarding all issues relating to the Holocaust, anti-Semitism, and totalitarianism. One of the crucial factors clearly referred to time and again within processes and initiatives to 'come to terms with the past' was the particular and aggressive form of German nationalism. Therefore, these debates on the German collective self-definition also contributed to decreasing levels of national identification.

One of the fundamental citizenship provisions of the German Basic Law has often been invoked as evidence of Germany's ethnic understanding of nation, but it can also be interpreted in another way. Article 116 states that former expatriates under Nazi rule, refugees, and displaced persons of German nationality (Volkszugehörigkeit) and their descendants, who lived within the territorial borders of 1937, have a privileged access to immigration and citizenship. But at least the original intent was very similar to the aims of Article 16 in trying to correct and react to historical injustice. Because persons belonging to these groups are of German ethnic origin but also because it was assumed that they were victims of persecution and expulsion during and after World War Two owing to their German origin, they were granted privileged access to entry and German citizenship – without further conditions because of the constitutionally guaranteed status.[18] Consequently, after the fall of the Iron Curtain, when rising numbers of re-settlers applied for access, it was legally possible for the German government to adjust the privileged status of re-settlers of German ethnic origin. Now re-settlers were treated increasingly like other immigrants and were expected to make efforts to integrate and to learn the German language (cf. Levy 2002). It is noteworthy that in 1993 the government introduced a new law (Kriegsfolgenbereinigungsgesetz), establishing that those wishing to immigrate from countries other than the former Soviet Union have to give proof of individual discrimination (Dietz 2002, 30). Thus, the assumption of a collective persecution and discrimination because of ethnicity was dropped when the authoritarian regimes in Eastern Europe began their transformations to democratic rule and made headway in establishing minority rights at least partially.

In the parliamentary debates on citizenship reform the proponents of dual citizenship, the Social Democrats, the Greens, PDS, and also the FDP, expressed a republican understanding of nation. They viewed both open access (under certain conditions) to membership according to the will of the applicant and congruence of residents and citizens as a precondition of democracy.[19]

Logically, if the claim that the restrictive aspects of German citizenship law and the delay of reform are related to an ethnic concept of nation, we would expect to find it among arguments put forth by Christian Democrats. However, with respect to the subjective component, the Christian Democrats also have a republican

---

18 Of course, with the escalation of the Cold War, ideological arguments also played a role in the admission of ethnic German re-settlers. The emigration of re-settlers from socialist countries could be used as evidence of the superiority of the West German system (Ronge 1997, 125).

19 The differences between these political parties concern minor aspects such as the duration of stay or other conditions deemed necessary for citizenship acquisition on the one hand and the content of social and cultural pluralism – which structured the kind of moral arguments to a certain degree – on the other hand.

understanding of the nation. For potential applicants to citizenship, they lay strong emphasis on the subjective will of the immigrant. This is, of course, a central feature of a republican understanding of citizenship in opposition to an objective definition according to descent. Their objection to dual citizenship is not based on the principle of descent. Rather it is based on the idea that renunciation of citizenship serves as a sort of loyalty oath reflecting the internal willingness and readiness of the individual immigrant to be part of the German political community. In line with this position the Christian Democrats have accepted a compromise with the Social Democrats with respect to a changing asylum law which introduced for the first time the right to naturalization under certain conditions.

As far as democratic congruence is concerned, the coalition government led by the CDU/CSU stated as early as 1984 that 'no state in the long run can accept that a significant number of the population stands outside of the state's loyalty duties for generations'.[20] Moreover, in the 1993 and 1999 parliamentary debates the Christian Democrats agreed to a modern citizenship law reform which would make it easier to naturalize and to acquire German citizenship for the second and third generation of immigrants. In their statements they repeatedly mentioned that it is necessary to overcome the outdated German citizenship law of 1913. According to their arguments, objections to an introduction of *jus soli* are not justified on ethnic or cultural grounds. Instead, the rejection of the *jus soli* principle was based on legal and constitutional reasons and on its problem of over-inclusiveness.[21] The latter was regarded as a potential danger because unambiguous state loyalty of citizens was considered important. In this respect the *jus sanguinis* principle was viewed as more trustworthy because it can be assumed that German parents are more likely to pass on to their children the norms, values, and a sense of belonging to the state. It is also worth noting that the Christian Democrats in their 1999 draft law demanded more restrictive conditions concerning the loss of citizenship. This fact also contradicts an ethnic concept of nation if it is rightly assumed that ethnic nations are inclined to uphold ties with citizens abroad.[22]

Christian Democrats made very few explicit references to the self-concept of nation. The most important expressive argument about the character of state membership was folded in with a legal argument. The CDU claimed that dual citizenship contradicts the very essence of citizenship (Wesen der Staatsangehörigkeit). This argument was put forward together with a quotation of the German constitutional court, defining citizenship in a very abstract manner as a 'comprehensive legal relationship from

---

20 See German Parliament, Printed matter 10/2071, 1984.

21 Concerning inherent problems of over-inclusiveness and under-inclusiveness of an *jus soli* for the second generation of immigrants, see Aleinikoff and Klusmeyer 2002, 12ff.

22 For instance, in this draft law the CDU/CSU proposed the automatic loss of German citizenship after ten years of continuous residence abroad and also in cases of foreign born persons at the age of 21 when continuously residing abroad. Because of the principle of avoiding statelessness in both cases the loss of German citizenship, however, should have been conditional on having another citizenship (German Parliament, Printed matter 14/535, 1999).

which certain rights and duties emerge'.[23] This statement was cited, invoked, and subsequently interpreted by politicians of the CDU/CSU in four of eight speeches during the deliberations on the two draft laws in parliament in 1993 and 1994. Occasionally, it has also been pointed out that every people is a community of fate (Schicksalsgemeinschaft). Therefore, exit and entry could not simply be a matter of individual preference and mood. However, the term 'community of fate' was not elaborated according to descent and hence in an ethnic interpretation of nation. Rather, this interpretation was explicitly connected to a judgement of the constitutional court. The statements could be read as the reasonable claim that citizenship is something very important which should not be devalued by confusing it with membership in voluntary associations like clubs, where exit and entry is predominantly a matter of individual choice according to utilitarian expectations.

Another explicit reference to national self-understanding which is worth noting is the open acceptance of the republican idea of nation in the final parliamentary debate about the citizenship law reform in May 1999. In his speech, the legal expert Rupert Scholz (CDU) confirmed a republican understanding of nation as a 'daily plebiscite', according to Ernest Renan. The same term was invoked by Interior Minister Otto Schily (SPD) as a justification for the new citizenship law. Agreeing with Schily's description Scholz defined nations as communities of both shared experience and shared will. However, Scholz framed the consent to the respective law reform as an essentially democratic question. He contended that shared will would mean the clearly articulated desire to continue a common life. In enacting this contentious law this community of shared experience and will would not be able to integrate in a mutually accepting way.[24]

In sum, we assert that arguments and statements of the Christian Democrats in parliament did not resonate with a belief system of 'ethnic nationhood'. For their part, the Social Democrats and the Greens used the notion of ethnic nationalism as a symbolic term of political struggle in order to blame their political opponents. The more left-wing parties from time to time attacked the Christian Democrats by insinuating that their real motives in blocking citizenship law reform could ultimately be traced back to their ethnic conceptualization. Occasionally, the proponents of reform added that the *jus sanguinis* principle has an inherent ethnic character, although it is undoubtedly a very common element of citizenship acquisition. Ultimately, the issue was framed as a choice between the way backwards to ethnic origin or to a future-oriented republican modernity, which is reflected in making a clear decision between either *jus sanguinis* or *jus soli*. The SPD and the Greens framed objections against *jus soli* by the CDU as a general refusal to overcome the legal relics of the Nazi past and the Holocaust.

---

23 See BVerfGE 83, 37 (1990).

24 Another Christian Democratic politician argued that nations could only survive in the future if they understood themselves as houses with open doors and windows and if they were oriented towards integration instead of separation. At the same time he referred to Yugoslavia as a warning example of a dangerous misunderstanding of nationalism (Jürgen Rüttgers, parliamentary speech, Legislative Period 14, Session 40, 1999-05-07, 3420).

In some scholarly treatment of the subject it has been argued that the ethno-cultural conception of nation still plays an important role within the range of values adhered to by the Christian Democrats. Because of the overall discursive climate, however, they would shrink away from stating such a view openly but rather frame it in a different, and innocuous vocabulary in order to attract electorates who have anxieties about and serious reservations concerning the cultural differences of immigrants (Sarcinelli and Stopper 2005). Certainly, although such a 'hidden agenda' of ethno-nationalism is difficult to examine, it cannot be precluded, because our analysis is limited to the statements made within official contexts and parliamentary and public debates. Nevertheless, the almost complete absence of respective official references in recent debates points to a fundamental transformation of the predominant understanding of nationhood in Germany. Researchers studying the ethno-cultural basis of the German nation within the context of citizenship law debates in former times were still able to derive their results from official documents such as legal texts, parliamentary debates, and public statements (*cf.* most prominent: Brubaker 1992). Furthermore, the 'hidden-agenda' thesis has be confronted with the fact that the Christian Party is indeed usually the most powerful but not the only political party in Germany and numerous internal party discussions on questions of integration and naturalization took place within this party in recent years.

Assimilation or Multiculturalism

While the stance on dual citizenship is influenced by the concept of nation, it might also be influenced by the existing immigrant integration regime and its justification. Whereas from a republican perspective dual citizenship should be accepted in order to reach a congruence of residents and citizens as far as possible and to avoid 'internal statelessness', the multicultural argument for acceptance of dual citizenship follows from recognition of the original cultural affiliation of immigrants.[25] Integration policies that take into account the original culture, language, and religion of immigrants are normally justified by the claim that the recognition of one's own culture is a precondition of individual freedom and a secure sense of identity and that it has beneficial consequences for immigrant integration as well (*cf.* Kymlicka 1995).

In Germany, however, the term 'multicultural society' has been used in an extremely vague and confusing manner because it is tied to nearly every political statement referring to the broad field of immigration and integration. Proponents used it predominantly to refer to the overdue recognition of Germany as an immigration country and associated it in that sense with several policy proposals. But it was very rarely connected to institutional patterns of multicultural integration as opposed to assimilation.[26] Nevertheless, elements of the institutional recognition of culture as '*de facto* multiculturalism' (Joppke and Morawska 2003, 8ff.) exist in Germany,

---

25 Concerning the ideal-typical structure of both argumentations, see Gerdes 2000.

26 Good examples are the articles of former General Secretary of the Christian Democrats Heiner Geißler (1996). Similar indeterminate statements can be found within the internal

especially in connection with religious freedom, an interpretation arising partly as a reaction to the persecution and extermination of the Jews in Nazi Germany.[27] Equal religious rights for Muslims, along with certain special exceptions,[28] are predominantly interpreted by political actors and imposed by administrative and constitutional courts as an aspect of their civil right to religious freedom.

Within the debates among the proponents of citizenship law reform there have been very few references to the beneficial aspects of a multicultural mode of integration. An implicit multicultural argument was that the acceptance of dual citizenship would be an adequate way of recognizing the 'dual identity' of the immigrant population in Germany. This was sometimes accompanied by the claim that the renunciation of a previous citizenship is psychologically difficult and could ultimately lead to severe conflicts within immigrant families if family members have different citizenships. However, it must be added that the accentuation was on the assumed motivations of the persons concerned to naturalize and not explicitly on recognition of bi-national or bi-cultural identity.

By contrast, some members of Christian Democratic parties, especially from the Bavarian Christian Social Union, regarded general acceptance of dual citizenship as an aspect of an emerging multicultural society and equated it with the emergence of 'parallel societies, linguistic islands and unlegislated areas'.[29] On occasion, leading politicians of the CSU, such as Günther Beckstein and Edmund Stoiber, claimed that dual citizenship would transform immigrant groups into national minorities. They

---

discourse and programme of the Green Party (cf. Bethschneider 1990; Tanz and Bethschneider 1990; Cohn-Bendit and Schmid 1992).

27 The extensive interpretation of religious freedom as, simultaneously, freedom of faith, of confession, and of practice (Article 4, Basic Law [German constitution]) has many aspects. To mention only a few: not only aspects of worship (sacred rites) in a more narrow sense but also religious customs as an aspect of a religious way of life are protected by the German constitution and judicial interpretation (cf. BVerfGE 32, 98, 106). The point of reference as to whether or not a certain practice is to be considered an expression and act of religious faith is first and foremost the self-understanding of the persons concerned. Religious freedom cannot be related to the sheer number of adherents or the social relevance of a certain religious persuasion (cf. BVerfGE 33, 23, 29). The German conception of religious neutrality, unlike the French, can be best described as a sort of positive neutrality or non-identification: the state has a responsibility not only for granting formal and private freedoms but also for providing the conditions for the realization of religious practices (cf. Bielefeldt 2003, 27f.; Kälin 2000, 135). In contrast to other basic rights religious freedom can be restricted only with reference to other basic freedoms, rights, or values which have a constitutional status.

28 For instance, administrative courts ruled in a number of cases that Muslim girls could legitimately claim a release from sport or swim lessons in public schools (BVerwGE 94, 82). Another example is the decision of the constitutional court in 2002 according to which ritual slaughter for Muslims must be allowed in specific situations on religious grounds, because the same exemption applies to members of the Jewish Community (BVerfGE 1 BvR 1783/99).

29 Interview with Michael Glos, chief of the CSU-country-group, German TV ARD ('ARD-Tagesthemen', 1999-01-06). The same tone is prevalent in published articles of leading politicians of the CSU on multiculturalism (cf. Stoiber 1989; Beckstein 1991).

would stand to obtain more expansive rights, such as official recognition of their language and the opportunity to establish their own ethnic parties. In sum, the right wing of the Christian Democratic parties succeeded in framing the issue as the very opposite of integration.[30]

Integration

The word used most often in both parliamentary and public debates was 'integration'. Consequently, the dominant contested issue was whether or not certain aspects of citizenship law reform in general and dual citizenship specifically would serve to facilitate or hinder the integration of immigrants. The term 'integration' itself, however, is extremely ambiguous and could be assigned various meanings (*cf.* Brumlik 1984; Bauböck 2001). For instance, in an abstract sense the term could be used to signify the insertion of new elements in an already existing whole. But it could also be related to the reproduction and interaction of the different parts within a given unity. Whereas the concept of nation covers the latter, the question of assimilation or multiculturalism concerns the former. The German debate on citizenship law reform is characterized by an overlapping of arguments und understandings of both overall integration and integration of immigrants, which explains the principled nature of the political debate and the persistent conflict structure.[31]

Both political camps ascribed different roles for state, society, and the individual immigrants in the process of integration.[32] The discursive conflict structure within the German debate on citizenship law reform can be summarized as shown in Figure 2.1.

According to the view of the proponents of *jus soli* and the acceptance of dual citizenship, immigrant integration is the responsibility of all actors involved. The readiness of the state and the receiving society to accept immigrants has to converge with the willingness of immigrants to integrate. The proponents tied the main

---

30   One could argue that these accounts of references to disintegration and parallel societies in the public discourse contradict our general thesis denying an ethnic-national self-definition in Germany. However, equally intense campaigns are waged without such references in a number of other states not usually thought of as characteristically ethno-cultural, for instance, the Netherlands (*cf.* de Hart this volume, chapter 3).

31   The more immigrant integration is regarded as a fundamental social and political problem, the greater the likelihood that aspects of social integration of immigrants and overall societal integration overlap in political debate. Then the basics of collective identity and political community and certain continuities and traditions of interpretation with regard to basic rights are at issue. Those general belief systems have been termed 'philosophies of integration' (Favell 1998). But whereas Favell, comparing Britain and France, describes overall national framework conditions enabling and constraining political action and justification, for the German context it is typical that two philosophies of integration within a single nation-state compete.

32   Such a perspective corresponds with familiar conceptual approaches according to which different political belief systems can be distinguished in relation to the distribution of roles, orientations, performances, responsibilities and duties they attribute to three broader realms of social integration, namely family, market, or civil society and the state (*cf.* Offe 2000).

Figure 2.1   Belief Systems of Political Parties: 'Integration'

	Immigrants	Society	State
Christian Democrats (Free Democrats)	• Loyalty; • Socio-economic-cultural integration.	• Static orientations; • Concept of societal solidarity.	• Focus on core state functions; • Focus on effective legitimacy.
Social Democrats/ Greens/PDS (Free Democrats)	• Equal rights; • Political integration.	• Institutional malleable orientations; • Concept of political solidarity.	• Focus on extensive and changing state functions; • Focus on democratic legitimacy.

arguments for eased naturalization conditions to political and social equality. Full legal and political inclusion of immigrants by means of citizenship law was viewed as both a moral question of equal and basic individual rights and a precondition of successful social integration. The equality argument was linked to different lines of reasoning: First, such moral arguments concerned above all the legal equality of those who continuously live within the state's jurisdiction. Citizenship and naturalization would be a precondition both of having full and equal rights and of having status as equal members of society in the eyes of the German population. In this view, equal legal and political status within a nation-state determines in certain important respects the social positions of persons. Second, it was argued that long-term residents have a right to feel at home in the place where they continuously live. An opportunity to acquire a new citizenship without giving up the previous citizenship is considered from this perspective not as a matter of right but also as an issue of a feeling of belonging to and identification with the political community. A third variant was a specification of the famous 'no taxation without representation' claim of the American Revolution. In this sense, it has often been said that those who have already for years fulfilled their duties as workers, as tax payers, and as contributors to social insurance schemes have a legitimate claim to all corresponding rights of citizenship. Fourth, with regard to the privileged access of East European re-settlers to German citizenship, which could not be made conditional on certain criteria for constitutional reasons, it was considered a matter of fairness to ease the conditions of citizenship acquisition for former guest-workers as well. Because German re-settlers are not obliged to give up their previous citizenship, tolerance of dual citizenship should also extend to other immigrant groups. Fifth, easier conditions of naturalization for long-term resident third-state nationals would be necessary because non-German EU-citizens have more rights than extracommunitari, especially voting rights at the local level. Because of the 1999 constitutional court's decision against alien voting rights there was no other route to political equality for third country nationals other than naturalization. Sixth, there was a counter-argument against the claim of the Christian Democrats that dual citizenship must be interpreted as a privilege. The Social Democrats and the Greens argued that dual citizenship could be seen instead as the elimination of an already existing privilege of Germans to work and settle in all other countries of the European Union, which is denied to all third country nationals.

Interestingly, the advocates of the government citizenship bill saw the moral aspect of equality of citizens as the basis for the expressive dimension of the identity of the political community. Loyalty of immigrants to state and society could essentially be expected as a result of successful legal and institutional integration. Moreover, integration is viewed as a matter of performance of different actors. The role of the state is to influence in a favourable way both the orientations of immigrants and the orientations of the domestic population. Immigrants would need offers and support by state institutions. Eased conditions of naturalization and hence high acquisition rates would send an important signal to the xenophobic sectors of society. The left-wing parties already reinforced their efforts to press for citizenship law reform after and because of the increased violent attacks on immigrants in 1993 and 1994 as a result of the heated political and public debate on asylum law. Integration through citizenship is viewed as important not only because of the corresponding rights, but also because of its high symbolic value regarding membership directed to both the immigrant and domestic populations. Furthermore, an adequate citizenship law reform could change the self-understanding of the political community leading to the recognition of Germany as a *de facto* immigration country. In sum, the proponents of citizenship law reform relied on what can be called the formative or socializing effects of political institutions.

The opponents of dual citizenship, on the other hand, used the term integration synonymously with or at least in relation to the loyalty of immigrants. Thus, the term integration was used predominantly in an expressive sense and was neither connected to the moral dimension of equality nor to legal inclusion. According to this view, integration is seen through the perspective of the demands of the state. Integration in this sense is first and foremost a performance and duty of the respective immigrants and their families. They must first demonstrate readiness to integrate on their own. Once a high degree of integration in economic, social, and cultural spheres of society as a result of individual efforts and orientation can be discerned, full political membership by citizenship can be granted. Only this type of social integration can provide a basis for assuring a sufficient degree of loyalty to the state. State offers are certainly necessary but are warranted only when the immigrants themselves show tangible efforts.[33] The opponents do not consider citizenship law as an appropriate instrument of integration. Rather, citizenship acquisition and political participation can be granted if social integration is brought to a close. Thus, the citizenship law has to contain reliable criteria, indicators of a comprehensive and successful social integration. The argument was that the different facets of social integration – for instance in kindergartens, schools, neighbourhoods, sports clubs, and within friendships – are generally neglected by the advocates of citizenship law

---

33 This view can also be found in the proposed CDU programmes of immigrant integration within the more recent discussion about a new immigration law. Proposed integration policies of the CDU/CSU are comparatively much more strongly tied to sanctions than to incentives.

reform in favour of a one-dimensional perspective on naturalization. The view in this camp is that naturalization should depend on a verifiable integration in the form of German language proficiency and basic knowledge of the German constitution. Here, the overall point of concern was that the debated draft legislation did not specify sufficient criteria indicating social integration. Indeed, the granting of dual citizenship would not only be unfavourable to the process of integration but also constitute a serious obstacle to integration. The opponents advanced three distinct arguments to support this claim: First, dual citizenship grants the possibility of return to the home country at any time and therefore hinders an unambiguous orientation towards the new country. This permanent possibility of return for immigrants could lead to evasion of duties and shirking responsibilities of citizenship. Second, renunciation of a previous citizenship is the central proof of authentic willingness to integrate on the immigrants' part and hence can serve as a sort of loyalty oath. In any case, naturalization without obligation to renounce the previous citizenship is detrimental to integration because it excuses immigrants from further efforts to integrate and releases them from taking a clear decision to one or another state and country. Third, dual citizenship is also a threat to integration because it undermines the 'basic societal consensus' and ignores the will of the overwhelming majority of the German people. This follows from the claim that dual citizenship is a privilege for immigrants who would have full access to two countries and all rights corresponding to the citizenship status.

Unlike the proponents, the opponents not only neglected moral arguments – with the exception of the privilege argument – they also frequently used instrumental arguments, especially regarding public safety, and legal arguments concerning security within single law. This finding suggests that the opponents considered issues of law and order and hence questions of upholding nation-state sovereignty of far greater importance than did the proponents. The main instrumental issue was the security interest of the state. With respect to the internal dimension, the opponents claimed that deportation in cases of serious criminal offenses would no longer be possible if the person concerned also holds German citizenship. Regarding the external dimension of state security they argued that other states could exercise influence within the German polity by 'using' their dual nationals as instruments of their particular policy interests (cf. Kadırbeyoğlu this volume, chapter 5). To grant exceptions on dual citizenship would always mean that the respective other state could influence the numbers of dual citizens, for instance by making it impossible to renounce citizenship.

The ideas of immigrant integration are intricately linked to overall societal integration. Instead of an ethnic concept of nation the Christian Democrats adhered to a more 'communitarian' idea of political community,[34] in two different variants. First, it is the basic right of the already existing political community to regulate

---

34 According to the ideal-typical classification of different concepts of citizenship from Bauböck the position of the Christian Democrats consequently must be assigned to the republican and not to the nationalist variant (see Bauböck 1998, 32ff.).

access of newcomers and therefore a matter of state sovereignty to define the instances of citizenship acquisition. Legitimate interests and rights of individuals must be respected but only if weighed against the more serious legitimate right to self-determination of the political community and the state (*cf.* Walzer 1983; chapter 2).[35] Second, overall integration of society cannot be regarded as the exclusive task of political institutions. Societal integration goes far beyond political loyalty in a more narrow sense, such as obedience to existing laws and the constitution. Rather, social cohesion and internal solidarity are based on a mixture of social, economic, and cultural elements which are viewed as a precondition of political integration. Instead of demanding cultural integration as the Christian Democrats do, it is more useful to refer to aspects of civil society, as for instance certain capacities of individual and collective self-organization in everyday life, which are regarded as necessary in modern democratic and market societies.[36] Placing an emphasis on societal integration is meant to underscore certain personal qualities like self-reliance and personal responsibility which could be reasonably expected from immigrants.[37] Moreover, existing orientations and practices of the indigenous population are seen to a certain degree as fixed or static. Thus, the existing civic culture is seen as a sort of constraint to political action. Attempts to reform citizenship law must take into account already existing orientations of the population.

For their part, the Social Democrats, the Greens, and the PDS hold that societal integration can and must be influenced by political measures in a substantive as well as in a symbolic way. The proponents of dual citizenship take precisely the opposite

35 Walzer, of course, argues from a normative standpoint that the right of the political community to decide on how much and which members it will admit is confined to immigration and border control. Regarding admission to citizenship long-term residents have a legitimate claim to became equal members. Thus, according to Walzer, the commingling of immigration and integration issues on the part of the Christian Democratic Parties is morally illegitimate. However, the Christian Democrats would respond, that they do not deny the principal claim to naturalization of residents after a certain period of stay, but only refuse to accept dual citizenship at the same time.

36 This view resonates with recent more general programmatic statements of the Christian Democrats. In various programmatic documents they refer to an often cited sentence coined in 1967 by a former judge of the constitutional court, after which the free and secular state builds upon preconditions which it could not guarantee on its own account (Böckenförde 1991, 112). Such remarks generally have been tied to a revival of the principle of subsidiarity, emphasizing individual capacities for active citizenship, i.e. to act on one's own responsibility, participate in civil associations, and get involved in self-help groups if necessary (*cf.* CDU-Basic Programme 'Freedom in Responsibility' 1994; Konrad-Adenauer-Stiftung 2003). In self-interpretations of the basic programme we find explicit references to communitarian thoughts and authors (*cf.* Kluxen-Pyta 1997; CDU Chair-Commission 2000). Theoretically, this perspective could be best described as a neo-Tocquevilleian view (*cf.* Bellah et al. 1985).

37 Such a perspective strongly corresponds with reform concepts of the Christian Parties regarding the welfare state. Therefore, the message addressed to immigrants is that citizens are or should be able to undertake sufficient initiatives for vocational training and job search, and to take on responsibilities and commitments for family members in need of care and the like.

standpoint according to which political integration influences the patterns of social integration. To rely on some sort of a pre-political cohesion is seen as incompatible with the facts of cultural and social pluralism in modern states and societies. Thus, overall political integration has to bear the main burden of internal cohesion. Loyalty is defined first and foremost by political and legal equal membership. Nation-state membership is tied to some sort of 'constitutional patriotism'[38] which means an individual identification with the constitution, democracy, the rule of law, and its corresponding institutions. Constitutional patriotism rejects the idea of citizens' affiliation with a culturally defined community.

These observations reveal that both contending political camps obviously had different understandings of political legitimacy. In emphasizing democratic congruence, constitutional patriotism, and equal political rights of participation, the Social Democrats, the Greens and segments of the Free Democrats and the PDS clearly espoused a concept of democratic legitimacy as the basis of political unity. These ideas, which come close to what can also be called input-legitimacy or procedural democracy, presumed the vast congruence of subjects and objects of political rule, i.e. that those who are subject to the law should be citizens and eligible to full political participation. By contrast, the Christian Democrats were primarily concerned with a concept which could be called output-legitimacy, focusing on upholding the capacities of the sovereign state, its intervention capacities, and the ability of its representatives to perform political core functions such as guaranteeing public and social security. Thus, they view political legitimacy predominantly as the empirical consent of the established citizenry.[39]

Conclusions

The puzzling result of the debates on the German citizenship law enacted in 1999 and valid since 2000 – a very liberal *jus soli* regime and a rather restrictive regulation regarding tolerance of dual citizenship – can essentially be explained by the factors inherent in the institutional and discursive opportunity structures. It can

---

38 By using the word 'constitutional patriotism' the proponents of citizenship law reform refer to a term which has been coined by Sternberger (1982) and Habermas (1987, 173).

39 Another interesting, but more implicit, difference concerned the universe of options available to individuals and the state. The opponents adhered to a more idealistic concept. They were oriented towards a comparison of two main alternatives: classical mono-citizens and dual citizens. Considering this alternative, especially regarding loyalty, mono-citizens logically will be preferred. On the other hand, the proponents of dual citizenship took into account a more extensive range. The alternative exists between mono-citizens, dual citizens, and non-citizens with continuing legal residence. If one assumes that naturalization is in the last instance a decision of the individual person, who presumably is not willing to acquire citizenship by giving up her previous citizenship, the more real choice is restricted between dual citizens and non-citizens. Logically, again regarding the prospect of loyalty, this alternative clearly would prefer dual citizens (*cf.* Neuman 1994). Yet such a pragmatic view of the issue was not openly discussed.

be interpreted as a political compromise, partly unintended, between very different interpretations of the nature of the relationship between the state and its citizens, the function of citizenship law, the integration of immigrants, and societal integration. The persistent dividing line between the relevant political parties was drawn well before the enactment of the law and fuelled by incentives created by the competitive party system and Germany's federal structure. This political structure invites the articulation and mobilization of dissent in trying to gain electoral support. With respect to the discursive opportunity structure, the debate on citizenship law reform in Germany was from the beginning of a very principled kind. Since the first debate in 1993/1994, main political actors such as the Social Democrats, the Greens, and the Free Democrats presented arguments that combined the moral and expressive dimensions. They argued in favour of introducing *jus soli* and giving up the renunciation requirement in order to increase the comparatively low naturalization rates in Germany. In moral terms they regarded naturalization as a precondition of equality; in expressive terms they viewed it as necessary to reach congruence between the resident population and the people as the basis of democracy. On the other side of the divide, the Christian Democrats combined legal-expressive and expressive-instrumental types of arguments. The dominance of instrumental arguments was due to both the strategic opportunity for a symbolic use of arguments in order to (re-)gain electoral support and their belief system on integration which delegates the main duties to the individual immigrant. Immigrant integration and hence naturalization were viewed predominantly from the perspective of the state and centred on questions of loyalty and positive contributions of immigrants.

Within the German discourse on citizenship law reform two fundamentally different understandings of citizenship were intertwined: 'citizenship-as-legal-status', meaning full legal membership in a particular political community conferring basic individual rights, and 'citizenship-as-desirable-activity', meaning citizenship as a function of one's actual participation in civil society (Kymlicka and Norman 1994). Whereas the proponents understood citizenship primarily as a legal status the opponents referred to citizenship as a desirable performance necessary for the common good. The Christian Democrats rejected dual citizenship precisely on the grounds that they viewed it as conferring rights without sufficient duties.

Hence, just as in other states, objections against dual citizenship were raised within a republican context rather than based on an ethno-cultural version of nationhood. Irrespective of country-specific features and traditions, such objections voiced by politicians[40] and political scientists[41] were cast in the language of duties, obligations,

---

40 The recent revisions of citizenship law with regard to dual citizenship in the Netherlands especially were justified in a similar way, emphasizing citizenship activities, responsibilities, and obligations (de Hart this volume, chapter 3). The same features apply to arguments against the general tolerance of dual citizenship made by conservative politicians in Sweden during the last debate on citizenship law reform (Spång this volume, chapter 4).

41 For instance, the basic structure of arguments against dual citizenship accentuating duties and commitments as a precondition for having citizenship rights is also very similar in

virtues, and commitments. Citizens generally are expected to possess and develop certain capacities of self-reliance, personal responsibility, and primary identification with the existing nation-state. Immigrants should use and invest their resources within the boundaries and to the benefit of the common good of the political community where they want to be citizens. Dual citizenship is regarded as a serious obstacle to such orientations, because it is held to undermine national sovereignty, akin to processes such as globalization, transnationalization, and sub-national identities. Therefore, the somewhat well-intentioned illusion of left-wing politicians and theorists that a changing understanding of the nation in the direction of republicanism would be the ultimate solution for the political inclusion of immigrants (cf. Kurthen 1995, 934f.) is seriously misleading. For some time, the German case has not been as exceptional as was assumed for so many years, and it is appropriate to say that the Germans are predominantly republicans now. However, arguing from a republican point of view does not necessarily entail a liberal stance on dual citizenship. Moreover, in arguing for an alternative belief system we do not claim that this leads inevitably to more liberal conditions of legal and political integration of immigrants. On the contrary, the ideas of societal integration on the part of the opponents of the recent citizenship law reform which are aimed at shifting the balance of rights and duties of prospective citizens are also very amenable to legitimizing a restrictive citizenship law regime. From this point of view a conservative belief system inspired by communitarian thoughts can serve as a sort of modern surrogate for a former ethnic nationalism.

Nevertheless, it stands to reason that tolerance of dual citizenship will grow in Germany. Some crucial mechanisms in liberal democratic states could favour an increased tolerance, especially the proliferation of exception groups. Since liberal and democratic nation-states recognize basic individual rights, they are internally compelled to grant certain exceptions. For instance, this is necessary in those cases when governments refuse to release their citizens, and in several cases of gender equality, especially when parents pass their citizenship to their children. The German case reveals, as indicated especially in the expert hearings in 1999, that trouble would obviously arise in trying to continually construct new groups who are treated unequally with respect to allowances of dual citizenship. The discussion and implementation of the new German citizenship law raise questions of inequality, which normally must always be justified on reasonable grounds legally and politically. On the one hand, the more substantial and extensive the interpretation of individual rights and the more related they are to possession of citizenship, the more exceptions have to be granted. On the other hand, this leads to a proliferation of 'exception groups'. If additional exception groups are constructed in the name of European integration or as an expression of certain special inter-state relations, as in the case of Germany and France, the issue becomes complicated even further. For instance, it was pointed out in the expert hearings in 1999 that the clause allowing dual citizenship with member states of the EU in general on the basis of reciprocal

---

the US, deemed as one of the most republican countries of all, as visible in related discussions of political scientists (see for example Renshon 2001; Huntington 2004).

Figure 2.2   Germany: Chronological List of Dual Citizenship-Related Legislation

Date	Legislation	Insitutional and Discursive Opportunity Structures
1949	**German Constitution** (Basic Law): Protecting human dignity against contingent political majorities; strong system of judicial review.	Because of a possible judicial review, political actors have always been sensitive regarding the compatibility of political measures with constitutional provisions.
	Article 16 prohibits the deprivation of citizenship as a reaction to expatriation practices of the Nazi Regime.	Article 16 of the Basic Law has been invoked repeatedly by legal experts and politicians as ruling out the possibility of general tolerance of dual citizenship.
	Adaptation of **German Citizenship Law** of 1913, based on *jus sanguinis*.	Initially interim solution with regard to the political aim of German reunification.
1974	**Constitutional Court**: Decision that citizenship of children must be passed on by fathers and mothers in equal conditions, but stating that dual citizenship is in principle an 'evil' to be avoided in aid of both states and individuals.	Since then it has become common understanding that avoiding dual citizenship is an important principle which could be overruled only by higher-ranking constitutional values.
1990	**Constitutional Court**: Ruling out local voting rights for resident non-citizens, but recommending facilitation of naturalization by reforms of citizenship law in order to reduce the gap between subjects of the law and citizens.	Since then, for political parties advocating measures of legal and political inclusion of immigrants the only political option was to ease naturalization rules by altering the citizenship law.
1993	**Partial Citizenship Law Reform**: Introduction of as-of-right naturalizations under specified conditions.	Achieved within a broader compromise; the introduction of as-of-right naturalizations was an additional opportunity for the Christian Democrats to argue against the tolerance of dual citizenship.
1999	**Adoption of a new Citizenship Act**: Entered into force from 1ˢᵗ January 2000; upholding the prohibition of dual citizenship in general, but providing for many exceptions.	The final unintended compromise, fuelled by the competitive party structure and the system of federalism, introducing at the same time a very liberal *jus soli* and a still restrictive stance against dual citizenship, mirrors the conflicting positions.

consent[42] would lead to an additional instance of discrimination against third-country nationals. Moreover, what about the inequality of *jus soli* dual citizens on the one hand vs. *jus sanguinis* dual citizens on the other, with respect to the obligation to give up the previous citizenship? Furthermore, differences in opportunities regarding maintenance of original citizenship of immigrants who naturalize in Germany and Germans who naturalize elsewhere can be detected. Within the EU there are second-

---

42 In the meantime this provision of mutual acceptance of dual citizenship is generally valid in relation to Belgium, France, Great Britain, Greece, Hungary, Ireland, Italy, Malta, Poland, Portugal, Slovakia, and Sweden, and, in cases of certain categories of persons, with the Netherlands and Slovenia.

generation third-state immigrants who have a range of choices in upholding their original citizenship. There are also, compared to other groups, fewer opportunities to obtain a permit to maintain original citizenship for foreign spouses of Germans at naturalization. Concerning the German case, it is not unlikely that some aspects of unequal treatment resulting from the implementation of the 'option model' and other provisions of the new citizenship law will bring some cases of unequal treatment before the constitutional court. This could lead to further steps being taken towards granting dual citizenship. Furthermore, if naturalization rates remain low, because giving up one's previous citizenship turned out to be the main obstacle against naturalization, it may also be politically necessary to revise the citizenship law of 1999 once again.

References

Aleinikoff, T. A. and Klusmeyer, D. (2001), 'Plural Nationality: Facing the Future in a Migratory World', in Aleinikoff, T.A. and Klusmeyer, D. (eds), 63-88.

Aleinikoff, T. A. and Klusmeyer, D. (eds) (2001), *Citizenship Today: Global Perspectives and Practices* (Washington, D.C.: Carnegie Endowment for International Peace).

Aleinikoff, T. A. and D. Klusmeyer (2002), *Citizenship Policies for an Age of Migration* (Washington D.C.: Carnegie Endowment for International Peace).

Alter, P. (1985), *Nationalismus* (Frankfurt am Main: Suhrkamp).

Bade, K. J. (ed.) (1996), *Die multikulturelle Herausforderung* (München: Beck).

Bauböck, R. (1998), 'The Crossing and Blurring of Boundaries in International Migration: Challenges for Social and Political Theory', in Bauböck, R. and Rundell, J. (eds), 17-52.

Bauböck, R. (2001), 'Integration von Einwanderern – Reflexionen zum Begriff und seinen Anwendungsmöglichkeiten', in Waldrauch, H. (ed.), 17-52.

Bauböck, R. and Rundell, J. (eds) (1998), *Blurred Boundaries: Migration, Ethnicity, Citizenship* (Aldershot: Ashgate).

Bayaz, A., Damolin, M. and Ernst, H. (eds) (1984), *Integration. Anpassung an die Deutschen?* (Weinheim/Basel: Beltz).

Beckstein, G. (1991), 'Einheit in kultureller Vielfalt', in Micksch, J (ed.), 40-7.

Bellah, R. N., Madsen, R., Sullivan, W. M., Swidler, A. and Tipton, S. M. (1985), *Habits of the Heart: Individualism and Commitment in American Life* (Berkeley: University of California Press).

von Beyme, K. (1999), *Das politische System der Bundesrepublik Deutschland* (Opladen/ Wiesbaden: Westdeutscher Verlag).

Bielefeldt, H. (2003), *Muslime im säkularen Rechtsstaat: Integrationschancen durch Religionsfreiheit* (Bielefeld: transkript).

Böckenförde, E.-W. (1991), 'Die Entstehung des Staates als Vorgang der Säkularisation', in Böckenförde, E.-W. (ed.), 92-114.

Böckenförde, E.-W. (1991), *Recht, Staat, Freiheit* (Frankfurt am Main: Suhrkamp).

Bös, M. (2000), 'Die rechtliche Konstruktion von Zugehörigkeit. Staatsangehörigkeit in Deutschland und den USA', in Holz, K. (ed.), 93-118.

Brubaker, R. (1992), *Citizenship and Nationhood in France and in Germany* (Cambridge, Mass./London: Harvard University Press).

Brumlik, M. (1984), 'Was heißt Integration? Zur Semantik eines sozialen Problems', in Bayaz, A., Damolin, M. and Ernst, H. (eds), 75-97.

Castles, S. and Miller, M. (1993), *The Age of Migration: International Population Movements in the Modern World* (London: Macmillan).

Cohn-Bendit, D. and Schmid, T. (1992), *Heimat Babylon. Das Wagnis der multikulturellen Demokratie* (Hamburg: Hoffmann und Campe).

Die Grünen (ed.), *Die multikulturelle Gesellschaft. Für eine demokratische Umgestaltung in der Bundesrepublik* (Bonn).

Dietz, B. (2002), 'East Western Migration Patterns in an Enlarging Europe: The German Case', *The Global Review of Ethnopolitics* 2, 29-43.

Dworkin, R. (1978), *Taking Rights Seriously* (Harvard: Harvard University Press).

Edelman, M. (1971), *Politics as Symbolic Action: Mass Arousal and Quiescence* (Chicago: Markham).

Faist, T. (1994), 'How to Define a Foreigner? The Symbolic Politics of Immigration in German Partisan Discourse', *West European Politics* 17, 50-71.

Faist, T. (ed.) (2000), *Transstaatliche Räume. Politik, Wirtschaft und Kultur in und zwischen Deutschland und der Türkei* (Bielefeld: Transkript).

Favell, A. (1998), *Philosophies of Integration: Immigration and the Idea of Citizenship in France and Britain* (London: Macmillan).

Gauger, J.-D. (ed.) (1997), *Philosophie als Argument* (Sankt-Augustin: Konrad-Adenauer-Stiftung).

Geißler, H. (1996), 'Bürger, Nation, Republik – Europa und die multikulturelle Gesellschaft', in Bade, K.J. (ed.), 125-46.

Gerdes, J. (2000), 'Der doppelte Doppelpass. Transstaatlichkeit, Multikulturalismus und doppelte Staatsbürgerschaft', in Faist, T. (ed.), 235-98.

Goes, N. I. (1997), *Mehrstaatigkeit in Deutschland* (Baden-Baden: Nomos).

Gosewinkel, D. (2001), *Einbürgern und Ausschließen. Die Nationalisierung der Staatsangehörigkeit vom Deutschen Bund bis zur Bundesrepublik Deutschland* (Göttingen: Vandenhoeck & Ruprecht).

Green, S. (2001), 'Citizenship Policy in Germany: the Case of Ethnicity over Residence', in Hansen, R. and Weil, P. (eds), 24-51.

Habermas, J. (1981), *Theorie des kommunikativen Handelns* 2 vols. (Frankfurt am Main: Suhrkamp).

Habermas, J. (1987), 'Geschichtsbewusstsein und posttraditionale Identität. Die Westorientierung der Bundesrepublik', in Habermas, J. (ed.), 161-79.

Habermas, J. (ed.) (1987), *Eine Art Schadensabwicklung* (Frankfurt am Main: Suhrkamp).

Habermas, J. (1991), 'Vom pragmatischen, ethischen und moralischen Gebrauch der Vernunft', in Habermas, J. (ed.), 100-18.

Habermas, J. (ed.) (1991), *Erläuterungen zur Diskursethik* (Frankfurt am Main: Suhrkamp).

Habermas, J. (1992), *Faktizität und Geltung* (Frankfurt am Main: Suhrkamp).

Hailbronner, K. (1992), *Einbürgerung von Wanderarbeitnehmern und doppelte Staatsangehörigkeit* (Baden-Baden: Nomos).

Hammar, T. (1990), *Democracy and the Nation State* (Aldershot: Avebury).

Hansen, R. and Weil, P. (eds) (2001), *Towards a European Nationality* (Basingstoke: Palgrave).

Heckmann, F. (1992), *Ethnische Minderheiten, Volk und Nation* (Stuttgart: Enke).

Hoffmann, L. (1992), *Die unvollendete Republik. Zwischen Einwanderungsland und deutschem Nationalstaat* (Köln: PapyRossa).

Holz, K. (ed.) (2000), *Staatsbürgerschaft. Soziale Differenzierung und politische Inklusion* (Wiesbaden: Westdeutscher Verlag).

Huntington, S.P. (2004), *Who Are We* (New York: Simon & Schuster).

Joppke, C. (1999), *Immigration and the Nation Sate: The United States, Germany and Great Britain* (Oxford: Oxford University Press).

Joppke, C. (2000), 'Mobilization of Culture and the Reform of Citizenship Law: Germany and the United States', in Koopmans, R. and Statham, P. (eds), 145-61.

Joppke, C. and Morawska, E. (2003), 'Integrating Immigrants in Liberal Nation-States: Policies and Practices', in Joppke, C. and Morawska, E. (eds), 1-36.

Joppke, C. and Morawska, E. (eds) (2003), *Toward Assimilation and Citizenship: Immigrants in Liberal Nation-States* (Houndsmill: Palgrave-Macmillan).

Kälin, W. (2000), *Grundrechte im Kulturkonflikt* (Zürich: NZZ-Verlag).

Kluxen-Pyta, D. (1997), 'Philosophische Implikationen im Grundsatzprogramm der CDU', in Gauger, J.-D. (ed.), 11-25.

Koopmans, R. and Statham, P. (eds) (2000), *Challenging Immigration and Ethnic Relation Politics: Comparative European Perspectives* (Oxford: Oxford University Press).

Kopperschmidt, J. (1989), *Methodik der Argumentationsanalyse* (Stuttgart-Bad Cannstadt: Fromann-Holzboog).

Kurthen, H. (1995), 'Germany at the Crossroads: National Identity and the Challenges of Immigration', *International Migration Review* 29, 914-38.

Kymlicka, W. (1995), *Multicultural Citizenship* (Oxford: Oxford University Press).

Kymlicka, W. and Norman, W. (1994), 'Return of the Citizen: A Survey of Recent Work on Citizenship Theory', *Ethics* 104, 352-81.

Lepsius, M. R. (1990), 'Nation und Nationalismus in Deutschland', in Lepsius, M. R. (ed.), 232-46.

Lepsius, M. R. (ed.) (1990), *Interessen, Ideen und Institutionen* (Opladen: Westdeutscher Verlag).

Levy, D. (2002), 'The Transformation of Germany's Ethno-Cultural Idiom: The Case of Ethnic German Immigrants', in Levy, D. and Weiss, Y. (eds), 221-35.

Levy, D. and Weiss, Y. (eds) (2002), *Challenging Ethnic Citizenship* (New York/Oxford: Berghahn).

von Mangoldt, H. (1993), 'Öffentlich-rechtliche und völkerrechtliche Probleme mehrfacher Staatsangehörigkeit aus deutscher Sicht', *Juristenzeitung* 48, 965-74.

Meier-Braun, K.-H. (2002), *Deutschland, Einwanderungsland* (Frankfurt am Main: Suhrkamp).

Micksch, J (ed.) (1991), *Deutschland – Einheit in kultureller Vielfalt* (Frankfurt am Main: Otto Lembeck).

Münz, R. and Weiner, M. (eds) (1997), *Migrants, Refugees, and Foreign Policy* (Providence/Oxford: Berghahn).

Neuman, G. L. (1994), 'Justifying U.S. Naturalization Policies', *Virginia Journal of International Law* 35, 268-77.

Oberndörfer, D. (1991), *Die offene Republik* (Freiburg/Basel/Wien: Herder).

Offe, C. (2000), 'Civil Society and Social Order: Demarcating and Combining Market, State and Community', *Archives Européenes de Sociologie* 36, 71-94.

Plessner, H. (1982), *Die verspätete Nation* (Frankfurt am Main: Suhrkamp).

Renshon, S.A. (2001), *Dual Citizenship and American National Identity* (Washington, D.C.: Center for Immigration Studies).

Ronge, V. (1997), 'German Policies Toward Ethnic German Minorities', in Münz, R. and Weiner, M. (eds), 117-40.

Sarcinelli, U. (1989), 'Symbolische Politik und politische Kultur', *Politische Vierteljahreszeitschrift* 30, 292-309.

Sarcinelli, U. and Stopper, J. (2005), 'Doppelte Staatsangehörigkeit und Demokratie: zwischen Kulturnation und Verfassungspatriotismus', in Schröter, Y. M., Mengelkamp, C. and Jäger, R. S. (eds), 68-96.

Schröter, Y. M., Mengelkamp, C. and Jäger, R. S. (eds) (2005), *Doppelte Staatsbürgerschaft – ein gesellschaftlicher Diskurs über Mehrstaatigkeit* (Landau: Verlag Empirische Pädagogik).

Sternberger, D. (1982), *Verfassungspatriotismus* (Hannover: Niedersächsische Landeszentrale für politische Bildung).

Stoiber, E. (1989), 'Liegt Deutschlands Zukunft in einer multikulturellen Gesellschaft?', *Botschaft und Dienst* 2, 19-22.

Thränhardt, D. (1993), 'Die Ursprünge von Rassismus und Fremdenfeindlichkeit in der Konkurrenzdemokratie. Ein Vergleich der Entwicklung in England, Frankreich und Deutschland', *Leviathan* 21, 336-57.

Toulmin, S. E. (1958), *The Uses of Argument* (Cambridge: Cambridge University Press).

Trenz, E. and Bethschneider, M. (1990), '"Multikulturelle Gesellschaft" Umfassende demokratische Umgestaltung', in Die Grünen (ed.), 8-19, 88-93.

Waldrauch, H. (ed.) (2001), *Die Integration von Einwanderern. Ein Index der rechtlichen Diskriminierung* (Frankfurt am Main/New York: Campus).

Walzer, M. (1983), *Spheres of Justice. A Defence of Pluralism and Equality* (New York: Basis Books).

Winkler, H.A. (1991), 'Nationalismus, Nationalstaat und nationale Frage in Deutschland seit 1945', *Aus Politik und Zeitgeschehen* 41, 12-24.

Documents

Parliamentary Documents: Motions and Draft Legislations on Citizenship Law Reform, Foreigner Law and Integration

Federal Parliament
Printed matter 10/2071, 1984 (Christian Democrats).
Printed matter 11/4268, 1989-03-23 (Social Democrats).
Printed matter 11/4464, 1989-05-03 (Greens).
Printed matter 12/1714, 1991 (Greens).
Printed matter 12/4533, 1993-03-10 (Social Democrats).
Printed matter 12/5684, 1993-09-16 (Social Democrats via Bundesrat).
Printed matter 13/259, 1995-01-19 (Social Democrats).
Printed matter 13/423, 1995-02-08 (Greens).
Printed matter 13/2833, 1995-10-30 (Social Democrats).
Printed matter 13/3657, 1996-02-01 (Greens).
Printed matter 13/8157, 1997-07-02 (Social Democrats via Bundesrat).
Printed matter 14/296, 1999-01-19 (Free Democrats).
Printed matter 14/532, 1999-03-16 (Christian Democrats).
Printed matter 14/533, 1999-03-16 (Social Democrats, Greens, Free Democrats).

Printed matter 14/534, 1999-03-16 (Christian Democrats).
Printed matter 14/535, 1999-03-16 (Christian Democrats).

Bundesrat
Printed matter 402/93, 1993-06-09 (Social Democrats).
Printed matter 745/95, 1995-11-03 (Social Democrats).
Printed matter 180/97, 1997-03-11 (Social Democrats, Free Democrats).

Parliamentary Debates, Federal Level, Minutes
Legislative Period 12, Session 155, 1993-04-29, pp. 13196-13213.
Legislative Period 12, Session 189, 1993-11-11, pp. 16272-16278.
Legislative Period 12, Session 225, 1994-04-28, pp. 19404-19415.
Legislative Period 14, Session 28, 1999-03-19, pp. 2281-2319.
Legislative Period 14, Session 40, 1999-05-07, pp. 3415- 3477.
Legislative Period 14, Session 40, 1999-05-07, pp. 3420 (Rüttgers, parliamentary speech).

Expert Hearings
Minutes, expert hearing at the Committee on Internal Affairs, Session 75, 1993-09-27.
Minutes, expert hearing at the Committee on Internal Affairs, Session 12, 1999-04-13.

Party Documents
CDU, Party Platform (Grundsatzprogramm): 'Freiheit in Verantwortung', 1994.
CDU, Chair Commission (Präsidiumskommission) 'Spielraum für kleine Einheiten': 'Starke Bürger. Starker Staat', Discussion Paper (Diskussionspapier), 2000.
Konrad-Adenauer-Stiftung, Board of Trustees (Kuratorium): 'Aufbruch in die Bürgergesellschaft: Weniger Staat – mehr Eigenverantwortung', Platform Paper (Grundsatzpapier), 2003.

Newspapers

Articles on dual citizenship, dual nationality and citizenship law from December 1998 – June 1999
Frankfurter Allgemeine Zeitung.
Süddeutsche Zeitung.
Die Tageszeitung.
Die Welt.

Television

News and News Magazines, from January 2ⁿᵈ to January 18ᵗʰ 1999
ARD: 'Tagesschau', 'Tagesthemen'.
RTL: 'RTL-Aktuell', 'Nachtjournal'.
ZDF: 'Heute', 'Heute-Journal'.

TV Talkshows Federal level
ARD: 'Sabine Christiansen': 'Politschlacht ums Ausländerrecht', 1999-01-10.

ARD: 'Presseclub': 'Doppel-Pass: Der Streit um die doppelte Staatsbürgerschaft', January 1999.

SAT 1: 'Talk im Turm': 'Wieviele Ausländer verträgt Deutschland noch?', 1998.

ZDF: 'Halb Zwölf': 'Doppelpass', 1999-01-10.

TV Talkshows Regional level

Bavarian TV 3: 'Münchner Runde': 'Integration per Gesetz? – Streit um doppelte Staatsbürgerschaft', 1999-01-11.

Hessen TV 3: 'Vorsicht Friedmann': 'Kampf um die doppelte Staatsbürgerschaft', 1999-01-12.

North German TV 3: 'Talk vor Mitternacht': 'Doppelte Staatsbürgerschaft: Gefahr für Deutschland?', 1999-01-11.

Chapter 3

The End of Multiculturalism: The End of Dual Citizenship? Political and Public Debates on Dual Citizenship in The Netherlands (1980-2004)

Betty de Hart[1]

Abstract

Beginning on 1st January 1992 immigrants who wanted to naturalize in the Netherlands were no longer required to renounce their original citizenship. In 1997 the renunciation demand was reinstated. The Dutch citizenship Law of 2000 made the acquisition of Dutch citizenship more difficult, while at the same time it has become easier for Dutch emigrants to retain dual citizenship. This article explains these contradictory consequences, on the one hand for immigrants and on the other hand for Dutch emigrants, by focusing on the development of Dutch integration policies. Integration policies have changed in recent years from a pragmatic pluralist approach to a more principled assimilationist approach. This shift in integration policies is explained by the changing concept of nationhood in the Netherlands, which became more expressive, or what might be seen as republican with increasingly strong ethno-cultural voices.

Introduction

In 1991 the Dutch government coalition of Christian Democrats (*CDA*) and Social Democrats (*PvdA*) abolished the renunciation requirement for naturalization. Starting on 1st January 1992, immigrants who wanted to naturalize were no longer required to renounce their original citizenship. In 1997, after years of debate in parliament, the

---

1   The author wishes to thank Thomas Faist, Bielefeld University, the coordinator of the project 'Multiple Citizenship in a Globalizing World', and other participants in the project for their comments and suggestions. The author also wishes to thank Kees Groenendijk of the University of Nijmegen (the Netherlands) for his guidance and comments throughout the research. Nils Coleman took care once more of the English.

renunciation requirement was reinstated. The Dutch Citizenship Law of 2000, which came into force on 1st April 2003, has made the acquisition of Dutch citizenship more difficult. At the same time it has become easier for Dutch emigrants to retain Dutch citizenship and hold dual citizenship.

This chapter discusses and attempts to provide explanations for the development of Dutch legislation and policy concerning dual citizenship. On what ground was the renunciation requirement abolished and how was its subsequent reinstatement defended? How can a policy concerning dual citizenship which has different and contradictory consequences for immigrants and Dutch emigrants be explained?

To answer these questions, this chapter provides an analysis of political debates since 1985, the point at which the renunciation requirement first came under discussion. In explaining the development of policy regarding dual citizenship, a central issue is whether it was the Dutch concept of 'nation' that was determining the outcome, or whether there were other factors at play. This chapter demonstrates that from the 1980s access to naturalization and dual citizenship was initially dealt with in a pragmatic manner, with the objective being the effective integration of immigrants. The prevailing notion at the time, in a shared understanding between the political left and right, was that the integration of immigrants had to be fostered by granting immigrants a strong legal position. Naturalization was perceived as a means to further such integration. Efforts were taken to make access to Dutch citizenship easier. During this period, naturalization became a right instead of a favour. The duration of procedures was shortened considerably and the decision-making process was transferred from police and judicial authorities to municipal authorities, who from that point onwards would provide advice to the Immigration and Naturalization Service (*IND*). The abolishment of the renunciation requirement in 1992 can be seen as a next step in the effort to make naturalization for immigrants easier. In the period between 1992 and 1997, naturalization rates rose considerably while 80 per cent of the naturalized immigrants retained their first citizenship.

During the 1990s, however, this pragmatism made way for a more formalistic approach. The Dutch government's and political parties' approach towards integration of immigrants changed. Gradually, in a newly built consensus between left and right, naturalization was no longer seen as a means to further integration, but as the 'crowning' of a completed integration process. This can be explained in the context of a shift away from multicultural policies to more assimilationist policies. In contrast to the 1980s, a higher degree of cultural adaptation was expected, and dual citizenship came to be seen as a cultural issue. The result was that the renunciation requirement was reinstated in 1997 and access to naturalization was made more difficult by means of the new Citizenship Law 2000.

Thus, arguments within the ideological system of 'integration' are important if one is to explain the development of renunciation policy. However, as this chapter attempts to demonstrate, arguments on the issue of dual citizenship should also be placed within the ideological system of 'nation'. During the period under consideration, the Netherlands shifted from a vague and implicit, so to speak 'empty', concept of nationhood at the beginning of the 1980s to a more explicit concept of nationhood. This development first became clear in 2001, under the reign of the Purple government of the Social Democrat (*PvdA*), the conservative-liberal *VVD*, and the progressive-liberal *D66*. In this period, the Dutch republican model of nationhood not only became more explicitly republican, it also came under pressure by ethno-cultural voices in political and public debates on citizenship. This development became increasingly important after the remarkable changes in Dutch politics following 9/11 and the killing of the populist politician Pim Fortuyn in May 2002. The provisional result of these changes is that the current Balkenende II government (CDA, VVD, D66) considers dual citizenship as undesirable and intolerable. Plans to ban dual citizenship are underway.

The above developments and the present intention to ban dual citizenship could be explained as a clean break in the Dutch thinking about integration and dual citizenship. After all, the Netherlands were perceived as a pacesetter for multicultural policies. In this chapter I argue that it would be more accurate to interpret the current state of play as the result of a path-dependant process (Gerdes, Rieple and Faist, this volume, chapter 2), and a continuation of Dutch integration policies, which have defined immigrants as ethnic and cultural 'others', in new terms.

In order to explain the final outcomes of the political debates on dual citizenship, it is necessary first to describe the development of the Dutch version of multiculturalism and its relationship to both integration policies and the Dutch concept of nationhood. I will then outline the political opportunity structure, including a description of Dutch consensus policy. The discussions of integration policies, nationhood, and the political opportunity structure will help us understand the arguments used within political debate on dual citizenship. After reviewing the political debates, the media debate will be analyzed. In concluding, I will offer possible explanations for the current outcomes of the political process.

Multiculturalism and Integration

As mentioned above, the Netherlands are often viewed as a pacesetter of multicultural policies (e.g. Vermeulen and Penninx 2000, 3). More recently, the shift from multiculturalism towards a more assimilationist approach has also been noted (Joppke and Morawska 2003, 2).

In the aftermath of World War Two, the Netherlands had to respond to the immigration from the former Dutch colony of Indonesia, followed by the immigration of Mediterranean guest-workers in the 1950s and 1960s, and immigration from Surinam, the Dutch colony that became independent in 1975. During the 1970s, the Dutch government developed a two-track policy aimed at both integration and the return of immigrant guest-workers to their home country. Dutch society in general and the government in particular became more aware of the ambiguous attitudes among Dutch citizens towards immigrants after the terrorist actions carried out by Moluccans during the 1970s. In 1978, during a debate on the Moluccan minority group, the PvdA asked for a coordinated policy which would concern all minority groups (Fermin

1997, 79). At the request of the Dutch government in 1979, the Scientific Council for Government Policy (*Wetenschappelijke Raad voor het Regeringsbeleid*, 1979) presented its influential report, *Ethnic Minorities*, in which it advised the government to accept the fact that immigrants would remain permanently in the Netherlands, and to develop a policy aimed at the equal participation of minorities in society. With the government's acceptance of these recommendations, the Dutch minority policy became a fact. In 1983 the government presented a Memorandum on minority policy. This Memorandum focused on immigrants as *groups*, explaining their disadvantaged social and economic position as a consequence of cultural differences (van Walsum 1998, 2). Minority policies would be designed to allow for cultural pluralism (for example, education for immigrant children in their native language) as a means to stimulate emancipation and integration. A strong legal position for immigrants was considered of paramount importance for furthering integration. Hence, in the 1980s many initiatives were taken to improve the legal position of immigrants, and to promote naturalization. On the whole, however, these policies were never based on a principled multiculturalism. Rather, they were based on a pragmatism that would later be labelled as multiculturalism in public and scientific discourse.

The consensus on minority policy that emerged during the 1980s broke down during the 1990s. Starting in 1991, with the famous Luzern speech by the political leader of the VVD, Frits Bolkestein, Dutch minority policies became increasingly contested.[2] The idea emerged that ethnic minorities had been treated too liberally; that they had been 'pampered' without imposing demands. Opportunities that had been granted to minorities in the enjoyment of certain 'cultural rights', were now considered to be an obstacle to integration. Consistent with the growing popularity of neo-liberal ideas in the 1990s more generally, the group approach was replaced by an individual approach. The emphasis was no longer on rights, but on the obligation of individuals as citizens. In 1998, so-called newcomer programmes were introduced, which required individual immigrants to take language and civic knowledge courses. During this period, ethnic minorities were renamed non-western *allochtones* in political discourse.[3]

An influential essay by the Dutch publicist Paul Scheffer (2000) entitled 'The Multi-cultural Tragedy', the events of 9/11 2001, and finally the influence of the populist politician Pim Fortuyn gave rise to an atmosphere of increasing tension. In this atmosphere the idea emerged that minorities had not only been pampered, but that the integration of minorities had failed. Integration of non-western *allochtones*, now referred to as 'Muslims', was no longer to be encouraged, but demanded. Immigrants had to express loyalty to the Dutch constitutional state and Dutch cultural norms and

---

2   In this speech Bolkestein explicitly addressed the question whether an Islamic background was compatible with Dutch citizenship.

3   Officially, an *allochtone* is any person of whom at least one of the parents is born abroad. The term *allochtone* was first used by the scientific Council for Government Policy in 1989 and taken over by the government. Later, the distinction between western and non-western *allochtones* became common.

values. A lack of integration in individual cases may be sanctioned, to which end the Balkenende II government has developed several instruments. Such instruments include the obligations for non-western family members to integrate abroad, before and as a condition for, joining their family in the Netherlands. Furthermore, a permanent residence permit will not be granted in cases where the integration standard is not met, and strict standardized exams of knowledge of the Dutch language and Dutch society have been introduced as requirements for naturalization.

Although this short description of the development of Dutch integration policies shows an obvious change, two features remain constant. The first is the idea that 'good', integrated immigrants can be 'made' through government policy. This feature fits with the long-standing Dutch tradition of educating citizens about the meaning of community and morality. The second constant feature is that culture is viewed as the cause of the problems that individuals and immigrant groups as a whole experience in relation to integrating into Dutch society. According to the scholar Jan Rath (1991), Dutch minority policy has constructed 'ethnic minorities' as a category of persons who are not considered fully-fledged members of the Dutch imagined community – a social construction that revolved around socio-cultural signifiers. This reasoning remained the starting point for the more individual and obligatory approach towards the integration of immigrants which has been developing since the 1990s. As we will see below, the construction of ethnic minorities as culturally and socially different has played an important role in the political and public debate on dual citizenship. Overall, dual citizenship was treated as a cultural issue, and as relevant only to ethnic minorities, which is arguably the reason why the possibility of holding dual citizenship as a rule was finally rejected.

Nation

Scholars typically distinguish a republican from an ethnic conception of nationhood (Brubaker 1992). A republican understanding of nationhood is based on the premise that government in a republic is in principle the common business of the citizens, conducted by citizens for the common good. The inclusion of all permanent residents into the nation is seen as a basis for civic-mindedness. Access to citizenship is based on the subjective avowal of loyalty to the nation on the part of individuals. In this sense republicanism strives to ensure an optimum of equal opportunities regarding political participation for all those residing within national boundaries. An ethnic understanding of nationhood also holds that government is based on popular consent and participation. In contrast to republicanism, however, the nation is focused on the idea of a common culture. Inclusion in the nation may then be traced to such factors as common descent, cultural tradition, shared language, and lineage (Faist this volume, chapter 1).

The Dutch scholarly standpoint overall is that the Netherlands lacks an elaborated concept of nationhood or national identity. That does not mean that it does not exist, but that it remains implicit. As several authors point out 'Dutch national identity has no name, it exists expressly in the denial' (*Raad voor Maatschappelijke ontwikkeling* 2003, 9). During the 1990s, however, a new feeling of Dutch nationhood surfaced, prompted by what the Dutch philosopher Baukje Prins (2003) calls the 'new realism'. Prins mentions four features of the 'new realism': The author presents himself as someone who dares to face the facts about immigrants, and thus to speak frankly about facts that others have tried to cover up. Second, the author presents himself as a spokesperson for ordinary – autochtonous people. Third, his or her frankness is presented as 'typically Dutch', a feature of Dutch identity. The fourth feature is a resistance against the 'left' and its embrace of political correctness, which has attempted to ignore the problems associated with immigrants. Bolkestein and Scheffer can be considered as exponents of this 'new realism'. This 'new realism' has not only influenced political and public debates, but also Dutch government policy. After 2001, it became commonplace for politicians to talk 'openly and frankly' (i.e. negatively) about immigrants. In 2003, the Blok Commission was installed at the initiative of the Socialist Party, tasked with studying not *if* but rather *why* integration of immigrants had failed.

During the 1990s subsequent governments placed new emphasis on republican traits, explaining the duties of active citizenship and loyalty to the Dutch constitutional state. This republican concept of nationhood can be found in the 2001 Government Memorandum 'Integration in the Perspective of Immigration':

> Citizenship means having a part and participating in Dutch society as an autonomous person. Immigrants are offered sufficient possibilities to use their rights and to fulfil their social obligations, but they have to prove themselves. They have sufficient room to develop their identity and to express their religious beliefs and convictions about life, within the framework of our country. It can be expected of them to contribute actively to this modern, open and dynamic society. … Every resident of the country has to respect the fundamental values of society, as laid down in the constitution, laws and rules and the generally accepted opinions of society. The values are carried by all citizens and codified again and again in democratic decision-making processes. (Government Memorandum Integration in the perspective of Immigration 2001, 55 and 60)

Over the years, in the political and public debate and in government policy, ethno-cultural voices became more common. The thought was that immigrants from non-western cultures, due to the distance between their culture and Dutch culture, do not fulfil the requirements of good citizenship. Non-western immigrants are not deemed modern or open-minded, and do not share the fundamental values and generally accepted opinions of the common Dutch culture. The perceived task of the Dutch government is to teach immigrants the traits which make up a good citizen, and to accept and assume their individual responsibilities. Immigrants should first prove that they are worthy of becoming residents or citizens, that they are deserving of the rights of citizens. The obvious contradiction is that on the one hand the assumption is that non-western immigrants do not possess the traits of a good citizen, while on the other hand the Dutch government is perceived to have the task of teaching immigrants these very traits.

Increasingly, solutions are not only sought in liberal democratic principles, but also in valorizing a shared Dutch culture, putting the republican model of nationhood under pressure. The emphasis is not on political participation, but on cultural behaviour and norms. Solutions are sought not only in the public domain, but also in the private domain. The current government Balkenende II recently announced its intention to introduce a legal obligation for all immigrants (meaning those from outside the EU, newcomers and residents, citizens and non-citizens) to take a civic integration exam (*inburgering*). Financial incentives include a partial refund of the costs of the exam after it is successfully completed, and an administrative fine in the event of failure.[4] The same line of thinking can be found in the integration plans of the respective political parties. The VVD, for example, suggests assigning a family guardian to immigrant families who do not speak Dutch at home and to limit their rights to educational choices for their children. D66 has argued for the withdrawal of Dutch citizenship from immigrants who have committed the crime of honour killing.[5] Green Left has pleaded for a ban on marriage migration for husbands who have abused their wives.[6]

To sum up, the trend since the beginning of the 1990s has been towards a gradually more expressive concept of Dutch nationhood, which is republican, with a strong emphasis on the obligations of immigrants and loyalty towards the Dutch constitutional state. Ethno-cultural voices have become stronger over the years, placing the emphasis on the obligations and loyalty of non-western immigrants, especially Muslims. Recently, the republican model seems to have come increasingly under pressure from these ethno-cultural voices.

Political Opportunity Structure

The described shift in thinking with regard to integration and nationhood was enabled by conditions within the political opportunity structure. Dutch political culture is characterized by a need to build consensus and reach compromises. The outcome of political decision-making processes, however, is not always the result of a true compromise in substance. Decision-making is not always based on policy which was adopted after careful preparation and consideration (Jacobs 1998, 261). In the period under scrutiny here, government coalitions were consecutively formed by the Christian Democrat CDA and conservative-liberal VVD (Government Lubbers I and II, 1982-1989), CDA and the Social Democrat PvdA (Government Lubbers III 1989-

---

4   *Government Memorandum* (2004), 'Herziening Inburgeringsstelsel', Tweede Kamer 2003-2004, 29 543, no. 2.

5   Memorandum on Integration of D66 '*De anderen, dat zijn wij*' (The others, that is us), The Hague 2004-04-05, 9. The Dutch Citizenship Law 2000 only allows withdrawal because of criminal behaviour in case of war crimes (genocide) and if the Dutch citizenship was obtained by fraud (Article 14).

6   *Memorandum on integration of Green Left*, 'Het hoofd koel, het hart warm', The Hague, March 2004, 23.

1994), and PvdA, VVD, and the progressive-liberal D66 (Purple Government I and II 1994-2002). The formation of the Purple government in 1994 marked the first time that a confessional party was absent from the government since 1918. The current government Balkenende II consists of CDA, VVD, and D66. Thus, CDA, PvdA, and VVD may be identified as the main political players throughout this period. The need to build coalitions among parties with very different ideologies has led to a political culture of pragmatic consensus-building, even in the case of moral issues. A study of the development of Dutch abortion policy, for example, showed that the liberal abortion policy was as much the result of moral tolerance as it was the result of political compromises between major political parties that did not want to remain involved in a political battle over the issue (Outshoorn 1993).

Consensus-building has also been stimulated by the relatively large number of small political parties represented in parliament, but which are hardly ever included in government coalitions. Most influential in this sense have been the small left-wing parties that united and formed Green Left in 1990, and the conservative-protestant Christian parties such as the Reformed Party (*Staatkundige Gereformeerde Partij* [*SGP*]) and the Christian Union. At times, opportunity coalitions with some of these smaller parties allow the passage of legislation that is not supported by one of the main government parties.

Consensus-building does not occur within an isolated political field. Also involved in policy-making are advice councils, scientists, and NGOs. The Dutch Scientific Council for Government Policy (*WRR*), for example, has produced several reports on integration policy, which, as we will see below, has had a significant influence on the policy concerning dual citizenship. Another example is the compromise reached in 1991 between CDA and PvdA that allowed for the holding of dual citizenship, a compromise enabled by a meeting between CDA Prime Minister Lubbers and the Director of the Dutch Foreigners' Centre (*NCB*), later MP Mohammed Rabae. They discussed the arguments in favour of dual citizenship. Later, in his statement before the Blok Commission, Rabae mentioned it as one of the successes of minority organizations. Professor of Sociology Han Entzinger, an acknowledged expert on immigration policy, was at the forefront of the civic integration policy (Entzinger 2003, 75). This analysis therefore also includes the relevant influence which advice councils and NGOs have exercised.

Political representation in the Netherlands in the 1980s already included an extreme right-wing party (*Centrum Democrats*). With one seat in parliament, isolated by the other political parties, and without a charismatic political leader, the Centrum Democrats (*CD*) never posed a significant threat to other parties, nor did it exert a notable influence on their viewpoints. This stands in contrast to the impact of the appearance of the populist (but not extreme-right) Pim Fortuyn on the national political scene in 2001. Pim Fortuyn was a flamboyant politician who attracted a large number of voters in a very short time frame. His assassination by a radical animal rights activist in May 2002 was followed shortly after by elections, which made the Lijst Pim Fortuyn (*LPF*) the second largest party in the country. The LPF was granted 26 of the 150 seats in parliament and provided four ministers to the government. The elections which followed the swift demise of the government Balkenende I diminished the LPF to eight seats in parliament. Despite the absence of Pim Fortuyn himself, and the fact that the LPF has been reduced to the ranks of the smaller parties in parliament, the impact on Dutch politics remains considerable. The political establishment was severely shaken by the initial election results in favour of the LPF. Politicians were left wondering about the underlying causes of this development and where they had failed in the perceptions of the public. They responded by accepting the answer that Fortuyn had provided before his death: so-called *regentenpolitiek* – a style of 'old' politics that failed to listen to the public and to learn what the people wanted. Part of this criticism was that politicians had ignored the problems of a multicultural society. The adoption of a discourse founded on the frankness and openness of 'new realism' in discussing societal problems, especially when touching upon immigration matters, presented a survival technique for politicians. Although some parties were affected more than others, parties across the political spectrum were required to adapt to the new political reality. This led to a clear change in the manner in which immigrants figured in political and public discussions.

Method and Material

Several sources were used in this study. The most important source consisted of the records of parliamentary debates concerning the issue of dual citizenship during the period 1980-2004. Debates on the introduction of legislation to amend the Dutch Citizenship Law were reviewed, as well as debates on dual citizenship unrelated to legislation or amendments of the law (such as for example the expulsion of imams and of Moroccan-Dutch juveniles after 2001). Also included were debates on the relevant international conventions.[7]

Reports of governmental advice councils and NGOs, which were mentioned in the above parliamentary debates, provided a second source of information. Reports by the media constituted a third source. A total of 289 articles from Dutch nation-wide newspapers during the period 1991-2003 were covered.[8] All articles with reference to the issue of dual citizenship were included, even where dual citizenship was not the main topic. In addition to articles pertaining to the situation in the Netherlands, articles on dual citizenship in Germany were also reviewed. As it turns out, the debate in Germany was one of the three main topics covered by the newspapers (55 articles).

---

7   Strasbourg Convention on the reduction of cases of multiple nationalities and on military obligations in cases of multiple nationalities of 1963, later amended by the Second Protocol of 1993; European Convention on Citizenship of 1997.

8   Newspapers included in the analysis were *NRC*, *De Volkskrant*, *Algemeen Dagblad*, *Parool* and *Trouw*. Of the largest newspaper, *De Telegraaf*, only the years 2002-2004 were covered, as it was not included in the databank system that I used (Lexis-Nexus).

Political Debates: Upholding the Renunciation Requirement (1985-1990)

A regulation for naturalization adopted in 1977 already allowed for exceptions to the renunciation requirement, formalizing an existing practice. Article 3 of the regulation stipulated that renunciation would not be required in cases where this 'cannot reasonably be expected'. The government clarified this provision by contending that it was aimed at situations where renunciation would have unnecessarily harsh consequences, such as for example where persons were faced with a moral dilemma, would experience problems of subsistence, or had grounds to be reluctant to contact the authorities of their country of origin (refugees).[9]

The discussion of the political debates starts with the amendment of the Citizenship Law in 1985, when the Netherlands amended their Citizenship Law and simultaneously ratified the 1963 *Strasbourg Convention on the reduction of cases of multiple nationalities and on military obligations in cases of multiple nationalities*.[10] Although the Strasbourg Convention was aimed at the prevention of multiple nationalities, multiple nationalities became more frequent as a result of the Citizenship Law of 1985. It allowed for dual citizenship of children of mixed marriages who, from 1st January 1985, not only obtained the citizenship of the father, but also the citizenship of the mother at birth. The government did not consider that this amendment contradicted the objective of preventing multiple nationalities, but rather sought to give weight to the principle of gender equality. The objective of prevention of dual citizenship was left to the individual, who now had to exhibit responsibility and a willingness to make a conscious choice in this regard. None of the political parties disagreed with the equal treatment of men and women. The PvdA inquired whether it would be advisable to require the child choose one or the other citizenship upon majority, in order to limit the frequency of dual citizenship.

For the second generation of immigrants, a right of option for Dutch citizenship was introduced. The second generation could acquire Dutch citizenship by a simple, unilateral declaration between the ages of 18 and 25, without costs or further requirements. The right of option also meant that the second generation of immigrants were not required to renounce their former citizenship. The third generation of immigrants have been Dutch by birth since 1953, when the *jus soli* basis for acquiring Dutch citizenship for the third generation of immigrants was introduced. Although the government wanted to replace this by an option right, the majority in parliament, including the conservative liberal VVD and Christian Democrat CDA, opposed this proposal and the third generation thus continued to acquire Dutch citizenship automatically.

Despite these amendments, which led to a growing number of persons with multiple nationalities, the government expressly opposed multiple nationalities in the case of naturalization. An immigrant who wanted to be naturalized had to renounce the

---

9   Hoofdafdeling Privaatrecht Afdeling Nationaliteit en Burgerlijke Staat, 10th March 1977, Staatscourant 1977-04-27, 4.

10 Tweede Kamer 16 946 (ratification of the convention) and 16 947 (citizenship law).

original citizenship. During the parliamentary debate, the State Secretary of Justice Korte-van Hemel (VVD) presented three arguments supporting the renunciation requirement. First, dual citizenship would lead to legal insecurity. Second, it would cause inequality between immigrants, who could have dual citizenship, and Dutchmen, who automatically lost Dutch citizenship upon naturalization in a foreign country. Her third and most important argument was that immigrants who wanted to be naturalized should be required to make a choice for the country with which they felt most connected.

PvdA, D66, and the small left-wing parties questioned the relevance of the renunciation requirement. They used an argument based on equality. They considered it unjustified that some immigrants would be allowed dual citizenship (for example the immigrants who were not allowed to renounce according to the law of their country of origin), while other immigrants would be required to renounce their original citizenship. Since dual citizenship was already allowed for some groups, for example for children of mixed marriages, why could it not also be allowed for others?

Those advocating dual citizenship found support in the principles of the government's official minority policy. During the first half of the 1980s, the idea that the labour immigrants who had come to the Netherlands in the 1950s and 1960s would one day return was still a relevant factor in the development of minority policy. As the PvdA pointed out, integration was a process that was not necessarily completed at the moment of application for naturalization. Hence, renouncing the former citizenship, which was the legal expression of the immigrants' bond with their former country, and part of their cultural identity, should not be required of the applicant. Dual citizenship might stimulate re-emigration of immigrants. The government, however, wanted to separate the issues of citizenship law and minority policy. The Secretary of State pleaded repeatedly with the MPs not to connect these issues.

In the debate surrounding the Dutch Citizenship Law of 1985, legislation also addressed the position of Dutch emigrants abroad. Although naturalization elsewhere led to the automatic loss of Dutch citizenship, in some cases the descendants of Dutch emigrants could retain Dutch citizenship. The law at the time was that Dutch emigrants could retain Dutch citizenship by a declaration before the Dutch consulate that they wished to do so, which was to be made every ten years (Article 7, Section 5 Dutch Citizenship Law of 1892). In the Citizenship Law of 1985, this was replaced by a provision leading to the automatic loss of citizenship for Dutch nationals who were born abroad, possessed dual citizenship, and had lived in the country of the other citizenship since reaching the age of 18. The government argued that the bond of these Dutchmen with the Netherlands would be either very weak or non-existent, and presented the amendment as a 'correction' of the growing incidence of multiple citizenship now that children could derive their citizenship from one of both parents. Hence, Dutch women could finally pass on their Dutch citizenship to their children, but the possibility for such children born abroad to retain dual citizenship was restricted.

The options for immigrants and Dutch emigrants to hold dual citizenship were viewed as a matter of equal treatment. The State Secretary wondered why MPs advocated dual citizenship for immigrants, but not for Dutch emigrants. Dutch emigrants expressed their wish to retain Dutch citizenship by sending countless letters to parliament. The Dutch lawyer MacKaay (1983), working and living in Canada, wrote an oft-cited article in the prominent Dutch legal journal, *Nederlands Juristenblad*, pleading for the acceptance of dual citizenship for Dutch emigrants. The PvdA and the small left-wing parties submitted motions allowing for dual citizenship for both immigrants and emigrants, but these motions were rejected.

The Citizenship Law of 1985 upheld the renunciation requirement, except in cases where 'this cannot reasonably be expected' (Article 9, Section 1, Sub b). In practice, a policy was developed that allowed for a number of exceptions. Renunciation was not expected of persons who could not waive their former citizenship because their other country of citizenship did not allow it. In 1987, the head of the department of Citizenship and Civil Status of the Ministry of Justice specifically mentioned Moroccans, Greeks, Iranians, and East Europeans as such citizenship groups. Another reason for exemption was a resulting loss of inheritance or property rights in the country of citizenship. At the time, this applied to Turkish immigrants and persons from Yugoslavia. Turks and Moroccans were the two major immigrant groups in the Netherlands. Exceptions like these were dealt with rather leniently. As a consequence, in the period before 1990 around 40 per cent of the immigrants who were naturalized were able to retain their original citizenship (Zilverentant 1987).

Abolishing the Renunciation Requirement (1990-1991)

The renunciation requirement became an issue of discussion again a few years later. In 1989, the Scientific Council for Government Policy *WRR*, recommended allowing dual citizenship for immigrants in its report 'Allochtonenbeleid' (*Immigrant Policy* 1989, 93-6). The WRR criticized the earlier minority policy and urged the government to promote the social integration of immigrants, which required the improvement of immigrants' legal positions. Hence, naturalization should not be made more difficult than strictly necessary. The council was of the opinion that legal and emotional considerations in not renouncing the old citizenship (yet) should be taken into account as much as possible. The council recommended consideration of the 'real objections' for persons of 'some Mediterranean countries'. The WRR report played an important role in opening up the discussion on dual citizenship. Initially, the Lubbers III government (PvdA and CDA, 1989-1994) rejected the recommendation to allow dual citizenship. The government thought it important to stimulate long-term immigrants to obtain Dutch citizenship without unnecessary difficulty, but did not advocate dual citizenship. The government pointed to the legal objections against dual citizenship and stated that only in individual cases could exceptions be made.

After questions from members of parliament, the government revised this position in a 'Memorandum on multiple citizenship and voting rights for immigrants'.[11] In this memorandum, the government proposed the total abolishment of the renunciation

---

11 Notitie Meervoudige Nationaliteit en Kiesrecht voor Vreemdelingen, Tweede Kamer 1990-1991, 21 971, no. 14.

requirement. It was considered a barrier to the naturalization of immigrants, for emotional factors relating especially to a sense of betrayal of, or breach with, the country of origin. It is important to note that the government did not fully support dual citizenship. It described its policy as a shift from the *prevention* to the *limitation* of dual citizenship. Since naturalization was now perceived as an adequate means to stimulate integration, this meant that voting rights for immigrants would not be expanded to the provincial and national level. In this sense, the memorandum was a compromise between the CDA and PvdA – the CDA gave up its earlier objections against dual citizenship; in exchange, the Social Democrats had to sacrifice their wish for the extension of voting rights for non-Dutch immigrants in parliamentary elections. Furthermore, the government rejected the introduction of a special law for equal treatment of immigrants. Immigrants who wanted full equal treatment had to naturalize. Hence, the government's 'embrace' of dual citizenship entailed a rejection of the so-called 'denizen-status' or postnational membership for immigrants (Faist, this volume, chapter 1; Soysal 1994).

The government's proposal met with resistance in parliament.[12] The conservative liberal VVD and the small protestant parties resisted dual citizenship altogether, although the VVD favoured a relaxation of the naturalization procedure. The Christian Democrats had serious doubts and were divided on the issue from the start. In 1990, the CDA spokesman for minority policies stated that the party did not have objections in principle to dual citizenship. Less than a year later he claimed that the CDA had always held the opinion that dual citizenship was highly problematic. The party favoured relaxation, but not abolishment of the renunciation requirement. In the same period, the journal of the party published an article supporting the plans to abolish the renunciation requirement.[13] In parliament, the CDA expressed sympathy for the problems that the renunciation requirement was causing for individuals. But the party was also concerned about conflicts of loyalty, and considered it the government's responsibility to protect immigrants from such conflicts. The other government party, PvdA, advocated dual citizenship. They saw it as an instrumental means to integration, but also pointed to the inequality between various immigrant groups: some were allowed to have dual citizenship, while others were not. The PvdA expressed time and again the opinion that the world had changed because of globalization and migration. Mixing loyalties and ties with more than one country had become a possibility in such a context.

The CDA and PvdA finally agreed on a compromise, formulated in a motion that in fact was ascribed different meanings by each party.[14] For the CDA the motion confirmed that the renunciation requirement would continue to exist, but would be applied more leniently. The PvdA explained the motion as providing the possibility

---

12 *58e Vergadering vaste commissie voor het minderhedenbeleid* (Parliamentary Document), 1991-09-09.

13 CDA-blad (1991-10-03), 'Pleidooi voor Afschaffing Afstandseis' in *Nieuwsblad voor Migranten*.

14 Tweede Kamer 1991-1992, 21 971, no. 19.

for an individual immigrant to choose, if desired, whether to hold on to or rescind the original citizenship. The State Secretary of Justice (Kosto, PvdA) agreed with the interpretation of the PvdA. He saw no difference between the government's memorandum and the motion. Aware of these differences in interpretation, PvdA, CDA, D66, and Green Left nonetheless accepted the motion. The abolishment of the renunciation requirement was introduced by changing the related policy with immediate effect, awaiting the necessary amendment of the Dutch Citizenship Law. Thereby, renunciation was no longer required in practice from 1st January 1992. It must be mentioned, however, that this amended policy applied only to immigrants. While immigrants were allowed to retain their former citizenship upon naturalization, Dutch emigrants still automatically lost Dutch citizenship upon naturalization abroad.

The effects of the new policy differed among the main immigrant groups in the Netherlands. For Turkish immigrants, the change in policy was of significance, as is illustrated by the increase in the numbers of naturalizations within this group. The situation for Moroccans, on the other hand, did not change as a result of the new policy. Since Morocco did not allow its citizens to waive their citizenship, Dutch citizenship law had already exempted them from the renunciation requirement before 1992. For persons from the former Dutch colony of Surinam there were no changes either, since Surinamese citizenship law caused the automatic loss of citizenship upon naturalization elsewhere.

Discussion of the Amendment of the Citizenship Law (1992-1997)

The government put forward legislation in order to formalize the new policy of 1992. It presented this legislation, holding the proposal of dual citizenship for immigrants, within the context of minority policy. After the Council of State, in its advice concerning this legislation, pointed out that this would imply the unequal treatment of Dutch nationals, the government also included dual citizenship for Dutch emigrants. The political debate, however, focused on immigrants and on the whole neglected the interests of Dutch emigrants. In clarifying the legislation, the Lubbers III government posited citizenship as an expression of connection, and not of undivided loyalty. In short, a person could have a bond with more than one country. Relations with a country could be political, social, economic, cultural, and emotional. The government expressed a rather vague notion of citizenship and nationhood:

> The question whether and to what extent the existence of these relationships is required cannot be answered in general terms. Which rights and obligations should be connected to the possession of Dutch citizenship cannot be answered either.[15]

Since the government did not perceive citizenship in ideological terms, room was left for a highly pragmatic, instrumental view of dual citizenship. Dual citizenship would provide an answer to the objections of immigrants against naturalization and

---

15 Tweede Kamer 1992-1993, 23 029, no. 6, p. 5.

thus further their integration. Integration and minority policy were considered most important. However, we should not neglect the more principled argument behind this pragmatic approach, namely that social integration of immigrants required a secure legal position.

During the following years, parliamentary discussion reflected the fact that opposition against dual citizenship grew stronger and the policy of 1992 became increasingly contested. The CDA and VVD expressed their objections against dual citizenship in increasingly explicit terms. They saw the rising numbers of naturalization not as a sign of success of the new policy, but as proof that abolishment of the renunciation requirement had made naturalization into a mere 'paper' formality. It allowed naturalization for people with very weak connections to the Netherlands. From this perspective, naturalization ought not to be a means for, but rather the 'crowning' of a completed integration process. The VVD feared that immigrants made instrumental use of dual citizenship and would collect nationalities as one would collect diplomas or credit cards. It would allow them to 'shop around' to see where they might be best off.

On the opposite side were PvdA, D66, and Green Left, who viewed dual citizenship as a means to further integration. This pragmatic, instrumentalist view of dual citizenship, however, focused on the cultural and social integration of immigrants rather than the political participation of immigrants. The Green Left was the only party that regularly put forward the issue of political participation, although PvdA and D66 still upheld their wish for the extension of voting rights for non-naturalized immigrants and would continue to do so up until 1997.

More and more, dual citizenship came to be viewed as an expression of ethnic and cultural identity. The left-wing parties and the Christian Democrats expressed sympathy for the emotional and cultural problems of immigrants when renouncing their original citizenship. This led to a certain degree of *culturalism*: culture was perceived as essentialist, primordial, homogeneous, objective, and connected to the common descent of a certain group (Tempelman 1999). The attitude of immigrants towards dual citizenship was explained primarily through their ethnic and cultural background. This culturalist approach can partly be understood by the fact that the discussion on dual citizenship started within the context of minority policy and its focus on ethnic and cultural difference. The PvdA and Green Left tried to present a more dynamic, multiple view of cultural identity. They held that a person could feel connected to two countries, and that immigrants who did not feel themselves 'fully-fledged' Dutchmen could still be socially integrated. Despite the efforts of these parties, the discussion remained focused on issues of cultural identity. Hence, dual citizenship became a cultural issue and seemed of importance only for certain non-western groups with a distinct culture, and not, or less so, for others.

In the same period, attention to the interests of Dutch emigrants grew. In 1995, the first Dutch emigrants lost Dutch citizenship as a consequence of the Citizenship Law of 1985. The government amended the provision of automatic loss of Dutch citizenship upon naturalization abroad, allowing for the retention of Dutch citizenship. Dutch emigrants 'bombarded' MPs with letters, as they had done before in the 1980s, pleading for the possibility of holding dual citizenship. Both left- and right-wing parties were in favour of dual citizenship for Dutch emigrants. The VVD, CDA, and SGP opposed dual citizenship for immigrants, but did not oppose dual citizenship for Dutch emigrants. The VVD at one point claimed to reject dual citizenship for Dutch emigrants. At another moment in the discussion, however, they tried to extend the exceptions for Dutch emigrants, allowing for dual citizenship. The left-wing parties also spoke out on behalf of Dutch emigrants. For these parties, however, the case of Dutch emigrants mainly presented an argument in pleading for dual citizenship for immigrants. If one did not oppose dual citizenship for Dutch emigrants, so they put it to the right-wing parties, how could one oppose dual citizenship for immigrants?

This argument for equality had been successful in leading to acceptance for dual citizenship in Sweden (Spång this volume, chapter 4). But it did not work in the Netherlands. The CDA and VVD saw dual citizenship of Dutch emigrants and immigrants as two separate matters. The VVD claimed it was the responsibility of the receiving country of Dutch emigrants to allow or ban dual citizenship. The CDA claimed that Dutch emigrants did not pose an integration issue. This last argument seemed the prevailing one. Placing arguments on dual citizenship within the rubric of integration made it possible to view the matter as two distinct issues. The objections raised against dual citizenship for immigrants were never mentioned in the debates on Dutch emigrants. The wish of Dutch emigrants to retain Dutch citizenship was never questioned, regardless of the motives involved, whether these were instrumental (loss of social security rights) or emotional.

Finally, although reluctantly, the Second Chamber accepted the new legislation. In the Senate, however, opposition was even stronger, and in fact the Secretary withdrew the bill before it would be rejected. This can be explained by several factors. The first lay in the political process. The VVD and CDA held a majority in the Senate. Since the CDA had become an opposition party in 1994, they no longer felt committed to the compromise they had reached some years earlier with the PvdA in the Lubbers government. The second factor was the growing media attention. For the first time since the political discussion on the renunciation requirement had started, the media paid serious attention to the outcomes of the debate. This attention focused on the political process. The 'shift' or 'turn' of the CDA in particular received a lot of attention and was heavily criticized. Politicians also took the political discussion into the public arena, by writing articles of opinion for the newspapers. Hence, as the issue became more publicized than before, the stakes for politicians increased.

The outcome of the discussion was also influenced by the publication of the yearly Social Cultural Planning Bureau's (*SCP*) report on minorities (SCP *Rapportage Minderheden*) in 1996.[16] In two pages devoted to naturalization, the SCP report published statistics that showed a considerable rise in naturalizations since 1990, most significantly by Turkish immigrants. The sections on naturalization were based on an earlier study on the subject that had been published in 1993, after the

---

16 The SCP was established by the government in 1973, tasked with conducting studies to provide information for the development of effective government policies.

renunciation requirement had already been abolished (van den Bedem 1993). At the time, the study received little attention. Now, however, the SCP report coincided with a heated political debate. The report questioned the assumption that naturalization was an indicator of the degree of integration of immigrants. According to the SCP, naturalization was the result of a balancing of advantages and disadvantages and had little to do with feelings of connection or social integration into Dutch society. Politicians referred frequently to the report during the 1996 debate. The opponents of dual citizenship saw their objections confirmed by the study's findings that immigrants who were said not to feel Dutch nevertheless had the option of naturalization open to them. The report seemed to confirm their idea that naturalization had become too easy. Of the advocates of dual citizenship, the Green Left, claimed that feeling Dutch was not the same as feeling connected to Dutch society. The government indeed denied that it was necessary to feel Dutch in order to become Dutch.

As the resistance against dual citizenship grew, the first government of the PvdA, VVD, and D66 (1994-1998) was forced to formulate the meaning of citizenship more explicitly. It resulted in the presentation of new arguments for a law that had in itself remained the same. Although the State Secretary of Justice (Schmitz, PvdA) still defended the proposed abolishment of the renunciation requirement, she did so with more restraint than before. She stated that dual citizenship should not be automatic, and that having only one citizenship was preferred. Immigrants should not choose dual citizenship without good reason and the authorities were to make sure that the choice for dual citizenship was a conscious and explicit one, although they were not required to evaluate the underlying motives as such. The State Secretary did not succeed in overcoming the objections against the legislation. Finally, in 1997, she withdrew it. The renunciation requirement was reinstated the same year, but the ministerial circular that reinstated it contained an even larger number of exceptions than before 1992. Their scope was so broad that the exceptions applied to a large percentage of the immigrants applying for naturalization.

Reinstating the Renunciation Requirement (1997-2001)

After the government had withdrawn the bill allowing dual citizenship, a new bill was drafted and sent to parliament. It contained a limited relaxation of the renunciation requirement, including the categories of persons contained in the Second Protocol of the Strasbourg Convention (partners and children of mixed marriages and second-generation immigrants). In defence of the new legislation, the government used mainly the same arguments that earlier supported the abolishment of the renunciation requirement, which were now justifying a relaxed 'renunciation-unless' policy.[17]

During the discussion on the revised bill, the larger political parties developed a more restrictive attitude towards naturalization in general, especially with regard to requirements concerning knowledge of the Dutch language and society. They

---

17 Tweede Kamer 1999-2000, 25 891.

stressed the importance of Dutch citizenship and did so in ethnic and cultural terms. During this period, the term 'loyalty' was used frequently. The CDA expressed the opinion that Dutch citizenship should be the object of pride, and should not be appropriated or discarded like an article of consumption. One had to feel Dutch. The CDA stressed the importance of loyalty and voted against the bill, while they considered the stricter standards for naturalization still too low. The discussion on language requirements resulted in the addition of a strict test of Dutch language skills and knowledge of Dutch society as a requirement for naturalization.

Whilst making it harder for immigrants to acquire Dutch citizenship, the legislation allowed for more possibilities to retain Dutch citizenship for Dutch emigrants. It abolished the rule stipulating the automatic loss of Dutch citizenship upon reaching majority after ten years of residence in the country of the other citizenship. Dutch emigrants who had lost their Dutch citizenship as a result of the Citizenship Law of 1985 could now re-obtain it under easier conditions. In addition, Dutch men and women who apply for the citizenship of their partner will no longer lose Dutch citizenship.

The new legislation was adopted in December 2000 and came into force on 1st April 2003. Although dual citizenship is still possible in many cases, acquisition of Dutch citizenship has become more difficult. Hence, the discussion on dual citizenship, which started with the intent to improve the legal position of immigrants, resulted in a new Citizenship Law that weakens this legal position in several respects, while it has become easier for Dutch emigrants to have dual citizenship.

Still, the question is whether anything had really changed after all the developments described here. After dual citizenship had been allowed in 1992, naturalization rates rose considerably. After the renunciation requirement was reinstated in 1997, naturalization rates did not drop, with the exception of Turkish immigrants. As before, most naturalized immigrants retained their original citizenship. Between 1995 and 1997 more than 80 per cent of those naturalized retained their original citizenship. In 2000, after the renunciation requirement had formally been reinstated, 77 per cent of the immigrants retained their original citizenship (Böcker and Tränhardt 2003). Based on this small decrease of three per cent, it would not be unreasonable to conclude that politicians had spent ten years fighting windmills.

The New Citizenship Law: Re-opening the Debate (2001-2004)

After the adoption of the new Citizenship Law of 2000 the discussion on dual citizenship continued. It also became more public.

In the period after 9/11 and after the LPF had become a government party, dual citizenship came to be seen in a new way: as a chance to expel undesired naturalized immigrants who could be stripped of their Dutch citizenship.[18] Dual citizenship offered an opportunity here. One example is the debate in 2002 on the expulsion of

---

18 In case the immigrant had only Dutch citizenship, de-naturalization was not allowed because of international conventions against statelessness and because it would become impossible to expel a stateless immigrant.

Moroccan-Dutch juveniles who had committed criminal offences. The debate started with an interview in a major newspaper by Minister of Immigration and Integration Nawijn (LPF) of the short-lived Balkenende I (CDA, VVD, LPF) government. He suggested withdrawing Dutch citizenship from these juveniles, so that they could be expelled to Morocco. He saw dual citizenship as posing a problem to integration, and considered withdrawing Dutch citizenship as an appropriate way to crack down on criminality among Moroccan-Dutch youth. Nawijn's suggestion met with a lot of criticism in the media and in the Second Chamber. Prime Minister Balkenende (CDA) distanced himself publicly from these statements and privately rebuked the minister. His main argument in rejecting Nawijn's plan was the constitutionally guaranteed equal treatment of all Dutch citizens.

Although Nawijn's suggestion never materialized, it illustrates an important change in thinking on dual citizenship. The idea is that immigrants, although naturalized or perhaps even born with dual citizenship, can be expelled to the country of origin because they did not behave according to Dutch cultural norms and values. It treats Dutch nationals differently based on their lineage. This line of thinking on dual citizenship reappeared in debates on imams who were thought to be working against the integration of immigrants, and in the proposal to withdraw Dutch citizenship from dual citizens convicted of honour killing.[19]

The first months of 2004 witnessed a re-opening of the debate on dual citizenship. The CDA submitted a motion, together with Hirsi Ali (VVD) and Nawijn (LPF), requesting the government to amend the law, so that *allochtones* from the third generation could have only Dutch citizenship.[20] The motion was accepted with the support of the VVD, CDA, Christian Union, SGP, and LPF.[21] The publication of the report of the Blok Commission, which evaluated Dutch minority policy, proved a further incentive to re-opening the debate. During the weeks surrounding the report's publication, all parties presented integration plans, containing *inter alia* positions on the issue of dual citizenship. Only the PvdA and D66 still jointly supported dual citizenship. The Green Left did not want to ban dual citizenship. Although initially the Ministers of Justice and Alien Affairs and Integration stated that a legal regulation stipulating that third-generation *allochtones* may have only Dutch citizenship would be a breach of international law, the ministers also promised a memorandum on citizenship issues and dual citizenship, and a reconsideration of the renunciation requirement of Article 9 section 1b of the Citizenship Law.[22] Later, in the government reaction to the report, Minister Verdonk of Immigration and Integration (*VVD*) said that she not only wanted to ban dual citizenship for the third generation, but found dual citizenship undesirable more generally, because it would undermine integration. She announced plans to combat dual citizenship.

---

19 For example the debate about an Amsterdam mosque that distributed books with homophobic texts, Handelingen Tweede Kamer, 2004-04-28, 72-4714.

20 Tweede Kamer 2003-2004 (2003-11-03), 29 200 VI, no. 81.

21 Handelingen Tweede Kamer (2003-11-18), 25-1714.

22 Tweede Kamer 2003-2004, 29 200 VI, no. 119, 3-4.

The Influence of Experts, NGOs, and Jurisprudence

In reviewing the influence of NGOs on the debate on dual citizenship, it is important
to note that, in the Netherlands, issues around immigration and integration are
generally addressed by immigrant organizations, and far less by the broader non-
immigrant organizations such as trade unions. Only one non-immigrant organization,
the Dutch Legal Committee for Human Rights (*Nederlands Juristen Comite voor de
Mensenrechten*), was active with regard to the issue of dual citizenship. The NJCM
report (1992), advocating the possibility of dual citizenship, did not play any role in
the debate in parliament. This lack of attention by non-immigrant organizations turned
dual citizenship into an issue for experts, and not for the general public. The Dutch
Centre for Foreigners published a report on the law of 1985. D66 in particular used
this report as an argument to plead for dual citizenship. In the 1990s, only the Turkish
Immigrant Organisation (*IOT*), the official representative of the Turkish community
to the Dutch government, was notably active on the issue of dual citizenship. While
representing one of the largest immigrant communities they had a clear interest in
the matter. The IOT wrote reports in 1990 and in 1996, arguing, respectively, for the
abolishment of the renunciation requirement, and against the reinstatement of the
renunciation requirement and extension of the range of exceptions to renunciation
(IOT 1990 and 1996). The main influence of this organization was felt in 1991
and on a more informal political level, when they advised Prime Minister Lubbers
(CDA) on how to argue against the objections of his party members with regard to
dual citizenship. In 1996 IOT successfully campaigned for the exception that allows
an applicant to retain the original citizenship in case of having to serve in the army
in his country of origin. This became one of the total of 13 exceptions which were
eventually accepted by parliament in 1997. The activities of immigrant organizations
were mentioned in parliament on occasion, but not nearly as frequently as were the
'thousands of letters' of Dutch emigrants. The parties that opposed dual citizenship
attempted to minimize the influence of minority organizations by claiming that
'signals' emanating from minority groups were insufficient in number or unclear.

The influence of immigrants became visible through the involvement of those
MPs of immigrant background in the PvdA, the Green Left, and even in the populist
LPF, who were all active participants in the debates in the Second Chamber.

The influence of case-law has been very limited. One exception is the *Micheletti*
decision of the European Court of Justice, which instigated a change in the regulation
of loss of Dutch citizenship. The government revised Article 15 of the draft Citizenship
Law, to determine that Dutchmen who were also members of another EU member
state and had taken up residence in that member state for a period exceeding ten
years would not lose Dutch citizenship.[23] Herewith, a further group of citizens was
allowed to hold dual citizenship.

---

23   Article 15, Section 1, Sub c Dutch Citizenship Law 2000.

The Media Debate on Dual Citizenship

Although it must be born in mind that the media debate that took place in the Netherlands on the issue of dual citizenship was not as fierce, for example, as it had been in Germany, two periods of relatively intense media attention may be distinguished: at the height of the legislative process in 1995, and at the time of discussions surrounding the issue of the expulsion of Moroccan-Dutch juveniles in 2002. The media debate on the latter issue was not highly polemical. In 1995, attention was focused not on the substance of arguments concerning dual citizenship, but rather on the political process and the position and attitude of political parties during the parliamentary debate. The first bulk of articles in the media concerned this political process.

Second, the Dutch media paid a lot of attention to the debate in Germany concerning the amendment of its citizenship law. As mentioned above, the situation in Germany with respect to dual citizenship was one of three major topics that featured in the Dutch media. News articles described the German debate as highly polemical and populist. A central issue was how Germany perceived itself: was it an immigration country or not, a society based on ethnicity or openness, a modern nation or a country with a nineteenth-century orientation, upholding a *Blut und Boden* citizenship law. Remarkably, the Dutch press went to great lengths to address the degree of ethnic connotations that characterized the German debate on citizenship law, while it mostly disregarded the ethnonationalism in the Dutch debate.

Instead, the Dutch media presented the Dutch debate on dual citizenship as a debate on integration. Both in general news reports and expert opinions, the assumption was that true integration of immigrants had not yet started. Even those authors who advocated dual citizenship claimed it would help immigrants 'to grow into Dutch society'[24] or to 'slowly move from one national and cultural identity into another'.[25]

The media dealt with the issue of dual citizenship from the perspective of Dutch society. The interests of persons directly affected by the rules on dual citizenship, immigrants and Dutch emigrants, were hardly addressed. Only the topic of military service was reported from the perspective of dual nationals, especially Turkish young men. During the period under consideration, a small number of articles focused on the problems of individual immigrants with dual citizenship. These pertained to the situation in the country of origin, where persons faced risks ranging from military draft, arrest, torture, or execution. The large number of letters from Dutch emigrants which landed at the doorstep of the parliament escaped media attention almost

---

24 Wil Tinnemans (expert) (1996-07-03), 'Dubbele nationaliteit laat allochtoon in ons land ingroeien' (Dual citizenship allows *allochtone* to grow into being part of our country), *De Volkskrant*.

25 Arnold Koper (columnist) (1995-05-20), 'Goddank werd om een paspoort niet gevraagd' (Thank God a passport was not asked for), *De Volkskrant*.

entirely. *Trouw* was the only newspaper that published material on the case of Dutch emigrants.[26]

Conclusions

Although immigration is often mentioned as one of the important factors leading to a more liberal approach to dual citizenship (Faist this volume, chapter 1), the Dutch case shows that this is not necessarily the case. In the Netherlands, the initial trend towards total acceptance of dual citizenship was replaced by a policy of 'renunciation unless'. As we have seen, the large number of exceptions still allows for dual citizenship in about three quarters of all naturalizations. The new Citizenship Law which came into force in 2003, however, has made access to Dutch citizenship much harder for immigrants. The first statistics on the revised Dutch Citizenship Law show a considerable drop in the numbers of naturalizations of about 40 per cent, which is likely due to the required computerized test of Dutch language and knowledge of Dutch society.[27] In 2004, the decrease will likely be even more dramatic. We have also seen that at the same time dual citizenship has become more accessible to Dutch emigrants. Explanations for these contradictory results have been sought in the development of Dutch integration policies. The issue of dual citizenship was discussed within the 'integration' belief system. The result was that arguments used for and against dual citizenship which focused on the issue of integration excluded the interests of Dutch emigrants, which did not fit within this belief system.

Second, placing arguments within the integration belief system meant that change from a pragmatic cultural pluralist approach to a more principled assimilationist approach impacted policy concerning dual citizenship. Acceptance of dual citizenship as a rule did not agree with an assimilationist approach. As indicated, the shift in integration policies can be explained by the changing concept of nationhood. For a long time, the Netherlands had what was considered an 'empty' concept of nationhood. This 'empty' concept of nationhood left room in the 1980s for a fluid policy and for a pragmatic approach to the subject of dual citizenship. In the late 1990s the expressive dimension of citizenship gained importance. It became expressly republican, with a strong emphasis on the obligations of citizens. At the same time, it was strongly connected with the discourse on minority policies that focused on the cultural identity of immigrants. This combination of republicanism with increasingly strong ethno-cultural voices explains why the policy of acceptance of dual citizenship was left in 1997, and why access to naturalization has been made harder.

That the still relatively liberal practice of dual citizenship of 'renunciation unless' could be preserved and that the government did not choose an even more restrictive policy may be explained by the political opportunity structure. The PvdA

---

26 6 articles between 1993-1996.

27 To fulfil the new strict Dutch language requirement for reading, writing, speaking, and comprehension applicants are subjected to a three-hour test in an educational institution.

Figure 3.1   **The Netherlands: Chronological List of Dual Citizenship-Related Legislation and Events**

Date	Legislation/Event	Change In Discursive Opportunity Structures
1983	Government Memorandum on Minority Policy.	Start of minority policy. Citizenship law becomes instrument of integration policy.
1985	New Dutch Citizenship Law of 19 December 1984; ratification of Strasbourg Convention on the Reduction of Cases of Multiple Nationality of 1963.	Citizenship Law includes renunciation requirement.
1989	Advice Report of the Scientific Council for Government Policy 'Immigrant Policy'.	Advice to allow dual citizenship for immigrants.
1992	Amendment circular.	Dutch government decides to cease applying renunciation requirement for immigrants in order to further naturalization.
1993	Publication WODC-research ('Wetenschappelijk Onderzoek- en Documentatiecentrum' / Research and Documentation Centre of the Dutch Ministry of Justice).	On naturalization behaviour of immigrants.
1996	Publication report on minorities by Social Cultural Planning Bureau.	Concludes that naturalization motives are instrumental.
1996	Ratification and entry into force of Second Protocol on the Strasbourg Convention on Reduction of Cases of Multiple Nationality.	Allows dual citizenship for spouses of Dutch citizens and second generation immigrants.
1997	Amendment circular.	Re-introduction of renunciation requirement.
2000	Paul Scheffer essay on 'The Multicultural Tragedy'.	Public discussion about integration policy.
2002	Murder of Pim Fortuyn.	Intensified politicization of immigrant integration and immigrant citizenship.
2003	1st April, amended Dutch Nationality Law comes into force.	Upholds renunciation requirement with exceptions, introduces naturalization exam.

in parliament had the same spokesman during the 1990s (MP Apostolou, of Greek descent and probably a dual citizen himself), who advocated dual citizenship and tried to reach the maximum result under the circumstances. But the acceptance of this relatively liberal policy did not come only from the Social Democrats, but also from the VVD and CDA. Although there was discussion on some exceptions such as financial damage and military service, on the whole, the major parties accepted the policy of 'renunciation unless'. Furthermore, the discussion was limited to dual citizenship in the case of naturalization, while dual citizenship acquired at birth or in the case of option was largely taken for granted. Hence, all parties accepted the reality of large numbers of dual citizens.

Some actors (PvdA and the Green Left, the Turkish immigrant organization IOT) have suggested that the position of the VVD and CDA was informed by populism and symbolic politics. One argument could support this suggestion: Right-wing parties accepted a policy that would lead to a large number of dual citizens, although verbally they opposed dual citizenship. This could be seen as symbolic politics:

sending a message to voters that the parties were tough on immigrants. But more likely their attitude could be perceived as pragmatic, since to a large extent the incidence of dual citizens could not be prevented.

This does not mean, however, that polemics and populism were entirely absent from the Dutch political debate. The discussion on dual citizenship could be seen as part of this more general debate. The new consensus seems to be that integration policies had failed and a new and 'firmer' handling of ethnic groups was necessary. In the period after 2001 in particular, the debate on dual citizenship became more public.

The new emphasis on the obligations of citizens instead of on rights is not limited to immigrants, but also extends to criminality, social security, public order, and so forth. This can be explained by the growing popularity of neo-liberal ideas in the 1990s. The rediscovery of the 'citizen' in Dutch politics was above all about the citizen as a *moral being*, more than as a political participant (Koenis 1997, 20). This moral citizen fits with a long Dutch tradition of educating citizens, including immigrants, to community and morality (Rath 1991). Recent developments have re-opened the debate on dual citizenship. It is too early to speculate about how this will work out in the future.

References

Becker, U. (ed.) (1993), *Nederlandse politiek in historisch en vergelijkend perspectief* (Amsterdam: Het Spinhuis).

Böcker, A., Thränhardt, D. (2003), 'Einbürgerung und Mehrstaatigkeit in Deutschland und den Niederlanden', (Special issue Migration im Spannungsfeld von Globalisierung und Nationalstaat), *Leviathan* 31, 117-34.

Brubaker, R. (1992), *Citizenship and Nationhood in France and Germany* (Cambridge: Harvard University Press).

Entzinger, H. (2003), 'The Rise and Fall of Multiculturalism: The Case of the Netherlands', in Joppke, C. and Morawska, E. (eds), 59-86.

Fermin, A. (1997), *Nederlandse politieke partijen over minderhedenbeleid 1977-1995* (Amsterdam: Thesis Publishers).

Jacobs, D. (1998), *Nieuwkomers in de politiek: het parlementaire debat omtrent kiesrecht voor vreemdelingen in Nederland en België 1970-1997* (Gent: Academia Press).

Joppke, C. and Morawska, E. (2003), 'Integrating Immigrants in Liberal Nation-States: Policies and Practices', in Joppke, C. and Morawska, E. (eds), 1-36.

Joppke, C. and Morawska, E. (eds) (2003), *Towards Assimilation and Citizenship: Immigrants in Liberal Nation-States* (Basingstoke: Palgrave MacMillan).

Koenis, S. (1997), *Het Verlangen naar Gemeenschap. Over Moraal en Politiek in Nederland na de Verzuiling* (Amsterdam: Van Gennep).

Koper. A. (1995-05-20), 'Goddank werd om een paspoort niet gevraagd' (Thank God a passport was not asked for), *De Volkskrant.*

Mackaay, E. (1983), 'Verlies van het Nederlanderschap voor emigranten', *Nederlands Juristenblad* 58, 1319-22.

Nederlands Juristen Comité voor de Mensenrechten (1992), 'Commentaar op de Nota Rechtspositie en sociale integratie minderheden en de Nota meervoudige nationaliteit/ kiesrecht voor vreemdelingen', *NJCM-bulletin* 16:1, 85-96.

Outshoorn, J. (1993), 'Abortus als politiek strijdpunt', in Becker, U. (ed.), 257-80.

Prins, B. (2002), 'Het lef om taboes te doorbreken. Nieuw realisme in het Nederlandse discours over multiculturalisme', *Migrantenstudies* 18:4, 241-54.

Rath, J. (1991), *Minorisering*: de *sociale constructie* van '*etnische minderheden*' (Amsterdam: Sua).

Scheffer, P. (2000-01-29), 'Het multiculturele drama', *NRC Handelsblad.*

Sociaal Cultureel Planbureau (SCP) (1996), *Rapportage Minderheden. Bevolking, Arbeid, Onderwijs, Huisvesting* (Rijswijk: Sociaal Cultureel Planbureau).

Soysal, Y. N. (1994), *Limits of Citizenship: Migrants and Postnational Membership in Europe* (Chicago: University of Chicago).

Tempelman, S. (1999), 'Duiken in het Duister. Een Gematigd Constructivistische Benadering van Culturele Identiteit', *Migrantenstudies* 15:2, 70-82.

Tinnemans, W. (1996-07-03), 'Dubbele nationaliteit laat allochtoon in ons land ingroeien' (Dual citizenship allows *allochtone* to grow into being part of our country), *De Volkskrant.*

van den Bedem, R. (1993), *Motieven voor Naturalisatie. Waarom Vreemdelingen uit Diverse Minderheidsgroepen Wel of Niet Kiezen voor Naturalisatie* (Arnhem: WODC).

van Walsum, S. (1998) 'Changing Images of Migration: Changing Images of the Nation', Paper presented at *Critical Legal Conference* (Lancaster).

Vermeulen, H. and Penninx, R. (2000), *Immigrant Integration: The Dutch Case* (Amsterdam: Het Spinhuis).

Zilverentant, F. T. (1987), 'Twee jaar Wet op het Nederlanderschap', *Migrantenrecht* 2:7, 185-87.

Documents

Advice Organs

Raad voor Maatschappelijke Ontwikkeling (2003), 'Nationale Identiteit in Nederland. Internationalisering en Nationale Identiteit' (Den Haag).

Scientific Council for Government Policy *WRR* (1989), report: 'Allochtonenbeleid' (Immigrant Policy), 93-6.

Wetenschappelijke Raad voor het Regeringsbeleid (2001), 'Nederland als Immigratieland' (Den Haag).

Wetenschappelijke Raad voor het Regeringsbeleid (1989), 'Allochtonenbeleid' (Den Haag).

Wetenschappelijke Raad voor het Regeringsbeleid (1979) 'Etnische Minderheden'(Den Haag).

Non-Governmental Organizations

Inspraakorgaan Turken (1990), 'Dubbele nationaliteit ook voor Turkse immigranten. Een advies aan de Nederlandse regering' (Den Haag).

Inspraakorgaan Turken (1996), 'Herinvoering van de afstandseis in het nationaliteitsrecht' (Den Haag).

Government Memorandums'

Government Memorandum, 'Integratie in de Context van Immigratie', Tweede Kamer (Lower Chamber) 2001-2002, 28 198, no. 2.
Government Memorandum, 'Herziening van het inburgeringsstelsel', Tweede Kamer (Lower Chamber) 2003-2004, 29 543, no. 2.
Government Memorandum 'Meervoudige Nationaliteit en Kiesrecht voor Vreemdelingen', Tweede Kamer (Lower Chamber) 1990-1991, 21 971, no. 14.

Parliamentary Documents

58e Vergadering vaste commissie voor het minderhedenbeleid, 1991-09-09

Newspapers / Magazines:

Algemeen Dagblad, 1991-2003.
De Telegraaf, 2002-2004.
De Volkskrant, 1995-05-20; 1996-07-03; 1991-2003.
Nieuwsblad voor Migranten, 1991-10-03; 1991-2003.
NRC, 2000-01-29; 1991-2003.
Parool, 1991-2003.
Trouw, 1991-2003.

Chapter 4

Pragmatism All the Way Down?
The Politics of Dual Citizenship
in Sweden

Mikael Spång

Abstract

This chapter gives an overview of the policy process and the political debate leading up to the acceptance of dual citizenship in Sweden in 2001. Understandings of state and nation, integration policies, and features of the political system are explored in order to explain the policy output. In my view the following factors are important for explaining the acceptance of dual citizenship in Sweden:

1. the extensive *de facto* toleration, together with minor differences between *denizens'* and citizens' rights and obligations, which are related to central features of immigrant integration policies;
2. the simultaneous focus on *denizens* in Sweden and Swedish nationals abroad and the stress on treating them equally in the 1990s debate; and
3. the combination of consensus and bloc politics, which delayed acceptance in the 1980s and early 1990s, but facilitated agreement on changing the law in the late 1990s.

Introduction

Dual citizenship has been a legally recognized option in Sweden since 2001 (SFS 2001, 82). This represents a change of principles and at the same time an acknowledgment of an already existing practice. Swedish citizenship legislation has since the first naturalization regulation of 1858 been based on the principle of avoiding dual citizenship, but from the late 1970s an extensive *de facto* toleration developed, leading by the late 1990s to the acquisition of dual citizenship by about 300,000 individuals (Sandesjö and Björk 1996, 19ff.; SOU 1999, 34, 173f.).

De facto toleration developed because of changes to the citizenship law, relaxed naturalization requirements, and administrative exemptions from the requirement of renouncing one's original citizenship when becoming a Swedish national (*cf.* Szabó

1997, chapters 1-3). The background to these changes can be traced to the 1970s, a time of increasing importance of gender equity in citizenship legislation and greater stress on equality and cultural pluralism in the new immigrant integration policy. At the same time, *de facto* toleration was seen as a passive acceptance and not linked to a change of principles. A more principled discussion about dual citizenship arose in the context of debates about extending voting rights to *denizens* for national elections. The Social Democrats and the Communists favoured this proposal in the late 1970s and early 1980s, but the centre-right parties opposed such a reform. Instead of pushing ahead with the reform, the Social Democrats began to look at dual citizenship as an alternative and suggested in 1991 that the principle of avoiding dual citizenship be abolished.[1]

The centre-right parties opposed this change as well and successfully delayed acceptance of dual citizenship in the late 1980s and early 1990s. When the issue was taken up again in the late 1990s, many of the centre-right parties had changed their views, which facilitated a broad consensus on the reform. The Conservatives were the only party in parliament that continued to argue for upholding the principle of avoiding dual citizenship. Central to the centre-right parties' shift from opposition to acceptance, and to a large degree endorsement, of the reform was that dual citizenship was discussed in relation to both Swedish nationals residing abroad and *denizens* in Sweden. The proponents argued that not only *denizens* but also Swedish nationals have deep and substantive ties with more than one country in today's globalized world. Allowing for dual citizenship was seen as a way to acknowledge these overlapping attachments.

Beside the focus on both *denizens* and Swedish nationals in the debate, political equality arguments as well as a certain form of pragmatism are important among the discursive factors explaining the outcome. Both equality and pragmatism are in part related to the welfare state programme and its underlying conception of state and nationhood. Integral to this conception has been an emphasis on the socio-political dimension of citizenship, both in relation to societal integration in general and immigrant integration more specifically. Among the institutional factors, the low level of legal differentiation between *denizens* and citizens should be stressed, as well as the extensive *de facto* toleration of dual citizenship. The combination of bloc and consensus politics, characteristic of Swedish politics, is also of importance for explaining the outcome, delaying acceptance in the late 1980s, and facilitating it ten years later.

In this chapter I discuss the political process leading up to the acceptance of dual citizenship in 2001. I begin by describing the policy process over the last two

---

1   During the period covered in this article the Social Democrats were in government up to 1976, between 1982 and 1991, and have been in government since 1994. The centre-right parties were in government between 1976 and 1982 and from 1991 to 1994. There are four centre-right parties represented in parliament: the Liberals, the Centre Party (formerly the Agrarian Party), the Christian Democrats, and the Conservatives (the Moderate Party). Between 1991 and 1994 the right-wing populist New Democracy was also represented in parliament.

decades and analyze the proponents' and opponents' argumentation. I then try to explain the policy process output by considering the discursive and institutional opportunity structures (Faist, this volume, chapter 1). This analysis involves taking into account characteristics of the political system and the debates and policies concerning immigrant integration as well as societal integration in general. I also discuss some aspects of the understanding of state and nation in Sweden and their impact on the dual citizenship debate.

The Policy Process

In 1979 the citizenship law was changed so that citizenship was to follow the mother, or the father if he was a Swedish national and married to the mother (SFS 1979, 139; Sandesjö and Björk 1996, 42ff.). This change can be seen as the first legal acknowledgement of dual citizenship for children, but the law was also amended in order to require that persons choose citizenship upon reaching maturity. This condition was to be regulated through treaties with other states, but no such agreements were concluded and the requirement was thus never implemented (Sandesjö and Björk 1996, 132ff.). The 1979 change signified a shift in attitude concerning dual citizenship. When the 1950 citizenship law (SFS 1950, 382) was prepared in the late 1940s it was noted that taking citizenship through the father was problematic from the point of view of gender equity, but making the law gender-neutral would increase the number of persons with dual citizenship (Szabó 1997, 25ff.). Avoiding dual citizenship was considered more important than making the law gender-neutral, a view that remained unchanged up to the late 1960s and early 1970s.

Naturalization requirements were relaxed in the 1970s; the length of required residence prior to application for Swedish citizenship was reduced, the subsistence requirement was relaxed, and the language proficiency test was abolished (*cf.* Szabó 1997, 54-79). As more and more individuals applied for citizenship, the assessment of when and how to uphold the requirement of renouncing one's other citizenship became both a political and an administrative question. An increasingly liberal practice developed over time, allowing for exceptions to or remittances of this condition in many cases, for example when it was impossible, or very difficult and costly, to renounce the original citizenship (*cf.* SOU 1984, 11, 131ff.; DsA 1986, 6, 55). The practice of *de facto* toleration led to about 100,000 persons acquiring dual citizenship in the mid-1980s, increasing to 150,000 persons in the early 1990s, and to about 300,000 persons in the late 1990s (SOU 1984, 11, 134; DsA 1986, 6, 54f.; SOU 1999, 34, 173f.).

In spite of the many cases in which the condition of renouncing the original citizenship was not upheld, the authorities saw tolerating dual citizenship as passive acceptance. When applicants cited the practical advantages of being dual nationals or reasons relating to family, feelings of loyalty, and so on, the application for Swedish citizenship was denied (Szabó 1997, 79ff., 141ff.). Both the view that toleration was a passive acceptance and the view that children becoming dual nationals should choose citizenship upon reaching maturity show that the principle of avoiding dual citizenship was still considered important and central.

A more principled debate about dual citizenship came about in the 1980s when the Social Democrats started to consider dual citizenship as an alternative to their proposal to extend *denizen*'s voting rights from local and regional to national elections, a suggestion that met with strong opposition from the centre-right parties. Voting rights in local and regional elections were recognized for immigrants permanently residing in Sweden in 1975 (*cf.* SOU 1975, 15), and the decision in parliament to grant voting rights to immigrants had been made unanimously. The possibility of taking another step in this franchising process and recognizing voting rights for immigrants even in national elections was discussed in the late 1970s and early 1980s (*cf.* Dahlstedt 1998; Hammar 1990, chapter 10; Bäck and Soininen 1996, 428-38). The majority, consisting of Social Democrats and the Communists, suggested in 1984 that voting rights should be recognized for immigrants in national elections (SOU 1984, 11). The centre-right parties, however, argued strongly against this reform, insisting that voting rights in national elections should be tied to being a Swedish national. The Social Democratic government did not choose to push the issue further and focused instead on dual citizenship as an alternative to extending voting rights.

The commission charged with discussing the extension of voting rights for *denizens* touched on the issue of dual citizenship and noted that it seemed to have few negative consequences, but suggested that the question had to be dealt with in more depth (SOU 1984, 11, 134f., 168).[2] This became the task of the 1985 citizenship commission, which reviewed several of the traditional problems of dual citizenship, such as difficulties concerning diplomatic assistance and military service, the risk of divided loyalties, and the principled problem of dual voting rights. The commission also looked into those aspects of tax and family law that related to dual citizenship (DsA 1986, 6).

The 1985 citizenship commission noted that the possibility of extending diplomatic assistance to dual nationals would be limited and dependant on other countries' willingness to cooperate. Military service in more than one country was also a problem, though in practice limited to a very few countries (Greece, Turkey and Yugoslavia) (DsA 1986, 6, 83ff., 103f.). The security risks of dual citizenship, with its possible implication of divided loyalties, were also discussed. The defence forces argued that dual citizenship for this very reason created problems with respect to assigning persons to several of the positions in the military and in UN service (DsA 1986, 6, appendix 6). The security police also stressed the possible loyalty problems of dual citizenship (DsA 1986, 6, 86ff., 104). The commission, however,

---

2   Almost all political issues are prepared and discussed in government and parliamentary commissions before propositions are presented to the parliament. Some commissions consist only of experts in the field investigated but most often party representatives and sometimes interest groups are included in the commissions. Much of the actual negotiation around political issues takes place in the commissions.

thought that it was difficult to draw any general conclusions about the loyalty and security problems. Loyalty to more than one state could certainly be a complicating factor, the commission agreed, but argued that it was not clear that dual citizenship itself was decisive in this respect (DsA 1986, 6, 104).

Dual voting rights posed a principled problem since it could be said to violate the principle of 'one person, one vote'. The commission recognized that this would be an unwelcome effect and considered it to be the most important argument against recognizing dual citizenship (DsA 1986, 6, 100f., 105). But there were also significant advantages in this respect, since more persons would be able to participate in politics, something that would also be beneficial for the integration of immigrants (DsA 1986, 6, 100ff., 122ff.).

The investigation conducted by the 1985 citizenship commission was important for several reasons. First, it undertook a comprehensive study of dual citizenship, including a broad set of social, family-, and tax-related issues. Second, it gave a generally positive account of dual citizenship, playing down the traditional problems of divided loyalties and so on, and emphasizing its probable positive effects on integration and political participation. Third, the commission introduced a novel guideline for the evaluation of dual citizenship: unless compelling arguments could be made *against* dual citizenship, it should be favoured as a principle (DsA 1986, 6, 10). All these aspects have proved significant for later discussions about dual citizenship. Of particular importance in my view was the guideline of evaluation, which shifts the burden of proof from those who argue in favour of a change in principle to those who argue against it. Given that avoiding dual citizenship has been a central principle, this guideline itself entails a significant change in point of view.

The 1985 citizenship commission's analysis was discussed in the late 1980s, and in 1991 the Social Democratic government proposed that the traditional view on dual citizenship needed to change (Regeringens proposition 1990/91, 195). The government explicitly related their proposal to the earlier controversy about extending voting rights to *denizens*, arguing that dual citizenship would be an alternative. The government acknowledged the problems of dual voting rights, but agreed with the 1985 citizenship commission that it was of little practical importance since few persons actually exercised their right to vote in elections in their home countries. This problem had, furthermore, to be weighed against the benefits of more persons being able to participate in politics. The government stressed that the principle of residence had become more and more central in policy and legislation and that citizenship correspondingly had lost much of its practical importance for persons' opportunities, rights, and obligations. The government also thought that the option of becoming a citizen was an important part of integration and that many immigrants wanted to retain their original citizenship when naturalizing in Sweden (Regeringens proposition 1990/91, 195, 89f., 93ff., 97).

The government concluded that 'very little speaks in favour of upholding the traditional view in Swedish legislation of avoiding multiple nationalities' (Regeringens proposition 1990/91, 195, 95, author's translation). It noted, however, that since recognizing dual citizenship would mean a major change of the principles on which legislation was based, it was necessary to investigate the issue further. Furthermore, changing the law should be coordinated with other Nordic and European countries, the government argued. Some measures could be implemented in a shorter time perspective though, in particular to extend the cases in which dual citizenship was tolerated (Regeringens proposition, 1990/91, 195, 96).

When the centre-right parties entered government in the autumn of 1991, they withdrew the 1991 proposition, partly because they wanted to retain the principle of avoiding dual citizenship (Parliament Records 1992/93, 37). The Social Democrats continued to argue for appointing a commission in the early 1990s (*cf.* Motion, 1992/93:Sf644). This was also suggested by some individual MPs from the centre-right parties (*cf.* Motion, 1993/94:U608 [Liberals]; Motion 1996/97: Sf622 [Conservatives]). On the whole, however, there was little discussion about the issue in the early and mid-1990s, but in 1997 a citizenship commission was appointed. The commission was to consider how the 1950 citizenship law could be adapted to the changing social and political circumstances, but not discuss whether or not dual citizenship should be recognized in principle. The Social Democratic government wrote in their directives that the principle of avoiding dual citizenship should be upheld and the commission's mandate was restricted to reviewing the existing practice of toleration (Kommittédirektiv 1997, 5). The political stalemate was probably one of the reasons that discussing the acceptance of dual citizenship was not part of the initial directives.

In discussing the toleration of dual citizenship, however, the members of the 1997 citizenship commission touched on the general arguments for and against dual citizenship and the commission agreed to ask the government for supplementary directives, to allow for opening the question (Interview with Lennart Strinäs, 2003-02-13). Such directives were also given in 1998 (Kommittédirektiv 1998, 50). In these the government instructed the commission to look at the general arguments relating to dual citizenship. Among the reasons for the supplementary directive, the government mentioned the existing practice of toleration and that the 1997 European Convention on Citizenship was neutral on the issue of dual citizenship. There had hence been significant changes in the European regulation of citizenship in recent years, the government contended (Kommittédirektiv 1998, 50). According to Lennart Strinäs, serving as secretary in the 1997 citizenship commission, the international trend of increasing acceptance of dual citizenship was important to the commission's discussion, but the 1997 European Convention was not of direct importance to the commission's analysis (Interview with Lennart Strinäs, 2003-02-13).

The 1997 citizenship commission analyzed the pros and cons of dual citizenship with respect to the same issues that had been addressed by the 1985 citizenship commission. The commission adopted the same general guideline as its predecessor, saying that dual citizenship was to be preferred unless compelling arguments could be made against it. The commission argued that the existing practice of toleration gave ample evidence for assessing whether there were, in practice, any major problems with dual citizenship (SOU 1999, 34, 203, 215).

In discussing the problem of dual voting rights the commission agreed with earlier assessments that it could be seen as a violation of the principle of 'one person, one vote', but that this had to be weighed against the benefits of making it possible for more *denizens* to become citizens in a complete political way. As the earlier investigation had noted, dual voting rights were less of a problem in practice since few persons actually voted in more than one country (SOU 1999, 34, 10ff., 142ff., 204ff.). The second issue concerned possible divided loyalties and the security problems this might involve. The police authorities had become less sceptical than they had been in the 1980s and thought that dual citizenship was not a decisive factor in this respect. The defence forces voiced similar concerns as they had done in the 1980s, arguing for keeping the principle intact (SOU 1999, 34, 157-63). The commission concluded that the security problems were most probably minor, and that the problems that might arise could be averted in the defence forces by not assigning dual nationals to specific missions (SOU 1999, 34, 209-11).

When discussing the potential risk in cases that persons might be forced to serve in the military in more than one country, the commission acknowledged that there could be such risks for individuals, but that they would very likely be small since most countries recognize that persons should have to serve in the military in only one country. Diplomatic assistance also posed a problem: the commission noted that diplomatic assistance was not completely foreclosed, but that it would depend on the goodwill of the country in question. The commission thought that it was important that persons becoming dual nationals also be informed in the future about the potential problems in this respect (SOU 1999, 34, 153ff., 207ff.).

In general, the 1997 citizenship commission looked on dual citizenship in a very positive light, arguing that the *de facto* toleration had so far not led to any major problems. The commission thought that concerns about dual voting rights and diplomatic assistance did not constitute compelling reasons against dual citizenship. The disadvantages had also to be weighed against the advantages, for example making it possible for persons to live and work in any of the countries of which they were citizens, and making visits and returns easier. Dual citizenship would also facilitate political participation and integration in general since becoming a citizen no longer had to involve any feeling of severing ties with the country of origin (SOU 1999, 34, 130ff., 202f., 212ff.).

The Social Democratic government followed the 1997 citizenship commission recommendation that dual citizenship be allowed (Regeringens proposition, 1999/2000, 147). The government made the same assessment; it also noted that much legislation and administrative practice were tied to residence and that as a consequence the importance of citizenship for most walks of life had decreased. Moreover, migration and globalization had led to the emergence of a multicultural society. In such a society more and more persons have 'genuine and deep' feelings of attachment to more than one country. Allowing dual citizenship would be a way to acknowledge these changes and would most likely facilitate integration; immigrants might otherwise hesitate to become citizens because of the requirement to renounce their original citizenship. This might hinder integration, the government contended (Regeringens proposition 1999/2000, 147, 16ff.).

While the 1997 citizenship commission had unanimously agreed to propose acceptance of dual citizenship, some members did so reluctantly. The Liberal member of the commission regretted the fact that citizenship legislation would now be changed, but conceded that the extensive *de facto* toleration made change necessary in order to reflect existing practice (SOU 1999, 34, 353). Some other representatives of the centre-right parties argued on more principled grounds in favour of dual citizenship, reflecting their change of view. The Conservative representative in the commission agreed with the commission's proposal as well, but in this he was at odds with the party. The Conservatives were the only party that argued for retaining the principle of avoiding dual citizenship in the debate that followed the commission's report (Parliament Records 2000/01, 70; Motion 2000/01:Sf3).

Some authorities and organizations also voiced criticism against the change, but most organizations and associations favoured accepting dual citizenship.[3] On the whole, dual citizenship did not become a politically contentious issue. It was not used by any party to mobilize support or politicize issues relating to migration and integration in spite of some opinion polls showing that the electorate was divided on the issue (*Dagens Nyheter* 1999-03-24). The proposition was first discussed in the relevant parliamentary sub-committees, and then debated in parliament on 21st February 2001. The new law was passed on the same day with 233 votes in favour, 69 against, and 3 abstentions. The Conservatives (with one exception) and one Christian Democrat voted against the new law. Two Christian Democrats and one Conservative abstained (Parliament Records 2000/01, 70).

Arguments in the Political Debate

The four issues dealt with in the government and parliamentary commissions were discussed in the public debate as well, but they were framed by more over-arching considerations (*cf.* Gustafson 2002; Gustafson 2004). Among the most discussed questions was whether dual citizenship meant a devaluing of citizenship, as the opponents claimed, or instead a way of strengthening it, as some of the proponents argued. Another issue debated was whether acquiring citizenship should be seen as a tool for the integration of immigrants, something the proponents argued, or as the end result of integration, which the opponents claimed. A much discussed aspect related to how migration and globalization had changed the character of attachment.

In the following section I discuss these issues and the arguments put forward, focusing on the roles played in the debate by pragmatic and principled (expressive and moral) arguments (Faist this volume, chapter 1). The proponents often combined equality arguments with those relating to changes of attachment due to migration

---

3   It is common practice that organizations, associations, and authorities can comment on commissions' arguments and proposals before the government presents their proposition to the parliament.

and globalization. Some stressed the importance of political equality, looking at the change of attachment as an aspect that reinforced the importance of recognizing dual citizenship, whereas others emphasized the change of attachment and used equality as a corollary argument. That dual citizenship would facilitate the integration of immigrants was an important aspect of the proponents' arguments, sometimes constituting a pragmatic context for arguing that the law should be changed.

Several proponents, especially the Social Democrats, the Left, the Greens, and many of the immigrant associations, viewed the change in law as a democratic reform. By acknowledging dual citizenship more persons would be able to participate in politics (*cf.* Parliament Records 2000/01, 70; The Cooperation Group for Ethnic Associations in Sweden, KU 1999/977/IM). The opponents' worries about dual voting rights were played down (Parliament Records 2000/01, 70). For example, the Centre Party had put forward the problems with dual voting rights as an important reason for their opposition in the early 1990s, but ten years later regarded this as a minor problem since few persons voted in more than one country (Motion 1990/91: Sf63; Motion 1998/99:Sf608). Other parties and organizations also used this more pragmatic reason, which was heavily criticized by the opponents, for supporting their principled argument about political equality (*cf.* Parliament Records 2000/01, 70; Regeringens proposition 1999/2000, 147; The Cooperation Group for Ethnical Associations in Sweden, KU 1999/977/IM; The Swedish Finnish Council, KU 1999/977/IM).

This blend of pragmatism and principles can be found in many of the proponents' arguments. The following statement by a Centre Party MP is characteristic:

> Citizenship is very important for the process of integration into Swedish society. It gives immigrants equal opportunities to be active in society ... Citizenship makes identification with the country in which one lives easier. Dual citizenship facilitates the process of integration and counter-acts the feelings of distress, guilt and alienation that many persons experience in their everyday lives. (Parliament Records 2000/01, 70, author's translation)

In this statement we find both moral and expressive arguments in favour of dual citizenship, linking a sense of belonging with equal rights and opportunities. These arguments are articulated in the context of a pragmatic concern with immigrant integration.

The second major argument put forward by the proponents drew upon the changing nature of attachment due to migration and globalization. In this line of thinking, the proponents contended that more and more persons sustained strong and genuine ties with two (or more) places and countries as a result of migration and globalization. Allowing for dual citizenship was seen as a way to acknowledge these changes (Parliament Records 2000/01, 70; Motion 1998/99:Sf635 [Greens]; Motion 1999/2000:Sf637 [Centre Party]; Motion 2000/01:Sf4 [Christian Democrats]). The proponents also emphasized that allowing dual citizenship was consistent with the ideas behind the immigrant integration policy (*cf.* Motion 1998/99:Sf635 [Greens]). For example, the Social Democratic Minister Ulrika Messing argued:

Integration is a matter of becoming part of a different cultural and social reality. But it is not a matter of having to give up one's earlier cultural identity. In a modern society that is ethnically and culturally plural, it is natural that persons have more than one identity … Everyone has the right to choose his or her own identity and to be respected for this. (Messing 2000, author's translation)

An important argument in this discussion was that changes to attachment mattered to Swedish nationals abroad as well as to *denizens* in Sweden. This point was critical for the centre-right parties' change of view, in part because the centre-right parties have traditionally stressed the rights of Swedish nationals living abroad. Furthermore, some associations representing Swedish nationals abroad played a role in making the importance of dual citizenship for Swedish nationals an issue in the debate (The Association for Swedes in the World, KU 1999/977/IM). At the same time it should be noted that the discussion about dual citizenship in regard to Swedish nationals was not related to earlier emigration from Sweden, which makes the discussion different from that in Poland (Górny, Grzymała-Kazłowska, Koryś and Weinar this volume, chapter 6).

Of some importance for the simultaneous focus on *denizens* and Swedish nationals was the example of the ice-hockey player who was not allowed to play in the 1998 Olympic Games since it turned out that he had naturalized in the US and thereby lost his Swedish citizenship (*cf. Aftonbladet* 1998-02-17). This case was often invoked by proponents as an example of how unreasonable and outdated the legislation was. One of the largest tabloid newspapers wrote in an editorial in 2000:

After all, we do live in a new time in which we often grow up in one place and then work and live in another place. But when the roles change and Uffe (the first name of the ice-hockey player – authors' remark) is replaced with Ahmed and the USA with Sweden, what seems obvious is no longer taken to be obvious and the principles are shifted. (*Expressen* 2000-12-02, author's translation)

Besides showing that dual citizenship mattered to Swedish nationals, the ice-hockey player example was often used as a pedagogical tool by those favouring dual citizenship to show the importance of taking up the perspective of the other. As such, it carried a certain moral weight, as expressed by some in the debate, for why accepting dual citizenship was a matter of fairness. Several persons had argued against allowing dual citizenship because they saw it as a privilege for immigrants. For example, Liberal MP Ana Maria Narti, who had initially opposed dual citizenship because she thought it meant creating a privilege, changed her position as it became clear that dual citizenship would be an option open to Swedish nationals who wanted to naturalize in other countries as well:

The question of dual citizenship is not only a question for immigrants. It is of course important for us who were born in another country. But as long as the discussion about dual citizenship centred on the new Swedes, as they are usually called, I opposed the idea of dual citizenship. One should not create privileges for a certain group. (Parliament Records 2000/01, 70, author's translation)

A similar type of argument was put forward by the Social Democratic Integration Minister Mona Sahlin, who stressed that dual citizenship was not foremost a question of immigrant integration, but a matter of 'rights and decency that has a general character' (Parliament Records 2000/01, 70, author's translation).

The changed nature of attachment was, furthermore, connected to a different interpretation of political allegiance and in that way related to political equality. The proponents argued that even though persons feel attached to several places this does not diminish the personal commitment to each one of those places. Sometimes this was put forward in terms of analogies that implied an expressive understanding of the political community. For example, Messing likened the feelings of attachment felt by people born in one country and then moving to another to those of someone about to become a parent for the second time who, despite wondering if the love for the newborn will be as strong as it was for the first child, discovers that the bond is equally strong the second time around (*Svenska Dagbladet* 1999-04-11).

Most of the time, however, the proponents used moral arguments for supporting their interpretation of attachment and allegiance, stressing that persons wanted to naturalize because of a conscious will to be part of the political community. Several opponents argued that many persons naturalized for practical reasons only and that allowing dual citizenship would lead to potential 'citizenship shopping' (Motion 2000/01:Sf3 [Conservatives]). Other parties and also immigrant associations criticized this view. For example, Messing said that:

> there is deeper thought behind such an act. At the last instance it is a conscious decision to be part of the national community. It is a matter of the will of the human being to take on responsibilities for the new society to which he or she has moved. It is also a matter of the resolve to be part of society and form its future together with other citizens. (Messing 2000, author's translation)

The opponents thought that the proponents exaggerated or over-interpreted the changes in attachment. The Conservatives argued that allowing dual citizenship meant devaluing citizenship and that it was important that the connection between individual and state, signified through citizenship, be upheld (*cf.* Motion 2000/01:Sf3; *Dagens Nyheter* 1999-03-11). That persons have attachments to more than one place did not change this normative consideration. Allowing dual citizenship, according to this argument, would undermine the specific connection between individual and the state and make citizenship into something similar to membership in an association in civil society (Parliament Records 2000/01, 70; Motion 2000/01:Sf3). Although it was mainly the Conservatives who articulated this type of argument in the late 1990s debate, it had been a central line of reasoning behind the other centre-right parties' opposition to dual citizenship in the 1980s and early 1990s as well (*cf.* Parliament Records 1992/93, 37).

Other opponents looked more favourably on the argument about the changes in attachment put forward by the proponents and thought that this included a vision worth striving for, but that it was not yet a reality (*cf. Dagens Nyheter* 1999-03-12; *Dagens Nyheter* 2000-04-28). The liberal morning newspaper *Dagens Nyheter*

(Daily News) thought that although many arguments in favour of dual citizenship were worthy of 'earnest consideration', the overall assessment of these arguments by the 1997 citizenship commission was problematic.

> It seems today too rash to give up the idea of one single citizenship. There is much that is still tied in with citizenship, both formally and factually. And it can be asked, is it not reasonable that somebody who wants to become a Swedish citizen must be asked to decide which political association primarily to be part of? (*Dagens Nyheter* 1999-03-12, author's translation)

This last point was a common argument among the opponents. Persons must be asked to make a choice, a choice that would itself signal the commitment to the political community. The Conservatives argued that having to renounce one's original citizenship signals such a commitment. It shows that one is prepared to take this step and understands and accepts its consequences (Parliament Records 2000/01, 70). For example the Conservatives' spokesperson on migration and integration issues, Gustaf von Essen, formulated it in the following way:

> Sure, the more immigrants that become Swedes the better, but one also has to renounce one's old citizenship, if possible. That really shows a willingness to become integrated and not to sit on two stools at the same time. (cited in *Dagens Nyheter* 1999-03-11, author's translation)

Most of the time these arguments were based on the importance of evidence of an individual's genuine interest in being part of the new political community. But more expressive arguments were also put forward, often based on various analogies. Some used the metaphor of marriage, suggesting that whereas persons could divorce and enter into a new relationship, this was a change from one single relationship to another (*cf.* Stenius 1999). Neither polygamy nor infidelity was generally accepted in society. Another metaphor used was that of adoption. Conservative Gun Hellsvik, the former Minister of Justice, argued that citizenship is akin to belonging to a family:

> You are part of the family from the beginning if you are born a Swede. If you get another citizenship later in life, it is really like being adopted. And we recognize adoption in principle as a matter of exiting your old family. (cited in *Dagens Nyheter* 1999-03-11, author's translation)

More pragmatic arguments were also put forward by the opponents. They doubted that dual citizenship would facilitate integration and argued that it may instead make immigrants more prone to uphold and strengthen their attachment to their former home countries. Dual citizenship exemplified a laissez-faire attitude that was not conducive to integration, the Conservatives argued (Parliament Records 2000/01, 70). The opponents also took a different view on how integration and citizenship are connected. Whereas the proponents thought that citizenship may be seen as a tool facilitating the integration of immigrants, the opponents argued that it was important that integration should be 'complete' before persons became citizens (*cf.* The Aliens Appeal Board, KU 1999/977/IM). The proponents' view implied a major change in policy, the opponents argued, that was not justified by any solid arguments (*cf.* Gustafsson 2000). This was just one of many examples of how the 1997 citizenship commission's report was shallow, imprecise, and inconsistent, in the opponents' view. The 1997 citizenship commission had brushed the principled objections aside. Reforming such important legislation as that of citizenship should not be based on practical advantages and shifting feelings of attachment, many opponents contended (*cf.* Gustafsson 2000; Gür 1999; *Svenska Dagbladet* 1999-03-25; *Svenska Dagbladet* 2000-01-10).

Although many proponents had argued in principled terms for a change of the law in the 1980s, it was the opponents this time who formulated their criticism in terms of principles. Those approving of dual citizenship seemed to be restricted to assessing its practical advantages and disadvantages, and approaches to some degree related to the guideline of evaluation mentioned earlier. Although it shifts the burden of proof to those who argue against dual citizenship, it also implies that the evaluation should be focused on the practical effects of the problems associated with dual citizenship. Because of this, arguments relating to, for example, the changing structure of attachment appear not as principled arguments but as pragmatic ones.

Still, a specific feature of pragmatic reasons is that they are made within an already established set of moral and expressive or ethical considerations (*cf.* Habermas 1991). Since many of the practical reasons for accepting dual citizenship did challenge the prevalent view, it is not strictly speaking correct to identify them as pragmatic reasons. As argued, they involved moral considerations, for example, with respect to the fairness of the reform, and expressive or ethical considerations, especially concerning the changed nature of attachment and belonging.

When comparing the dual citizenship debates of the 1980s to those of the late 1990s, a shift is apparent – from a national to a trans-state perspective (*cf.* Faist 2001). The debate of the 1980s focused almost exclusively on *denizens* in Sweden, and dual citizenship was conceived of as a mechanism of immigrant integration, either in more pragmatic terms or on the basis of the importance of political equality. Although this was also discussed in the 1990s, the national perspective was now supplemented with a more trans-state view on dual citizenship. The argument that attachment and allegiance had changed because of migration and globalization implies a trans-state perspective in which the importance of overlapping ties is stressed.

Explaining the Acceptance of Dual Citizenship

In order to explain the acceptance of dual citizenship in Sweden I have looked at the role of understandings of nationhood, the impact of integration policies and debates, and some of the characteristics of the political system. Since the rationale for focusing on these factors as well as the specific hypothesis related to them are taken up in the introduction to this volume, I will not repeat them here (Faist this volume, chapter 1).

Understandings of State and Nation

Understandings of state and nation did, as we have seen, play an important role in the debate about dual citizenship, for example with respect to the interpretation of attachments and allegiance. Yet, it is not easy to establish more specifically the relationship between these arguments and understandings of nationhood in Sweden. One of the reasons for this lies in the difficulty of characterizing nationhood in Sweden itself.

Nationhood is to a large degree mediated through the welfare state. The so-called 'people's home' (*folkhemmet*) was central to political understandings of state and nation in Sweden for the better part of the twentieth century. Introduced by conservatives around the turn of the century, the notion was taken up by the Social Democrats in the 1920s and formed the backbone for mobilizing support for what would become the welfare state project. The 'people's home' is to a high degree tied in with a modernizing zeal and the effort to create a cross-class support for the Social Democrats (*cf.* Ambjörnsson 1988; Berggren 2001; Hallberg and Jonsson 1996; Jonsson 2000, chapters 6-9; Korpi 1978, chapter 11). For a long time the 'people's home' was synonymous with modern Sweden, an example of a stable, democratic welfare state, and as such clearly a form of nationalism (*cf.* Ambjörnsson 2002; Ehn, Frykman and Löfgren 1993; Götz 2001).

The 'people's home' does not correspond neatly to either a republican or an ethno-cultural understanding of the nation. Instead we find elements that point in the one or the other direction (*cf.* Westin 2000, 44). The scholarly literature on the 'people's home' provides at least four different interpretations of the concept that have been made over the past decades. Until the 1970s, the 'people's home' was to a large extent seen as synonymous with the welfare state. In that view, which resembles a republican ethos, the 'people's home' expressed a form of solidarity guided by fairness, cooperation, and inclusion (*cf.* Inghe and Inghe 1968; Larsson 1994). This view has since then been problematized in several ways. Some have pointed out the gendered character of the 'people's home', others have stressed its connection with nineteenth-century forms of nationalism, and still others have argued that there is a connection between it and various race-hygienic ideas that became influential in the 1920s, especially as expressed in the sterilization programme of the 1930s and onwards (*cf.* Broberg and Tydén 1994; Frykman and Löfgren 1985; Hall 2000, chapter 3; Hammar 1964; Hirdman 1989; Molina 1997, chapter 3; Roll-Hansen 1997). Over the past two decades all these aspects of the 'people's home' and their meaning for contemporary Sweden have been much discussed.

These elements do not exclude each other, but rather add different facets to the 'people's home'. In this respect it may be useful to characterize the 'people's home' as a hegemonic project in which the various elements are articulated (*cf.* Billing and Stigendal 1994; Fryklund, Himmelstrand and Peterson 1988; Hallberg and Jonsson 1996; Jonsson 2000). It is beyond the scope of this article to go into the details of the hegemonic appeal of the 'people's home' since the 1930s. Suffice it to say that an intricate web of inclusion and exclusion has been formed over time.

Among the inclusive aspects that are of importance for explaining the acceptance of dual citizenship I would stress the socio-political as opposed to socio-cultural idea of citizenship understood in the concept of the 'people's home'. Among the excluding aspects, the use of several elements characteristic of such a socio-political understanding of nationhood and citizenship, including that of equality, can be mentioned. Equality can be used as a marker, differentiating between us and them when it comes to viewing immigrants as carrying traditions that are incompatible with individual freedom, equality, gender equity, and so on. Indeed, equality itself is often seen as a Swedish value in the political debate (*cf.* de los Reyes 2001; Molina 1997), and as such can be used to define outsiders, as the Dutch case clearly demonstrates (de Hart this volume, chapter 3).

Both the including and the excluding aspects of the 'people's home' are central to understanding several of the policies usually discussed in terms of the welfare state. It is also in this mediated way that the relation between the 'people's home' and dual citizenship can be analyzed. The socio-political character of citizenship meant that the integration of immigrants was located within the over-all societal integration project of the welfare state. In contrast to many other policy fields related to immigrant integration, however, there are relatively few examples of an excluding use of equality and allegiance arguments in the dual citizenship debate. For example, the discussion in the Dutch case about *denizens'* and citizens' differing capacities to be good citizens did not play any significant role in the Swedish debate (de Hart this volume, chapter 3).

Integration Policies and Debates

Between the 1940s and the 1960s there was a common understanding that labour migrants would return to their home countries after a couple of years, but there existed no explicit guest-worker system in Sweden (*cf.* Lundh and Ohlsson 1994). This reflects the way in which the socio-political understanding of citizenship together with over-all societal integration through the welfare state had an impact on migration policies. The unions' response to labour migration – not opting for the protection of domestic workers – is also noteworthy. This response was facilitated by the way the unions were tied in with the welfare state project in general (*cf.* Lundh 2002; Lundqvist 2002).

The prevalent idea in the 1940s and 1950s was that immigrants should assimilate, which was also the dominant idea when the debate about immigrant integration started in the 1960s. Gradually, however, cultural-pluralist understandings became more and more prominent in the debate (*cf.* Diaz 1993, chapter 2; Hedin 1966). When the Social Democratic government announced in the late 1960s that socio-economic equality would be at the centre of integration policies, they also made clear that many features of earlier policies had embodied an assimilationist ideal that now needed to change. A commission was appointed to outline a new, more multicultural or pluralist integration policy. It presented its results in 1974 (SOU 1974, 69).

The new integration policy, adopted by parliament in 1975, was based on three principles: equality, freedom of choice, and partnership or cooperation. The central-pluralist element of the policy was the freedom of choice principle (Borevi 2002, chapter 3; Westin 1996; Widgren 1982; Ålund and Schierup 1991). Simply put, this principle entailed the idea that immigrants should be able to choose whether they wanted to retain and develop their own cultural and ethnic identity or assimilate to a Swedish cultural identity (SOU 1974, 69, 95f.). The third principle, partnership, entailed mutual respect and tolerance between immigrants and the native population, but also, and more ambitiously, measures with the intent to make them equal partners in society. Public support for immigrant associations and religious congregations, mother-tongue education in schools, and the like were some of the measures introduced in order to facilitate the possibility of choice and partnership (*cf.* Borevi 2002, chapters 4-6; Westin 1996).

Liberalized naturalization rules, local and regional voting rights, and the further equalization of rights, opportunities, and obligations between *denizens* and citizens make up an important set of institutional factors that have facilitated the acceptance of dual citizenship. In discursive terms, the role of cultural pluralism should be stressed. The familiarity of pluralist arguments from the debate about immigrant integration probably made it easier for the proponents to draw upon them in the debate about dual citizenship as well. Perhaps it also facilitated the acceptance of these arguments, though it should be noted that freedom of choice has been the most controversial of the principles underlying immigrant integration policies. Because of these controversies surrounding it, this issue could have been a way for opponents to mobilize support for their side. It is also interesting to note that cultural-pluralist arguments figured less in the debates about immigrant integration during the 1990s. The focus on freedom of choice gave way in the 1990s to a combination of the need by immigrants to adapt, and an emphasis that all policies should reflect and promote diversity in society (*cf.* de los Reyes 2001; Södergran 1998; Ålund and Karlsson 1996).

One reason that opponents of dual citizenship did not use cultural-pluralist arguments to mobilize opinion against its supporters was most likely that these arguments were applied not only to *denizens* in Sweden but also to Swedish nationals living abroad. This twist to the pluralist argument in the late 1990s debate was in my view critical for the discursive opportunity structure. In this context one should also make note of the role played by internationalization and globalization arguments played. Per Gustafson (2002, 476) has highlighted these arguments in his analysis of the dual citizenship debate whereas I have focused more on the role of cultural-pluralist arguments in the debate. But it may be the case that these two types of argument work in tandem, making it possible to put forward the claim that cultural pluralism due to globalization mattered to Swedish nationals as well. This contrasts with the way in which this connection was played out in the Dutch debate (de Hart this volume, chapter 3).

Political System

The fact that the Social Democrats did not choose to push for recognition of dual citizenship in the 1980s shows that the search for consensus mattered considerably to the development of the issue. Trying to achieve consensus, especially in matters related to constitutional principles, defence, and foreign policy, is an important feature of Swedish politics, but should also be related to bloc politics. As we have seen, the dividing lines between the parties during the 1980s followed the two blocs, the socialist and the non-socialist parties respectively. In spite of the formal and informal coalitions between the Agrarian Party and the Social Democrats from the 1930s to the 1950s, Swedish politics has for a long time been divided along the lines of the two blocs. Bloc politics has been most significant in political matters related to the welfare state, such as social and economic policy.

The combination of consensus and bloc politics has to do with what the party system looks like. The Social Democrats have long been the dominant party, with around 40 per cent of the vote in elections, making it necessary for the centre-right parties to form a bloc in order to be able to challenge them. The dominant position of the Social Democrats is also related to consensus politics. With some exceptions the Social Democrats have been heading minority governments since the late 1950s and as a rule must look for coalition partners and majorities on broader or smaller sets of issues.

Given these features of the political system, the centre-right parties' opposition in the 1980s and their changed position during the 1990s was central to the political process. Had this shift not come about, the likelihood was low that the Social Democratic government would have pushed, with the support of the Left and the Greens, for a change of the law. The fact that the undertaking of a more comprehensive analysis of dual citizenship was not part of the initial directives to the 1997 citizenship commission reflects this. The stress on consensus has consequences for the opponents as well. In spite of polls indicating a divided public opinion, the Conservatives did not turn dual citizenship into a major political issue. One reason for this may be that the broad majority in favour of the proposal made it difficult for the Conservatives to influence the outcome.

Another reason for the lack of politicization may be the absence of an established right-wing populist party on the national level in the late 1990s. It is not unlikely that the opposition against dual citizenship would have been fiercer and more vocal had such a party been present at the national level, since the Conservatives would have had to openly compete with such a party for votes. Furthermore, a right-wing populist party would also have been a threat to the Social Democrats because it would most likely have drawn many voters from their ranks. Whether or not this would have changed the outcome is another question. But the impact of New Democracy in Sweden, a right-wing populist party in parliament between 1991 and 1994, on refugee and immigration discussions during the early and mid-1990s, and the role of established populist parties in other European countries, make it clear that the existence of such parties is important for other parties' positions.

Conclusions

The pluralist interpretation of attachment and belonging, relating to both *denizens* in Sweden and Swedish nationals living abroad, is among the important discursive factors facilitating the acceptance of dual citizenship. The simultaneous focus on *denizens* and Swedish nationals probably made it easier to accept the pluralist interpretation of attachment and the fact that dual citizenship would not affect political allegiance in a negative way. This focus also did away with the argument that accepting dual citizenship would mean creating a unique privilege for immigrants.

In sharp contrast, the Dutch debate focused on both *denizens* and Dutch nationals but as quite distinct categories (de Hart this volume, chapter 3). In the Swedish case, the emphasis on equality and fairness of the reform most likely played an important role in mitigating the idea of two distinct cases. Hence, the twist on cultural pluralist arguments in the debate about dual citizenship in Sweden must be understood in the context of the prominent role that equality and political participation arguments played in that debate. Both arguments are furthermore related to the way immigrant integration policies have been placed within the welfare state programme.

Turning to the institutional factors facilitating the acceptance of dual citizenship, the low levels of legal differentiation between *denizens* and citizens and the extensive *de facto* toleration should be highlighted. Both are related to the development of immigrant integration policies in the context of welfare state provisions and labour market regulation since the 1950s. Over time, *denizens'* and citizens' rights and obligations came increasingly to resemble each other. Further steps in the same direction were taken during the 1970s. As such, the process leading up to the acceptance of dual citizenship is clearly a path-dependant process in which lock-in effects can be noticed (Faist this volume, chapter 7). This path-dependence was partly reflected in a common argument in the debate of the 1980s: accepting dual citizenship was simply a logical step along the lines of easier naturalization, voting rights for *denizens*, and so on. At the same time, the question of accepting dual citizenship remained open until the centre-right parties changed their position. Some centre-right parties' representatives argued that dual citizenship had to be accepted because the principle of avoiding dual citizenship had been hollowed out by *de facto* toleration, but most representatives of the centre-right parties argued on principled grounds for accepting dual citizenship.

As the German and Dutch cases show, extensive *de facto* toleration does not necessarily lead to acceptance of dual citizenship in principle (Gerdes, Rieple and Faist this volume, chapter 2; de Hart this volume, chapter 3). The German political system is overtly competitive and this helps explain the outcome; Swedish politics, on the other hand, are characterized by a striving for consensus, a distinction that is important when explaining the differences between the Swedish and the German cases. But this does not explain the differences between the Swedish and the Dutch cases since consensus politics is of importance in both countries. In comparing the Dutch and the Swedish cases it would instead, in my view, be the simultaneous focus on *denizens* and nationals abroad, and the emphasis on their equal treatment, that

Figure 4.1   Sweden: Chronological List of Dual Citizenship-Related Legislation and Proposals

Date	Legislation and Proposals	Change in Institutional or Discursive Opportunity Structure
1858	First naturalization regulation	Principle of avoiding dual citizenship established.
1950	Citizenship Act	Principle of avoiding dual citizenship affirmed and considered more important than gender equity.
1979	Change of Citizenship Act	Citizenship Act changed so that citizenship is to follow the mother or the father if he is a Swedish national and married to the mother; gender equity considered more important than avoiding dual citizenship.
1985	Citizenship Commission	Commission considers dual citizenship less problematic than previously thought; argues that dual citizenship will be beneficial for the integration of immigrants.
1991	Proposition to Parliament	Social Democratic government suggests that principle of avoiding dual citizenship needs to be changed; proposition withdrawn by Centre-Right government in 1991.
1997-1999	Citizenship Commission	Commission suggests that dual citizenship should be accepted; centre-right parties except the Conservatives now agree to accept dual citizenship. The perspective of Swedish citizens naturalizing in other countries plays as important a role as the perspective of immigrants in Sweden. Extensive *de facto* toleration is also of importance to centre-right parties' changed view on dual citizenship.
2001	New Citizenship Act	Dual citizenship acknowledged in principle by parliament.

is of importance in explaining the difference. What distinguishes the Swedish case from the German and Dutch cases is that extensive *de facto* toleration was combined institutionally with consensus politics, and discursively with pluralism and equality, which facilitated a new interpretation of attachment and allegiance.

References

Almqvist, K. and Glans, K. (eds) (2001), *Den svenska framgångssagan?* (Stockholm: Fischer & Co.).

Ålund, A. and Karlsson, L. G. (1996), 'Svensk kulturpluralism i omvandling', *SOU [Statens offentliga utredningar] Vägar in i Sverige. Bilagor*, 1996:55, 57-70.

Ålund, A. and Schierup, C.-U. (1991), *Paradoxes of Multiculturalism. Essays on Swedish Society* (Aldershot: Avebury).

Ambjörnsson, R. (1988), *Den skötsamme arbetaren. Idéer och ideal i ett norrländskt sågverkssamhälle 1880-1930* (Stockholm: Carlssons).

Ambjörnsson, R. (2002), '(S)tädare i kapitalets korridorer', *Dagens Nyheter*, 2002-12-27.

Åsard, E. (ed.) (1996), *Makten, medierna och myterna. Socialdemokratiska ledare från Branting till Carlsson* (Stockholm: Carlssons).

Bäck, H. and Soininen, M. (1996) 'Invandrarna, demokratin och samhället', in *SOU [Statens offentliga utredningar] På medborgarnas villkor – en demokratisk infrastruktur*, 1996:162, 411-504.

Bauböck, R., Heller, A. and Zolberg, A. (eds) (1996), *The Challenge of Diversity. Integration and Pluralism in Societies of Immigration* (Aldershot: Avebury).

Berggren, H. (2001), 'Den framåtvända ängeln – nationalism och modernitet i Sverige under 1900-talet', in Almqvist, K. and Glans, K. (eds), 71-85.

Billing, P. and Stigendal, M. (1994), *Hegemonins decennier. Lärdomar från Malmö om den svenska modellen* (Malmö: Möllevångens samhällsanalys).

Borevi, K. (2002), *Välfärdsstaten i det mångkulturella samhället* (Uppsala: Acta Universitatis Upsaliensis).

Broberg, G. and Tydén, M. (1994), *Oönskade i folkhemmet. Rashygien och sterilisering i Sverige* (Stockholm: Gidlunds).

Dahlstedt, M. (1998), *Politiskt medborgarskap, integration och mångkulturell demokrati. Segregation, utanförskap och politiska reformsträvanden i Sverige från 70-tal till 90-tal* (Umeå: Partnerskap för multietnisk integration [PfMI]) 98:3.

de los Reyes, P. (2001), *Diversity and Differentiation. Discourse, Difference and Construction of Norms in Swedish Research and Public Debate* (Stockholm: The National Institute for Working Life).

Diaz, J. A. (1993), *Choosing Integration. A Theoretical and Empirical Study of the Immigrant Integration in Sweden* (Uppsala: Department of Sociology).

Ehn, B., Frykman, J. and Löfgren, O. (1993), *Försvenskningen av Sverige. Det nationellas förvandlingar* (Stockholm: Natur & Kultur).

Faist, T. (2001), 'Dual Citizenship as Overlapping Membership', *Willy Brandt Series of Working Papers in International Migration and Ethnic Relations* (IMER) 3.

Fryklund, B., Himmelstrand, U. and Peterson, T. (1988), 'Folklighet, klass och opinion i svensk politik under efterkrigstiden', in Himmelstrand, U. and Svensson, G. (eds), 617-46.

Frykman, J. and Löfgren, O. (1985), 'På väg – bilder av kultur och klass', in Frykman, J. and Löfgren, O. (eds), 20-139.

Frykman, J. and Löfgren, O. (eds) (1985), *Modärna tider* (Malmö: Liber).

Götz, N. (2001), 'Den moderna Tomtebolyckan', in Almqvist, K. and Glans, K. (eds), 103-16.

Gür, T. (1999), 'Dubbelt medborgarskap – andraklass svenskar', *Svenska Dagbladet*, 1999-03-13.

Gustafson, P. (2002), 'Globalisation, Multiculturalism and Individualism: The Swedish Debate on Dual Citizenship', *Journal of Ethnic and Migration Studies* 28:3, 463–81.

Gustafson, P. (2004), 'International Migration and National Belonging in the Swedish Debate on Dual Citizenship', Paper presented at the *Swedish Sociological Association* (Stockholm: Stockholm University), 2004-02-05/06.

Gustafsson, A. (2000), 'Problemen med dubbelt medborgarskap förbises', *Svenska Dagbladet*, 2000-09-14.

Habermas, J. (1991), 'Vom pragmatischen, ethischen und moralischen Gebrauch der praktischen Vernunft', in Habermas, J. (ed.), 100-18.

Habermas, J. (ed.) (1991), *Erläuterungen zur Diskursethik* (Frankfurt am Main: Suhrkamp).

Hall, P. (2000), *Den svenskaste historien. Nationalism i Sverige under sex sekler* (Stockholm: Carlssons).

Hallberg, M. and Jonsson, T. (1996), 'Per Albin Hansson och folkhemsretorikens framväxt', in Åsard, E. (ed.), 125-74.

Hammar, T. (1964), *Sverige åt svenskarna. Invandringspolitik, utlänningskontroll och asylrätt 1900-1932* (Stockholm: Statsvetenskapliga institutionen).

Hammar, T. (1990), *Democracy and the Nation State. Aliens, Denizens and Citizens in a World of International Migration* (Aldershot: Avebury).

Hedin, U. (1966), 'Pressen och invandrarna', in Schwarz, D. (ed.), 120-37.

Himmelstrand, U. and Svensson, G. (eds) (1988), *Sverige – vardag och struktur. Sociologer beskriver det svenska samhället* (Stockholm: Norstedts).

Hirdman, Y. (1989), *Att lägga livet till rätta – studier i svensk folkhemspolitik* (Stockholm: Carlssons).

Inghe, G. and Inghe, M.-B. (1968), *Den ofärdiga välfärden* (Stockholm: Tiden).

Jonsson, T. (2000), *'Att anpassa sig efter det möjliga'. Utsugningsbegreppet och SAP:s ideologiska förändringar 1911-1944* (Göteborg: Institutionen för idé och lärdomshistoria).

Korpi, W. (1978), *Arbetarklassen i välfärdskapitalismen* (Stockholm: Prisma).

Larsson, J. (1994), *Hemmet vi ärvde. Om folkhemmet, identiteten och den gemensamma framtiden* (Stockholm: Arena).

Lundh, C. and Ohlsson, R. (1994), *Från arbetskraftsimport till flyktinginvandring* (Stockholm: SNS Förlag).

Lundh, C. (2002), *Spelets regler. Institutioner och lönebildning på den svenska arbetsmarknaden 1850-2000* (Stockholm: SNS Förlag).

Lundqvist, T. (2002), 'Arbetskraftsinvandringen och facket. Debatt och historia i framtidsperspektiv', in Malmberg, B. and Sommestad, L. (eds), 107-39.

Malmberg, B. and Sommestad, L. (eds) (2002), *Befolkning och välfärd* (Stockholm: institutet för framtidsstudier).

Messing, U. (2000), 'Lättare få dubbelt medborgarskap', *Sundsvalls tidning*, 2000-07-30.

Molina, I. (1997), *Stadens rasifiering. Etnisk boendesegregation i folkhemmet* (Uppsala: Institutionen för samhällsgeografi).

Roll-Hansen, N. (1997), 'Missvisande om nordiska steriliseringar', *TLM* 3/4, 85-90.

Sandesjö, H. and Björk, K. (1996), *Medborgarskapslagen med kommentarer* (Stockholm: Publica).

Schwarz, D. (ed.) (1966), *Svenska minoriteter* (Stockholm: Aldus).

Södergran, L. (1998), '1990-talets invandrarpolitiska omprövning. Från invandrarpolitik till integrationspolitik', *MERGE Papers on Transcultural Studies* 2 (Umeå: Sociologiska institutionen).

Stenius, Y. (1999), 'Nog bäst med en nationalitet i taget', *Aftonbladet*, 1999-10-12.

Szabó, M. 1997), *Vägen mot medborgarskap. Studier i medborgarskapsbyte och integration* (Stockholm: Arena).

Westin, C. (1996), 'Equality, Freedom of Choice and Partnership: Multicultural Policy in Sweden', in Bauböck, R., Heller, A. and Zolberg, A. (eds), 207-26.

Westin, C. (2000), *The Effectiveness of Settlement and Integration Policies Towards Immigrants and their Descendants in Sweden* (Geneva: ILO).

Widgren, J. (1982), *Svensk invandrarpolitik* (Malmö: Liber).

Documents

Public Commissions

SOU (Statens offentliga utredningar) (1974:69), Invandrarna och minoriteterna. Invandrarutredningens slutbetänkande (Stockholm).

SOU (Statens offentliga utredningar) (1975:15), Kommunal rösträtt för invandrare Betänkande av Rösträttsutredningen (Stockholm).
SOU (Statens offentliga utredningar) (1984:11), Rösträtt och medborgarskap. Invandrares och utlandssvenskars rösträtt (Stockholm).
SOU (Statens offentliga utredningar) (1999:34), Svenskt medborgarskap. Slutbetänkande av 1997 års medborgarskapskommitté (Stockholm).
DsA (Departementsserien) (1986:6), Dubbelt medborgarskap (Stockholm).

Government Propositions

Regeringens proposition 1990/91:195 (1991), *Om aktiv flykting- och immigrations politik m.m.* (Stockholm).
Regeringens proposition 1999/2000:147 (2000), *Lag om svenskt medborgarskap* (Stockholm).

Government Directives

Kommittédirektiv (1997:5), *Översyn av lagen om svenskt medborgarskap* (Stockholm).
Kommittédirektiv (1998:50), *Tilläggsdirektiv till 1997 års medborgarskapsdirektiv* (Stockholm).

Laws

SFS (Svensk författningssamling) (1950:382), Lag om svenskt medborgarskap.
SFS (Svensk författningssamling) (1979:139), Lag om svenskt medborgarskap.
SFS (Svensk författningssamling) (2001:82), Lag om svenskt medborgarskap.

Parliament Motions

Motion 1990/91:Sf63 (Centre Party).
Motion 1992/93:Sf644 (Social Democrats).
Motion 1993/94:U608 (Liberals).
Motion 1996/97:Sf622 (Conservatives).
Motion 1998/99:Sf608 (Centre Party).
Motion 1998/99:Sf635 (Greens).
Motion 1999/2000:Sf637 (Centre Party).
Motion 2000/01:Sf3 (Conservatives).
Motion 2000/01:Sf4 (Christian Democrats).

Parliament Debates

Parliament Records 1992/93:37, 1992-12-03.
Parliament Records 2000/01:70, 2001-02-21.

Official Comments

The Aliens Appeal Board, *Utlänningsnämnden*, KU1999/977/IM.

The Association for Swedes in the World, *Föreningen svenskar i världen*, KU1999/977/IM.
The Cooperation Group for Ethnical Associations in Sweden, *SIOS – samarbetsorgan för invandrarorganisationer i Sverige*, KU1999/977/IM.
The Swedish Finnish Council, *Sverigefinska Riksförbundet*, KU1999/977/IM.

Interview

Interview with the judge of the Malmö district court (*rådman*) Lennart Strinäs (secretary to the 1997 citizenship commission), Malmö 2003-02-13.

Newspapers

Aftonbladet, 1998-02-17.
Dagens Nyheter, 1999-03-11.
Dagens Nyheter, 1999-03-12.
Dagens Nyheter, 1999-03-24.
Dagens Nyheter, 2000-04-28.
Expressen, 2000-12-02.
Svenska Dagbladet, 1999-03-25.
Svenska Dagbladet, 1999-04-11.
Svenska Dagbladet, 2000-01-10.

Chapter 5

National Transnationalism: Dual Citizenship in Turkey

Zeynep Kadırbeyoğlu[1]

Abstract

This chapter outlines the underlying causes of increased tolerance of dual citizenship in Turkey. The findings suggest that the proportion of Turkish citizens living abroad and their economic importance to Turkey are significant in explaining this phenomenon. There are various expatriate Turkish organizations, especially in Germany, which pressure policy-makers in Turkey to accommodate their needs to integrate in their host country without having to relinquish their rights to inheritance in Turkey. The findings presented in this chapter suggest that the major explanatory variable is the number of Turkish emigrants living abroad and their ties to Turkey.

Introduction

The last two decades have witnessed an increase in the numbers of dual citizens throughout the world and a growing tolerance of dual citizenship by nation-states. Analyses of changing attitudes regarding dual citizenship are provided by the works of, among others, Hammar (1989), Spiro (1997), Freeman and Ogelman (1998), and Aleinikoff and Klusmeyer (2001). These authors show that the reasons for shifts in perceptions regarding dual citizenship are multiple and vary depending on the country under analysis. Here, the case of Turkey will be analyzed in order to account for factors specific to an emigrant country. While the focus of this chapter is Turkey, the findings are relevant to broader concerns regarding an increasing tolerance of dual citizenship throughout the world, as well as to debates about globalization and migration.

1 The author wishes to thank Eyüp Özveren for his guidance throughout this research and writing. Thomas Faist and the participants in the dual citizenship workshops have provided valuable feedback on earlier versions of this chapter. The author is also grateful to Gamze Avcı and Kemal Kirişçi for their help and suggestions. Finally, Esra Derle and Selçuk Uğuz were of great help in facilitating access to resources and Jeffrey Cuvilier has done a great job in editing the chapter. The usual caveat applies.

The law currently regulating the acquisition and loss of Turkish citizenship was put into effect in 1964 (Law no. 403 *Turkish Citizenship Law* 1964). Originally, this law did not allow for dual citizenship. However, after changes to the law were accepted in 1981, dual citizenship became legal so long as the person acquiring a second citizenship informed the government (Keyman and İçduygu 2003); otherwise they can be stripped of their Turkish citizenship.[2] This chapter aims to account for the government's greater *de facto* and *de jure* tolerance of dual citizenship with reference to factors that include the official national self-understanding of Turkish identity, the proportion of citizens living abroad, the economic ties those citizens have with Turkey, and the roles different political and non-political actors play in influencing the process of increased acceptance of dual citizenship. Broader issues such as globalization and migration will be addressed in the conclusion.

Institutional Opportunity Structures

National Self-Understanding: Civic-Republican or Ethno-Cultural?

This section consists of a historical account of citizenship regulations and practices in Turkey presented with a view to clarifying the official national self-understanding in Turkey and to assessing whether this understanding is predominantly civic-republican or ethno-cultural in nature. We shall then on this basis try to evaluate the following claim: the more an understanding of nationhood is informed by republican concepts, the more tolerant the country will be of dual citizenship. Although in most cases ethno-cultural and civic-republican features are encountered together (see Spång this volume, chapter 4 for the Swedish case, and de Hart this volume, chapter 3 for an interesting mix of these two types), it is a useful exercise to go over the historical evolution of national self-understanding before examining tolerance of dual citizenship.

An analysis of the history of Turkish citizenship should begin with the last period of the Ottoman Empire. Whereas prior to the 1869 *Tabiyet-i Osmaniye Kanunu* (Ottoman Citizenship Law) the subjects of the Ottoman Empire were divided along religious lines, the new law recognized all residents of the Ottoman territories as nationals of the Empire. It was based on the *jus sanguinis* principle, but allowed for non-Ottoman children born in the Ottoman territories to apply for citizenship in the Empire when they reached adulthood (İçduygu et al. 1999).

The first constitution of the Republic of Turkey (1924) granted Turkish citizenship to all residents of the Republic irrespective of race or religion. The citizenship law of the Republic was accepted in 1928 and, like its Ottoman predecessor, it was based on the *jus sanguinis* principle but was complemented by a territorial understanding

---

2   This change was made possible by the 1981 amendment to the Law and permits Turkish citizens to acquire citizenship in another country without losing Turkish citizenship. This was also supported by the change in Article 23/III of the *Citizenship Law* now stating that it is legally possible to give permission for exit to citizens who wish to acquire another country's citizenship (Law no. 2383 *Türk Vatandaşlığı Kanunu 1981*).

(İçduygu et al. 1999, 193). Aybay (2001, 45) argues that behind this decision lay the desire to extend Turkish citizenship to as many people as possible.[3] The citizenship law of the early Republic is not easily characterized in terms of either the civic-republican or ethno-cultural models.

For example İçduygu, Çolak and Soyarık (1999) argue that the notion of citizenship was not defined solely in terms of ethnic background since the new Turkish citizenship was 'open to non-Turkish Muslim groups ... so long as they were willing to assimilate culturally and linguistically into the Turkish culture' (İçduygu, Çolak and Soyarık 1999, 195). Conversely, Kirişçi (2000, 1) argues that during the Republican era in Turkey, despite the presence of a formally established territorial and civic definition of national identity and citizenship, the ability to enjoy full citizenship rights was in practice related to ethnicity and religion. Kirişçi states that the analysis of groups that were given the right to settle in Turkey reveals how policies related to citizenship were put into practice. Specifically, in accordance with the Law on Settlement adopted in 1934, Turkey provided refugee and immigrant status to groups such as Muslim Bosnians, Albanians, Circassians, Tatars, etc. but declined to accept the settlement of groups such as Christian Orthodox Gagauz Turks and Shi'a Azeris. This policy effectively pre-screened those applying for citizenship and helped Sunnis to settle in Turkey, in spite of official statements that only those of Turkish descent and culture would be favoured (Kirişçi 2000).[4]

During the War of Independence there was a clear reference to the multicultural nature of Anatolia. However, after the Sheikh Said uprising of 1925,[5] there was no longer any reference made to the 'peoples of Turkey' and thus all citizens of Turkey were expected to adopt a Turkish identity (Ergil 2000, 125). Traces of official government ethnic-nationalism manifested themselves in the heavy capital tax levied primarily on Christian and Jewish minorities during World War Two[6] – non-Muslims were subjected to rates ten times higher than those of Muslims (Zürcher 1993, 208) – and in attitudes towards the Kurdish groups that resisted assimilation into the official Turkish identity.[7]

The current citizenship law dates from 1964 and has been modified several times since. The acquisition of citizenship for children of Turkish mothers or fathers is automatic whether the child is born in Turkey or outside – so clearly based on *jus sanguinis*. Children of non-Turkish citizens born in Turkey become Turkish citizens

---

3   It should not be forgotten that this was taking place in the context of sharp declines in the size of the population of Anatolia as a result of World War One.

4   Sunni Islam stands in opposition to Shi'a Islam and is considered to be the mainstream.

5   The Sheikh Said uprising was one of the first important rebellions against the state. The Sheikh gathered support on the basis of tribal and religious allegiance, and hence the insurgency was not exclusively one of Kurdish nationalism (Robins 1993, 660).

6   Officially the goal was to tax the windfall profits of the war. However, the manner of implementation led to a transfer of wealth from the non-Muslim population of the country to the emerging Muslim bourgeoisie (Neyzi 2002, 146).

7   For examples of the practices of citizenship in Turkey, see Bilgin 1997, Ünsal 1998, Oran 1999, and Yıldız 2001.

automatically if they cannot get the citizenship of their parents – the *jus soli* exception. Naturalization of immigrants is possible after five years of residence in Turkey. The conditions for application are the following: the individual should be an adult with the intention to settle in Turkey who speaks sufficient Turkish, has good moral conduct, causes no serious danger to public health, and has a profession that should provide for their livelihood and that of their dependents. There is one exception: individuals married to Turkish citizens may naturalize after three years of marriage if they fulfil the aforementioned criteria. Those who lose their citizenship due to marriage automatically become Turkish citizens. Therefore, the current citizenship law is predominantly ethno-centric when it comes to acquisition of citizenship by birth but allows immigrants to naturalize following five years of residence if they satisfy the criteria. The procedure for naturalization is lengthy and goes through the Ministry of Internal Affairs and the office of the Prime Minister. The decision to grant citizenship is given by the Council of Ministers (*Turkish Citizenship Law* 1964).

The historical evidence shows that citizenship policies of Turkey were civic-republican in nature – the first law gave citizenship to all those residing within the boundaries of the republic – but were flexible enough to accommodate the consequences of an ethno-cultural approach. The current law is very much based on the *jus sanguinis* when it comes to granting citizenship by birth. However, it cannot be argued that it is ethno-cultural because it allows for foreigners living in Turkey to naturalize following five years of residence. Therefore, at the individual level it follows the civic-republican path whereby the important issue is the decision to naturalize – even though the process is very lengthy and can sometimes be discretionary in practice. At the community level, however, even though the law does not explicitly refer to it, there is a conception of nationhood based on common descent and lineage – thus adding the ethno-cultural conception to the picture once again.

Given these considerations, one cannot clearly designate *Turkish citizenship law* as one or the other even though it is possible to trace civic-republican or ethno-cultural characteristics of the law. Tolerance of dual citizenship within Turkey appears to be inspired chiefly by ethno-cultural influences. Even though the hypothesis stated at the beginning of this section is refuted, the acceptance of dual citizenship in Turkey can be explained by another factor: the nature of relations between Turkey and its emigrants. In Turkey, as in cases of other emigration countries, an ethno-cultural understanding of nationhood may lead to greater tolerance of dual citizenship as the home country attempts to maintain ties to the second and third generations living abroad (see Górny, Grzymała-Kazłowska, Koryś and Weinar this volume, chapter 6 for similarities and differences with *Polonia* in the post-1990 Poland). The following section analyzes the link between tolerance of dual citizenship and the proportion of Turkish citizens living abroad.

Migrants and their Ties to the Sending Country

This section provides a brief overview of the history of Turkish migration to the Western industrialized countries, with a special focus on Germany. This will enable us to test the following hypothesis: the larger the proportion of citizens living abroad and the greater their economic ties to the country, the more likely will be the acceptance of dual citizenship. However, as the comparison of the case of Turkey with that of Poland (see Górny, Grzymała-Kazłowska, Koryś and Weinar this volume, chapter 6) indicates, the differences in the nature and history of emigrant groups affect the attitudes of the source-states towards dual citizenship.

The 1960s marked the beginning of an outflow of workers from Turkey. The post-war economic boom in Europe created increasing demands for labour, resulting in the recruitment of labour from southern European countries. A major recruiter of foreign labour was Germany, although there was no acknowledgment that this was a country of immigration throughout the 1950s and 1960s (Vogel 2000). In spite of this fact, it became one of the largest immigrant-receiving nations in Europe during the period after World War Two (Rotte 2000).

As of 2005, 3.1 million Turkish citizens were living in Europe. Together with another 530,000 Turkish citizens living in other parts of the world, Turkey's emigrant population numbers an approximate 3.6 million (TCCSGB 2005). In order to understand the economic significance of this population for Turkey, we should first examine the initial goals of the process of labour force exportation to Western European countries. According to Sayarı (1986) the main goals included fighting rising unemployment in Turkey and increasing foreign exchange reserves in order to cover trade deficits. A secondary goal, according to Sayarı (1986), was to increase the skill level of workers who would, then, through remittances, be able to increase the level of investment in small- and medium-sized companies in the emigrants' home towns in Turkey.

The remittances were of particular importance for Turkey. Sayarı (1986, 93) states that the share of workers' remittances in Turkey's foreign currency earnings had risen from 14 per cent in 1964 to an astonishing figure of 70 per cent in the early 1970s. During the 1980s, 24 per cent of Turkey's imports were covered by cash remittances and foreign exchange deposits of Turkish workers abroad (Kumcu 1989). This potential for foreign exchange was recognized early on and in the Second Five Year Plan (1968-1972) measures were proposed to increase the flow of remittances (Sayarı 1986).

Turkish workers in Germany were urged to maintain their ties to Turkey and not to undergo Germanization so that a constant flow of remittances could be guaranteed (Hunn 2001). Migrants were encouraged to remit their savings by means of special interest rates given to foreign currency saving accounts in Turkey and by certain privileges that were extended to emigrants who wished to import goods to Turkey (Sayarı 1986). More recently, direct investments by the second generation of Turkish emigrants, especially in the textile industry, are increasing in importance alongside remittances (Faist 1998, 213). In addition to economic investments, it is expected that Turkey will derive political benefits from the presence of Turkish migrants in Western Europe. The lobbying potential of this group has been seen as an asset by governments in Turkey, for instance, during debates in 1995 to amend to the *Turkish Citizenship Law* (TBMM 1995, 89-109).

Despite all these anticipated benefits there were also negative aspects to the migration process, two examples of which are religious politicians and Kurdish ethnic nationalism growing among the citizens of Turkey living in Western Europe (Sayarı 1986, 96). Whereas the Islamist groups filled in the social and cultural void left by the Turkish state – which was mostly interested in remittances – the Kurdish groups living in Germany demanded autonomy and more cultural and political rights in the homeland, if not actual independence.

During the period when dual citizenship was being debated in Germany there were concerns that supporters of the PKK (Kurdistan Workers Party) would be given citizenship; Edmund Stoiber of the CSU declared that permitting dual citizenship would allow at least half of the 11,000 PKK militants to become German citizens (*Hürriyet* 1999-01-16). Following Turkish pressure (*Hürriyet* 1999-01-16), Otto Schily – the German Interior Minister – stated that persons with connections to the PKK would be ineligible for dual citizenship (*Hürriyet* 1999-02-20). As the above discussion has demonstrated, the unintended consequences of the immigration process can pull the interests of the sending countries in opposite directions: whereas Turkey promoted dual citizenship among its citizens in Germany it strongly opposed the acquisition of dual citizenship by people connected to the PKK.

Overall, it can be argued that the proportion of citizens living abroad and the economic ties that they entertain with Turkey are a major reason for the tolerance of dual citizenship. This tolerance was in part brought about through the migrant associations' activities. The next sub-section examines the effects of these actors and organizations.

Migrant Associations and their Impact

A major factor in the analysis of Turkish policy on dual citizenship is the way in which organized groups intervene across borders on issues pertaining to dual citizenship and how they articulate their demands pro and con. The analysis of this factor follows on the previous section and, as will be demonstrated, reinforces the validity of the hypothesis developed therein. Turkish associations in Germany are the focus because they have been very active in attempting to bring about changes in policies pertaining to citizenship – as dual citizenship is still not allowed in Germany. Throughout this discussion it will be useful to keep in mind the contrast between the Polish case (see Górny, Grzymała-Kazłowska, Koryś and Weinar this volume, chapter 6), in which *Polonia*, as an organized collective effort, tried to affect the citizenship law in Poland despite the resistance of some segments of the Polish political system, as distinct from the Turkish case, where organizations were mainly confronted by resistance within their host states rather than the Turkish state.

The Turkish Immigrants Union (*Turkiye Gocmenler Birligi* – later called *Almanya Turk Toplumu-Türkische Gemeinde in Deutschland* [TGD]) was established in 1985. It is an umbrella body with around 200 member associations, including the German Turkish Academics Association Union, the German Turkish Students Association Union, and various occupational organizations. The *TGD* promotes the interests of the Turkish population of Germany vis-à-vis both the German and the Turkish governments by attempting to influence public opinion, and working to secure rights through legislative changes.[8]

The 1991 proposal for the amendment of the *Turkish Citizenship Law* was drafted by Aybay – a prominent law professor and citizenship specialist – after he had attended meetings in Germany at the invitation of the *TGD*. Once accepted in 1995, the amendment created the privileged non-citizen status. This status permits holders of a 'pink card'[9] to reside, to acquire property, to be eligible for inheritance, to operate businesses, and to work in Turkey in the same way as any citizen of Turkey. 'Pink Card' holders were only denied the right to vote in local and national elections (Law no. 4112 *Turkish Citizenship Law* 1995). Aybay states that the head of the *TGD*, Hakkı Keskin, a very old friend of his, invited him to find a solution to citizenship-related problems faced by Turkish people living in Germany (Interview no. 1). He makes it quite clear that the main issue was how to devise a mechanism that would allow people living in Germany to acquire German citizenship without losing their rights in Turkey.[10] This was the motivation behind the creation of the special non-citizen status (TBMM 1993, 203-6).

Germany still does not allow for dual citizenship apart from exceptional cases. The draft bill for the new German Citizenship Law contained a section accepting dual citizenship and most of the immigrant organizations were enthusiastic about this legislation.[11] The campaign conducted by the CDU/CSU against the inclusion of dual citizenship in the new law angered many such organizations (see Gerdes, Rieple and Faist this volume, chapter 2). There was a rally in Berlin on 6th February 1999, organized by the Anatolian Peoples' Cultural Associations Federation, with the following motto: 'Dual Citizenship is not a Courtesy but our Right'.[12] These groups were disappointed when dual citizenship was left out of the legislation.

The *TGD* organized a summit in July 2000 and produced a declaration pertaining to the problems and expectations of Turkish citizens living in Germany. The declaration stated that there were many problems in the practical use of the 'pink card' in Turkey as the bureaucracy was not informed about it. Therefore, people relinquishing their Turkish citizenship were facing problems in the use of the card. There was also a call for Turkey to stop evicting its citizens and to produce legislation that would make it impossible to force Turkish citizens to relinquish their citizenship. This would enable Turkish citizens to enjoy dual citizenship through an exception in the new German Law which states that in cases where the country of origin does not permit its citizens to relinquish their original citizenship Germany might allow dual

---

8 http://www.tgd.de, accessed 2006-04-26.

9 The 'pink card' is the document given to the people who have the special non-citizen status.

10 People who have acquired Turkish citizenship by means other than birth are ineligible to carry the 'pink card'.

11 http://www.buelten.de/mkilic1701imza.htm, accessed 2002-08-22.

12 http://www.kurtulus-online.com/eskisayilar/b-yolunda17/berlin.html, accessed 2002-08-23.

citizenship. The declaration also targeted the German government and asked for dual citizenship, asserting that the member associations of the *TGD* would continue to promote the acquisition of German citizenship among Turks residing in Germany.

Immigrant organizations in Germany and elsewhere in Europe support the tolerance and acceptance of dual citizenship and devise plans to pressure both the Turkish government and the governments of their host countries to make dual citizenship possible. It is possible to argue that the political opportunity structure – the economic and political interests of the home country and the political activism of immigrants in host countries – facilitated the adoption of a transnational perspective on dual citizenship. In other words, the cross-border life of Turkish emigrants is the most important determinant of tolerance of dual citizenship within Turkey. Discursive opportunity structures are also important in understanding increased tolerance of citizenship and the following section examines the parliamentary and media debates with this intention.

Discursive Opportunity Structures

Arguments and Ideas of the Political Actors

The realization that Turkish workers are not temporary guests in their host countries has led to significant amendments to the citizenship law in Turkey. The motives of politicians and bureaucrats have been shaped by the demands of emigrants who faced problems related to military service, property ownership, and lack of political rights in their countries of immigration. A fairly organized and quasi-official process was used to communicate the needs of citizens living abroad to Turkish officials.

This section examines the parliamentary debates related to citizenship issues and attempts to single out the arguments put forward in favour and against the acceptance of dual citizenship. The hypothesis that will be evaluated through the analysis of the parliamentary debates is the following: the distribution and accentuation of certain kinds of arguments by the political actors affect the tolerance of dual citizenship and this may be observed in citizenship law reforms. In order to test whether this hypothesis is valid, we will examine parliamentary debates concerning amendments to the *Turkish Citizenship Law* as well as the debates related to citizenship issues in general. The following paragraphs provide a chronologically ordered overview of the debates and the arguments presented in these debates.

A brief overview of the political party system in Turkey is necessary to understand these debates. The parties in Turkey are not well institutionalized in the sense that loyalty is to the party leader and not to the party programme – personalities attract more attention and more votes than the programme of the party (see among others Cornell 2001, 57; Sayarı 2002, 3). The political parties in Turkey do not differ from each other in their stance vis-à-vis dual citizenship and it is rare to find dual citizenship issues mentioned in party programmes, as in the Polish case.

Information gathered from experts interviewed for this study indicated that the seemingly liberal legalization of dual citizenship by the military government was in fact not such a mystery (Interviews nos. 1, 2 and 3). Fethi Akkoç identifies himself as one of the persons who understood the problems of Turkish citizens living in Germany and as having played an important role in the legislation of dual citizenship in 1981. According to his statement, his role then, as a journalist, was to talk to all the political parties in 1980 and to work for the passage of the law allowing dual citizenship (TBMM 1995, 61). This legislation was postponed because of the military coup and was introduced by the military government only after the coup.

The 1981 change was debated in a secret session by the *National Security Council* because it was initiated by the Ulusu Government, which was established after the coup.[13] Since no records were made of this session it is unknown whether there were arguments for and against the acceptance of dual citizenship in the debates, or what these might have been. The amendment also facilitated the processes for stripping individuals of their citizenship (*Cumhuriyet* 1981-02-15). The clause added to the law states that those who are outside the borders of Turkey and who have been charged with endangering the internal or external security of the country will be stripped of citizenship unless they return within three months during regular periods and one month under emergency rule (Law no. 2383 *Turkish Citizenship Law* 1981). Thus, while the changes are progressive in terms of allowing dual citizenship, they are in fact very anti-liberal in relation to people who fell afoul of the regime.

After the coup, 227 people lost their Turkish citizenship by means of this clause. However, in February 1992, the parliament removed this clause because it had violated human rights. Those who so desired were able to regain their citizenship and to have their property reinstated or receive compensation for the confiscated property (TBMM 1992, 53-5).

The next alteration connected with citizenship was the law regarding military service. In May 1992, the Law on Military Service (Law no. 1111 *Military Law* 1992) was amended to allow those who had performed military service in the country where they hold a second citizenship – and who satisfy the conditions of being born and residing in another country or having emigrated before the age of 18 – to be exempt from performing military service in Turkey provided that they presented official documents of their military service (Law no. 3802 *Military Law* 1992).

Parliamentary debates on issues of citizenship and/or problems of Turkish citizens living abroad have not been restricted to amendments of the laws pertaining to citizenship or military service. The events in Solingen, where five Turkish emigrants

---

13 After the military coup Bülend Ulusu was given the responsibility to form a technocratic government (http://www.tbmm.gov.tr/hukumetler/hp44.htm). Until the Advisory council was formed the *National Security Council* (NSC) sanctioned all decisions of the government. The members of the *NSC* were the four generals and one admiral who staged the coup. The minutes of the 1981-02-13 meeting of the *National Security Council* (38th Meeting, volume 1, 1981) indicate that the members of the Council voted in favour of debating the whole of the amendments related to the *Turkish Citizenship Law* no. 403 in a secret session. The debate lasted for approximately 2 hours.

died as a result of an arson attack on their house, were debated in the Turkish Parliament on 8th June 1993. During these debates, the *ANAP* (centre-right party) spokesperson emphasized the importance of having the right to vote in Germany. He pointed out that there are individuals who, despite having lived in Germany for the last 30 years, are still denied the right to vote. According to this argument, the right to vote is the key to finding a long-term solution for problems faced by Turkish persons residing in Germany. He claimed that in the current circumstances dual citizenship rights were of greater importance and the Turkish government ought to propose that Germany put this issue on its agenda (TBMM 1993, 189-92).

In the same debate, the *CHP* (centre-left party) spokesperson also highlighted the importance of dual citizenship and argued that Turkey should act to resolve the issues that had emerged on the Turkish side. He claimed that on average it took two years to obtain dual citizenship in Germany and that the time necessary to gain dual citizenship should be reduced (TBMM 1993, 199-200).[14]

The SHP (centre-left party) spokesperson claimed that in addition to the security aspects surrounding the Solingen events, political and legal issues should also be debated. He stated that obtaining equal rights in the political, economic, and social spheres by obtaining the German citizenship would not automatically prevent these attacks, but that extreme right parties would be more cautious about taking an anti-immigration stance as immigrants would form part of the electorate. His argument was that as long as Germany banned dual citizenship, the goal of the Turkish state should be to encourage emigrants to naturalize in Germany while maintaining their rights in Turkey (TBMM 1993, 203-6).

The last amendment to the *Turkish Citizenship Law* was made in 1995 and instituted what is known as the 'pink card' or the privileged non-citizen status. In statements on the reasons for this amendment, the government stressed the fact that it was a result – among other factors – of the actions of countries that refused to accept dual citizenship. The modified citizenship law permitted individuals who had relinquished their Turkish citizenship to acquire certain privileges in comparison to regular non-citizens (*Official Gazette* 1995-06-12). These were outlined in the previous section of this chapter.

During the parliamentary debates when this amendment was discussed, the spokesperson of the *ANAP* group argued that this law was what all factions of Turkish emigrants in Germany had been demanding for years. He claimed that these emigrants wanted to have political rights in Germany and that this amendment would ease their difficulties in acquiring the German citizenship. He also mentioned that Turkish emigrants would become a key electoral group in Germany, with some influence in the tight electoral competitions between the two main parties (TBMM 1995, 89-90).

---

14 Prior to 2000 Turkish citizens who relinquished their Turkish citizenship and obtained German citizenship could reapply for Turkish citizenship thereby bypassing the ban on dual citizenship in the *German Citizenship Law*.

The *RP* (religious-right party) spokesperson argued that this amendment would induce Turkish citizens to acquire the citizenship of their countries of residence (TBMM 1995, 90-91). The spokesperson for the *DYP* (centre-right party) group was also in favour of the amendment. He argued that Turkish legal procedures, which recognize dual citizenship, were slow and cumbersome, and that the debated amendment would solve all of the problems related to dual citizenship. In defending the amendment he also referred to the fact that there were approximately one million Turkish people who would be able to vote in Germany if they were citizens. He also mentioned the resolution of the military service issue through this amendment, as these privileged non-citizens would not have to perform military service (TBMM 1995, 92). The *CHP* group spokesperson stressed the need of Turkish emigrants in Germany to acquire social and economic rights. Like others who spoke before him, he also supported the amendment (TBMM 1995, 93).

A Member of Parliament (*MP*) justified the amendment by stating that the government had received hundreds and thousands of letters from individuals wanting to acquire German citizenship, urging the government to ease the procedures for relinquishing Turkish citizenship. He claimed that it was necessary for Turkish emigrants to be able to acquire German citizenship if they were to enjoy economic, social and political rights in Germany. The amendment in question would enable them to do this without threatening their rights in Turkey (TBMM 1995, 94). Another *MP* emphasized the benefits of this amendment by referring to the possibility of Turkish people who live in Germany becoming elected representatives in that country, thus strengthening the position of Turkey politically (TBMM 1995, 96).

During these debates an interesting concern was raised about whether this amendment would enable the 'Armenians, Jews, Greeks (Rum), etc.'[15] – who have relinquished their Turkish citizenship in order to acquire another citizenship – to come back to Turkey and reclaim property that had been confiscated when they changed their citizenship. This demonstrates that the tolerance of dual citizenship and special rights for those who had relinquished their citizenship was intended to apply exclusively to Turkish emigrants who had left the country under specific conditions; the amendment was never intended to include the minorities who left Turkey before 1981, and explicitly stated that the privileged non-citizen status would apply only to those who had acquired Turkish citizenship by birth and who had relinquished it by being granted permission by the Council of Ministers (Law no. 4112 Turkish Citizenship Law 1995; Law no. 403 Turkish Citizenship Law 1964). As mentioned earlier, this way of foregoing Turkish citizenship was made possible only after the amendments to the *Citizenship Law* in 1981.

Despite the fact that very few measures have been taken during the last 40 years of massive Turkish emigration to Western Europe, all major political parties expressed a wish to enhance the quality of life of emigrants. Most of the arguments were in favour of dual citizenship. Yet, it should not be forgotten that these arguments pertained

---

15 Speaker of the RP group (TBMM 1995, 103). Many other *MP*s have voiced their concern on this issue as well.

mostly to Turkish citizens living abroad and were introduced into the debate on dual citizenship as a way to demonstrate the willingness of political actors to improve the living standards of Turkish citizens residing abroad. The core reason for supporting dual citizenship, according to these arguments, was to enable Turkish people living abroad to achieve political and economic rights. In most cases this argument was seen as a means to improve the security and integrity of persons subjected to unfavourable conditions due to their inability to naturalize in their host countries. On several occasions, the argument was supported simply because it would potentially provide Turkey with lobbying groups that had voting rights in foreign countries. The arguments were pragmatic in nature as they were concerned with reaching an end (better living conditions for Turkish citizens and lobby groups for Turkey) without debating the assumptions, values, or norms that are related to dual citizenship.

When Turkish politicians comment on countries with significant Turkish emigrant populations, they tend to produce arguments based on principles of republican citizenship ideals. Their goal seems to be that these emigrants obtain the same rights enjoyed by other members of those communities of which they have become members. When *MP*s speak about the need for Turkish workers to naturalize in order to attain economic and political rights, their concern is how Turks are treated in other countries rather than the reciprocal rights of immigrants in Turkey.

Politicians in Turkey feel little need to respond to immigrant issues because such questions are not yet politicized, which is a common feature of countries that have only recently begun receiving immigrants (see Górny, Grzymała-Kazłowska, Koryś and Weinar this volume, chapter 6 for the similarities with Poland). In Turkey, there are not many organized immigrant groups able to place significant pressure on the government. The pragmatic nature of the debates on dual citizenship and the reactive policy-style has meant that reciprocation of tolerance towards immigrants in Turkey is left off the agenda.[16] In other words, if values that underlie the promotion of dual citizenship for Turkish emigrants were brought to the public sphere, they could lead to demands of reciprocity for immigrants in Turkey.

Having analyzed the debates that took place in the political arena we will shift our attention to the public sphere where the visibility, resonance, and credibility of certain arguments may be important factors in explaining the tolerance of dual citizenship. To this end, the next section examines the three major daily newspapers for news, articles, and reports on dual citizenship.

Legitimacy of Arguments: Visibility, Resonance, and Credibility

This section analyzes the political arguments and proposals on dual citizenship through a content analysis of the archives of *Hürriyet*, *Milliyet*, and *Cumhuriyet* between 1981 and 2002. I examine different categories of issues related to dual citizenship that were covered by the media as well as the visibility, the resonance, and the credibility of the arguments presented in these categories. Here we are testing

---

16 For taxonomy of policy styles see Richardson 1982.

the following hypothesis:[17] the more visible, resonant, and credible the arguments regarding dual citizenship, the higher the likelihood that the political process will work to facilitate it.

The coverage of issues related to dual citizenship in the media in Turkey seems to follow a particular trend. The legislative changes do not find much coverage in the daily newspapers. Instead they are announced as news – without much space devoted to them and almost no mention of them except by a very few columnists. Wider coverage of issues related to citizenship and workers abroad tends to follow a significant event. For example, the Solingen events, the changes to the *German Citizenship Law*, and the exclusion of Merve Kavakçı[18] from Turkish citizenship all marked the beginning of periods in which there was a greater number of articles on the issues of dual citizenship in the three daily newspapers.[19]

It should be kept in mind that none of the arguments about dual citizenship raise fundamental questions concerning its existence in Turkey. It is a fact that dual citizenship is legal in Turkey as long as the person acquiring a second citizenship asks for permission from the council of ministers. Therefore, the arguments presented are about why dual citizenship should be facilitated in other countries. However, it should also be noted that there are no serious discussions as to the benefits and problems of dual citizenship. Very few articles mention such problems as dual loyalties, dual military service, and double voting.

The first category is that of political, economic, and social rights. The articles and news stories in this category explicitly or implicitly refer to the necessity for Turkish people to be able to naturalize in their countries of residence in order to obtain the rights for which they have been longing. The number of articles in this category is 12 in *Hürriyet*, 6 in *Milliyet*, and 5 in *Cumhuriyet* during the period between 1980 and 2002.[20] The arguments presented in these articles resonate clearly with ideas about democracy and fairness. On several occasions there are also references to the multi-cultural nature of the countries where emigrants live. The arguments also resonate with the language of human rights and their violation in EU countries because of the impossibility in several EU member countries of acquiring citizenship without relinquishing the previous citizenship. An article from *Milliyet* focuses on political rights and argues in favour of double voting by stating that Turkish citizens living in Germany should have the right to vote in German and Turkish elections.

---

17 *Hürriyet, Cumhuriyet*, and *Milliyet* are the three daily newspapers selected because they represent different spectrums of the political arena and have had a nationwide circulation.

18 Merve Kavakçı was elected as an *MP* in 1999. When it was found out that she accepted US citizenship without informing Turkish officials she was excluded from Turkish citizenship. This issue will be elaborated upon later in this section.

19 This observation has been confirmed through the expert informant interviews (Interviews no. 2 and no. 4).

20 These numbers are minimums. Their importance lies in reflecting the types of arguments that were reflected in the media. The pre-1997 period was not analyzed comprehensively but covered based on dates of relevant events.

A columnist in *Hürriyet* argues that dual loyalty and dual belonging are difficult properties to achieve but that Turkish citizens living in Germany already belong to both nations. He claims that these people need to have dual citizenship, or at least voting rights in local elections, in order to participate in the solutions to the problems facing their localities (Mümtaz Soysal 1995). Another interesting article in the same paper is about a member of a Turkish nationalist group. This person applied for German citizenship and was subsequently rejected by German officials on the basis of nationalistic associations. The article quotes the vice-president of the *MHP* (Nationalist Action Party) who says that dual citizenship and nationalism do not contradict each other. The vice-president states that Turkish emigrants should have the right to own property in their countries of residence and that citizenship is a right of people who consistently contribute so much to the economy of the host countries (Turhan Alaverdi 2001).

The second category consists of news stories and articles about the *Citizenship Law* in Germany. The main concerns in 1998-1999 can be found reflected in 9 articles in *Hürriyet*, 11 in *Milliyet*, and 28 in *Cumhuriyet*. There was some initial enthusiasm during the period when the newly formed left coalition in Germany promised to include dual citizenship in the package of amendments to the *German Citizenship Law*. This did not prove to be the case, however, and the disappointment was reflected in these articles. There was condemnation of Ankara for not acting on behalf of its citizens while Germany was mistreating them. These articles are mostly factual but contain embedded arguments that resonate with ideas of fairness, democracy, and equal rights in society.

Another related category of articles dealt with the elections in Germany. Some of them were concerned with representatives to the local assemblies who are of Turkish origin, whereas others were concerned with the stance of the political parties vis-à-vis the Turkish population in Germany. The number of articles in this category was 8 in *Hürriyet*, 4 in *Milliyet*, and 12 in *Cumhuriyet*.

Most articles dealing with dual citizenship focused on Turkish emigrants. There are 6 articles in *Hürriyet*, 7 in *Milliyet*, and 3 in *Cumhuriyet* that dealt with the problems faced by immigrants to Turkey. The only immigrant groups to appear in the media were either the Network of Foreign Spouses or Muslim immigrants such as Bulgarian Turks. The Network of Foreign Spouses referred to ideals of fairness, while demanding more rights for individuals who are foreigners in Turkey. As to the Bulgarian Turks living in Turkey, politicians have encouraged them to vote in the elections in Bulgaria.[21] Some articles also referred to the unfairness of the situation in which some Bulgarian Turks, who had not been able to naturalize, were sent back to Bulgaria towards the end of the 1990s.[22]

The next category of news/articles concerns the exclusion of Merve Kavakçı from Turkish citizenship. She was elected to the parliament in Turkey in 1999, but

---

21 'Sofya'da bir Kurultay', *Milliyet* 2000-06-16; 'Soydaşa Green Card', *Milliyet* 1997-03-04; 'Menderes: "Çifte Vatandaşlık Kolaylaştırılsın"', *Milliyet* 1997-02-24.

22 'Menderes: "Çifte Vatandaşlık Kolaylaştırılsın"', *Milliyet* 1997-02-24.

between her candidacy and the election had taken US citizenship. In a critically important misstep, she failed to notify the proper officials that she was acquiring another citizenship. This was unearthed during the turmoil caused by her attempt, against the regulations of the institution, to wear the headscarf in parliament. Her Turkish citizenship was taken away and her position as a representative in the parliament dropped. The number of articles dealing with this issue and mentioning dual citizenship were 8 in *Hürriyet*, 2 in *Milliyet* (including one article about another person in a similar position), and 9 in *Cumhuriyet*. The arguments presented in these debates resonated mainly with the claims of dual loyalty and indicated that a person who has sworn loyalty to the United States of America could not be loyal to Turkey. At the same time, however, some articles referred to the internally contradictory nature of the Turkish state's position. The source of the confusion was the hostile attitude of Turkey towards a person who holds dual citizenship – whereas officials encouraged Turkish people living in Germany and other countries to acquire the citizenship of their country of residence. Nevertheless, there were columnists who made an attempt to justify this discrepancy. The main argument of Toktamış Ateş (*Cumhuriyet* 1999-05-29), for instance, was that dual citizenship is a justified right which should be given to people who wish to have equal rights in a country where they have been performing their duties such as paying taxes. Instead, he argued, Merve Kavakçı abused dual citizenship rights because she does not live in the USA.

The final category includes news reports relating to dual citizenship. These had no editorial content and were simply factual. There were 5 such articles in *Hürriyet*, none in *Milliyet*, and 6 in *Cumhuriyet*. Figure 5.1 gives an overview of the visibility of dual citizenship according to the categories of issues.

The arguments voiced in the media coverage tended to resonate with familiar ideas such as multicultural integration, democracy, fairness, voting rights, inheritance, property rights, and basic human rights. These ideas were expressed primarily in relation to ways that Turkish emigrants should be treated in their host countries, especially in Germany. In relation to Bulgarian Turks or Kosovar Turks, the arguments tended to resonate with an ethno-cultural understanding of nationhood. In contrast, the arguments voiced during the Merve Kavakçı incident focused mostly on the problematic nature of a member of parliament with dual loyalty.

These findings indicate that the hypothesis presented at the beginning of this section is supported by the media coverage analysis. It is possible to conclude, therefore, that the visibility, resonance, and credibility of arguments pertaining to dual citizenship increase the likelihood that the political process will work to facilitate it. It should not be forgotten, however, that most of these arguments were related to the question of dual citizenship not in Turkey but in other countries – primarily Germany. Thus the public debate did not feed back into the political process in terms of legalizing dual citizenship. Instead, the public debate made itself felt in the political process by informing politicians and bureaucrats about the problems of Turkish emigrants. Reactive policies were undertaken in order to find solutions to these problems.

Concluding Remarks

This chapter has focused on the increased tolerance of dual citizenship in Turkey and its underlying causes, with several complementary hypotheses put to the test in order to explain the underlying reasons for this tolerance. In the first part I analyzed Turkish national self-understanding and its influence on the tolerance on dual citizenship, arriving at the conclusion that national self-understanding in Turkey has a civic-republican appearance, but that citizenship policies of Turkey were mostly ethno-cultural in practice. The nature of national self-understanding, therefore, could be viewed as an explanatory factor behind the acceptance of dual citizenship in the sense that the motivation was to enhance the living standards and rights of individuals with Turkish origins living elsewhere. They were encouraged not to forget their roots, culture, or language despite becoming citizens of other states.

The findings suggest that maintaining vibrant economic links with citizens living abroad – especially those living in Germany – has been a constant concern for Turkish governments despite severe neglect of the social problems encountered by these people. Consequently, the proportion of Turkish citizens living abroad and their economic significance for Turkey has a considerable explanatory power in accounting for the increased tolerance of dual citizenship in Turkey. The research results show that there are a number of organizations and actors, especially within Germany, that pressure policy-makers in Turkey to accommodate their need to integrate into their host country without having to relinquish their rights to land ownership and inheritance in Turkey. The examination of the parliamentary debates concluded that most of the arguments voiced in the discussions favoured facilitating dual citizenship for Turkish citizens living abroad. Most of the discourse centred on the necessity for these emigrants to achieve political, economic, and social rights in their countries of residence. The findings tend to indicate that the major explanatory variable is the number of Turkish emigrants living abroad and their ties to Turkey.

The findings on the visibility, resonance, and credibility of arguments presented in the written media indicate that most of the material that was published in the three daily newspapers was supportive of dual citizenship. The arguments that were presented in the mass media resonated with the already prevailing ideas of democracy and fairness for Turkish people living in other countries.

Turkish governments have demonstrated their willingness to act on and take measures to deal with the practical problems experienced by the Turkish immigrants. In many cases the intentions were sincere even though official actions to solve the problems were either slow or non-existent. But delays or inaction did not stem from apathy to the real problems nor were they linked to the aim of using the issue strategically for political gain. Rather, there was a general lack of political incentive, because those persons living abroad who still have the right to vote in Turkey for all practical purposes cannot do so unless they return to Turkey during elections.[23]

---

23 The issue of voting during general elections in Turkey has been a widely debated issue. Legally it is possible for Turkish people living abroad to vote during elections from the

The Turkish experience indicates that the political activism of immigrants in their host countries combined with the economic and political interests of the sending countries are the major explanatory factors behind increased tolerance of dual citizenship. The Turkish case reflects a transnational perspective on dual citizenship predominantly as a result of the political, cultural, and economic interests of Turkey's emigrants abroad. Through Turkish emigration a transnational social space was created, which allowed border-crossing life-worlds for Turkish emigrants. In a way states had to tolerate the pluralization of ties to nations in order to deal internally with globalization (see Faist this volume, chapter 1 for further details about internal globalization). The acceptance of multiple ties to different nation-states is becoming increasingly common among states (see for example Spång this volume, chapter 4 for the Swedish case).

If we put the experience of Turkey into a larger context and compare what is happening there with trends throughout the world, several interesting observations can be made. This larger context brings to the forefront three factors that have become increasingly visible throughout the globe – even though some have been weakened in the post-September 11 world. The first one is globalization and includes features such as enhanced means of communication and more widespread use of transnational spaces for various issues (such as trade relations, environmental movements, and cultural exchange), which have changed the nature of links between emigrants and their home countries. All these features have, no doubt, increased the influence of Turkish immigrants but one should not romanticize their importance. There has always been communication between Turkish citizens living abroad – especially in Germany – and officials in Turkey.

The second and third factors, which have been widespread, are the increased importance of individual rights and the significance of multicultural integration policies. Prior to the second half of the twentieth century, states were not liberal democracies and did not have to justify the exclusion of certain groups. Now, there is more pressure to be inclusive. As could be observed from the debates in the Turkish Parliament and the media, when it comes to issues of dual citizenship and human rights, the focus tends to be solely on Turkish citizens living abroad. In those debates the issues of individual rights and multicultural integration of Turkish citizens living in immigrant receiving countries were at the core of the arguments supporting dual citizenship. Very few of the arguments mentioned the plight of immigrants in Turkey. While this may appear to be a puzzle, in reality it simply stems from the fact that the issue of immigration to Turkey and the rights of immigrants in Turkey have not yet

---

country where they reside. Because of practical problems such as placing ballot boxes in other countries and the insecurity of mail ballots, this has never been practiced. Fuat Boztepe, who is the head of the department in charge of workers abroad in the Ministry of Labour, stated that the greatest problem occurs in countries where there are a significant number of workers and the host country does not allow ballot boxes to be put in public spaces. Given the potential number of voters, placing ballot boxes only in the consulates and embassies does not provide a solution (Interview no. 3).

Figure 5.1   Turkey: Chronological List of Dual Citizenship-Related Legislation

Date	Legislation and Proposals	Change in Institutional or Discursive Opportunity Structure
1924	1st Constitution of the Republic of Turkey	Following the foundation of the republic all residents are considered citizens of the Republic of Turkey.
1928	Turkish Nationality Act (Act No. 1312/1928)	Based on *jus sanguinis* in order to attribute citizenship of Turkey to all those with 'Turkish descent'.
1934	The Law of Settlement (Law No. 2510/1934)	Muslim groups migrating from neighbouring countries were settled using this law and then given citizenship.
1964	Citizenship Act (*Turkish Nationality Law* No. 403/1964)	Based on *jus sanguinis*.
1981	Law No. 2383 on amendments to the *Turkish Nationality Law* No. 403 (acceptance of dual citizenship among other changes)	Labour migration to Europe started in the 1960s. It became clear that these emigrants were permanent residents of their host countries and hoped to acquire another nationality.
1995	Law No. 4112 on amendments to the Turkish Nationality Law No. 403 (Pink Card)	Acceptance of the special non-citizen status for those who have asked to relinquish their Turkish citizenship. Drafted and enacted based on the pressure from migrant associations (especially those in Germany where dual citizenship is not allowed). The change was supported by all political parties based on ideals of economic and social rights that could be obtained in host countries following naturalization.

become politicized. Furthermore, only a very few immigrant groups have organized and begun trying to pressure the Turkish state – for example, *die Brücke* which is a German-Turkish bridging organization, and the *Association of Foreign Wives*. Hence, if in the next 5 to 10 years immigration issues become more important and appears more frequently in the public-sphere, we might begin to see pressure applied to ensure that Turkish policies regarding immigrants are also based on individual rights and multicultural ideals.

References

Alaverdi, T. (2001), 'Delikanlı ülkücü Alman olur mu', *Hürriyet* 2001-08-18.
Aleinikoff, T. A. and Klusmeyer, D. B. (2001), 'Plural Citizenship: Facing the Future in a Migratory World', in Aleinikoff, T. A. and Klusmeyer, D. B. (eds).
Aleinikoff, T. A. and Klusmeyer, D. B. (eds) (2001), *Citizenship Today: Global Perspectives and Practices* (Washington, D.C.: Carnegie Endowment for International Peace).
Aybay, R. (2001), *Vatandaslik Hukuku* (Istanbul: Aybay Yayinlari).
Bilgin, N. (1997), *Cumhuriyet, Demokrasi ve Kimlik* (Istanbul: Bilgi Yayincilik).
Brubaker, W. R. (ed.) (1989), *Immigration and the Politics of Citizenship in Europe and North America* (Lanham: University Press of America).
Cornell, E. (2001), *Turkey in the 21st Century, Opportunities, Challenges, Threats* (Richmond, Surrey: Curzon Press).

Ergil, D. (2000), 'The Kurdish Question in Turkey', *Journal of Democracy* 11:3, 122-35.

Faist, T. (1998), 'Transnational Social Spaces out of International Migration: Evolution, Significance and Future Prospects', *Archives Europeennes de Sociologie* 39:2, 213-47.

Freeman, G. P. and Ogelman, N. (1998), 'Homeland Citizenship Policies and the Status of Third Country Nationals in the European Union', *Journal of Ethnic and Migration Studies* 24:4, 769-89.

Hammar, T. (1989), 'State, Nation, and Dual Citizenship', in Brubaker, W.R. (ed.).

Hunn, K. (2001), '"*Alamanya, Alamanya, Turk gibi Isci Bulamanya... Alamanya Alamanya, Turkten Aptal Bulamanya*" Labour Migration from Turkey to the Federal Republic of Germany in the Years of Official Labour Recruitement (1961-1973)', *German-Turkish Summer Institute Working Paper* No. 4/2001.

İçduygu, A., Çolak, Y. and Soyarık, N. (1999), 'What is the Matter with Citizenship? A Turkish Debate', *Middle Eastern Studies* 35:4, 187-208.

Keyman, E. F. and İçduygu, A. (2003), 'Globalization, Migration and Citizenship: The Case of Turkey', in Kofman, E. and Youngs, G. (eds).

Kirişçi, K. (2000), 'Disaggregating Turkish Citizenship and Immigration Practices', *Middle Eastern Studies* 36:3, 1-22.

Kofman, E. and Youngs, G. (eds) (2003), *Globalization: Theory and Practice* (London: Continuum).

Kumcu, M. E. (1989), 'The Savings Behavior of Migrant Workers: Turkish Workers in W. Germany', *Journal of Development Economics* 30, 273-86.

Kumcu, M. E. (2000), 'Sofya'da bir Kurultay', *Milliyet* 2000-06-16.

Kumcu, M. E. (1997), 'Soydasa Green Card', *Milliyet* 1997-03-04.

Kumcu, M. E. (1997), 'Menderes: "Cifte Vatandaslik Kolaylastirilsin"', *Milliyet* 1997-02-24.

Neyzi, L. (2002), 'Remembering to Forget: Sabbateanism, National Identity, and Subjectivity in Turkey', *Society for Comparative Study of Society and History* 2, 137-58.

Oran, B. (1999), *Ataturk Milliyetciligi: Resmi Ideoloji Disi Bir Inceleme* (Istanbul: Bilgi Yayinevi).

Richardson, J., Gustafson, G. and Jordan, G. (1982), 'The Concept of Policy Style', in Richardson, J. (ed.).

Richardson, J. (ed.) (1982), *Policy Styles in Western Europe* (Boston: Allen and Unwin).

Robins, P. (1993), 'The Overlord State: Turkish Policy and the Kurdish Issue', *International Affairs* 69:4, 657-76.

Rotte, R. (2000), 'Immigration Control in United Germany: Toward a Broader Scope of National Policies', *International Migration Review* 34:2, 390-422.

Sayarı, S. (1986), 'Migration Policies of Sending Countries: Perspectives on the Turkish Experience', *Annals of the American Academy of Political and Social Science* 485, 87-97.

Sayarı, S. (2002), 'Introduction', in Sayarı, S. and Heper, M. (eds).

Sayarı, S. and Heper, M. (eds) (2002), *Political Leaders and Democracy in Turkey* (Lanham, MD: Lexington Books).

Soysal, M. (1995), 'Cifte Vatandaslik Talimi', *Hürriyet* 1995-01-17.

Spiro, P. J. (1997), 'Dual Citizenship and the Meaning of Citizenship', *Emory Law Journal* 46:4, 1411-85.

Ünsal, A. (1998), *75 Yilda Tebaa'dan Yurttasa Dogru* (Istanbul: Turkiye Is Bankasi Yayinlari).

Vogel, D. (2000), 'Migration Control in Germany and the United States', *International Migration Review* 34:2, 390-422.

Yıldız, A. (2001), *'Ne Mutlu Turkum Diyebilene':* Turk Ulusal Kimliginin Etno-sekuler Sinirlari (1919-1938) (Istanbul: Iletisim Yayinlari).
Zürcher, E. J. (1993), *Turkey: A Modern History* (London: I.B.Tauris & Co Ltd).

Documents

Parliamentary Debates – TBMM (Türkiye Büyük Millet Meclisi-Grand National Assembly of Turkey)

Parliamentary Minutes, 1992-05-27, Period 19, Legislative Year 1, volume 12.
Parliamentary Minutes, 1993-06-08, Period 19, Legislative Year 2, volume 36.
Parliamentary Minutes, 1995-06-07, Period 19, Legislative Year 4, volume 88.
Official Gazette 1995-06-12.

Interviews

Interview no. 1: Prof. Rona Aybay – Lawyer and writer of a book on Turkish Citizenship Law – 2002-08-20.
Interview no. 2: Can Unver, Director General of External Relations and Services for Workers Abroad at the Turkish Ministry of Labor and Social Security – 2003-05-14.
Interview no. 3: Fuat Boztepe, Head of the Department of External Relations and Services for Workers Abroad at the Turkish Ministry of Labor and Social Security – 2003-05-14.
Interview no. 4: Dr. Ahmet İçduygu, Bilkent University, Department of Political Science – 2003-05-15.

Newspapers

Hürriyet 1995-01-17.
Hürriyet 1999-01-16.
Hürriyet 1999-02-20.
Hürriyet 2001-08-18.
Milliyet 1997-02-24.
Milliyet 1997-03-04.
Milliyet 2000-06-16.
Cumhuriyet 1981-02-15.
Cumhuriyet 1999-05-29.
Archives of *Hürriyet, Milliyet* and *Cumhuriyet* between 1981 and 2002.
TCCSGB (Türkiye Cumhuriyeti Çalışma ve Sosyal Güvenlik Bakanlığı-Ministry of Labor and Social Security) (2005), Bulletin 5:2 (Ankara: Ministry of Work and Social Security).

Chapter 6

Selective Tolerance? Regulations, Practice and Discussions Regarding Dual Citizenship in Poland[1]

Agata Górny, Aleksandra Grzymała-Kazłowska,
Piotr Koryś and Agnieszka Weinar

Abstract

This chapter is about the level of tolerance of dual citizenship and its determinants in Poland, an emigration country. We argue that, even though dual citizenship does exist in Poland, we cannot state with certainty that it is generally accepted. Tolerance applies to selected groups not including, in fact, immigrants. Formally, this tolerance is exemplified by the wide latitude the law gives authorities to make discretionary decisions. Determinants of that tolerance include an ethno-cultural understanding of the Polish nation and the Polish state's efforts to build and maintain a good relationship with *Polonia* all over the world.

Introduction

In the Polish tradition, citizenship and belonging to a nation are conceptually distinct. This distinction is rooted in the history of Central Europe, where nations have developed in only loose relation to the formation of contemporary states (Leoussi 2001). The partitioning of the Polish state between 1772 and 1918 brought about a dichotomy of the Polish nation and non-Polish state. This dichotomy was replicated, to some extent, in the Polish People's Republic (1945-1989) in the form of: (the communist) state and (non-communist) society (Brubaker 1996). The 1989 inception of the Third Democratic Republic of Poland revitalized the discussion of the relationship between citizenship and the Polish nation. One major element of this discussion is the issue of dual citizenship.

---

1 This chapter represents a summary of the most important findings from the study of the Polish case in the research project 'Multiple citizenship in a globalizing world. Germany in a comparative perspective'. A full analysis of data from the study can be found in Górny, Grzymała-Kazłowska, Koryś and Weinar 2002; 2003.

This chapter aims to analyze the level of tolerance of dual citizenship and its determinants in Poland. We argue that dual citizenship is tacitly (*de facto*) tolerated in Poland. What is at stake at the moment is its formal (*de jure*) acceptance, which would make citizenship matters independent of discretionary decisions of Polish authorities. Debates, even though limited, concern the question of abolishing the exclusiveness rule in Polish citizenship – the rule that Polish citizens holding foreign nationalities are ineligible for diplomatic protection from their other country of citizenship and must use Polish documents (passport, identity card, driver's licence, and so on) while in Poland.

It seems that the virtually unquestioned *de facto* tolerance of dual citizenship has arisen from the long history of large-scale emigration from Poland and from efforts to maintain contacts and good relations with Polish emigrants abroad. The strong and well-organized *Polonia*[2] is a significant lobby promoting this tolerance. Another important factor contributing to the tolerance is a wish to have the Third Republic of Poland compensate for some of the unjust and unfortunate policies from Poland's communist past. The dual citizenship question in this context intersects with the problem of returning Polish citizenship to people – foreign citizens at the moment – who were deprived of it by communist governments.

We also argue that, among other things, the relatively high *de facto* tolerance of dual citizenship in Poland stems from the fact that the main group of actual and potential dual citizens is, for now, emigrants. This practical tolerance is also supported by the fact that there is a large group of Polish-German citizens living in Poland, whose dual citizenship is tolerated. Particular treatment of this group is a consequence of German policy aimed at preserving citizenship rights of Germans who remained on Polish territory after World War Two. However, the introduction of formal/legal recognition of tolerance for dual citizenship would apply not only to Polish people, but also to other types of dual citizens. Controversies around introducing *de jure* acceptance of dual citizenship suggest that this recognition would meet with resistance in Poland.

Discrepancies between the tolerance of dual citizenship for emigrants and that for immigrants are not unique to Poland, as demonstrated by Dutch, German, and Swedish examples. They are embedded in a broad set of country-specific factors (*cf.* de Hart this volume, chapter 3; Spång this volume, chapter 4) and are difficult to explain in general terms. In our analysis of the Polish case, we assume that a conceptualization of nationhood and citizenship is a dimension of belief systems and that these belief systems provide a particular explanatory power for justifying such discrepancies, and hence the policy process and outcomes regarding dual citizenship in Poland.

---

2   The term *Polonia* is used in this article in a broad sense denoting the Polish minorities all over the world who have developed formal organizational structures. It applies to Poles, as well as to their descendants, who emigrated from Poland or found themselves on non-Polish territories due to shifts of state borders or deportation (i.e. territories of the former Soviet Union) (see Żukrowski 2001).

Our analysis starts with a presentation of the context for tolerance of dual citizenship in Poland. Using historical factors and political changes in the 1990s as a background, we describe the main actors and institutional opportunity structures of the debate on dual citizenship in Poland. Then, the analysis moves on to outline the legislative framework for tolerance of dual citizenship. An examination of political and public debates on dual citizenship then follows. The analysis is enriched with reflections about what limits the scope and frequency of debates on the issue and about the impact that political and public debates have on outputs concerning tolerance for dual citizenship in Poland. Finally, we draw conclusions about the nature of tolerance of dual citizenship in Poland and theorize about possible changes in this field in the future.

Method of Research and Analysis

The methodology involved a combination of different research techniques and types of analysis. We analysed published works on the history of the Polish nation, citizenship, and emigration from Poland. To determine the legislative framework concerning dual citizenship, we examined not only legislation in force, but also bills that have been discussed in the Third Republic of Poland. Their inclusion in the analysis was necessary to reveal the atmosphere surrounding dual citizenship in contemporary Poland, as the current Act on Polish Citizenship was introduced in the Polish People's Republic in 1962.

Besides analyzing tolerance of dual citizenship, we also examined attitudes to the Bill on a Special Status Law – in Poland called the Polish Charter – proposed in 1999. Rights that were to be given to the Polish minority abroad by this charter are not tantamount to citizenship but do represent 'semi-citizenship' rights and for many would be an acceptable substitution for Polish citizenship, thus for formal acceptance of dual citizenship in Poland for *Polonia*. Consequently, discussions on this particular legal solution were mingled with the problem of dual citizenship in terms of pros and cons used by disputants. Therefore, we argue that enriching our analysis with elements of these discussions is pivotal for understanding tolerance of dual citizenship in Poland, especially since similar Special Status Laws were introduced in Hungary and Slovakia – post-communist countries whose emigration rate is relatively high (*cf.* for example Fowler 2002).

In order to provide a better understanding of the institutional context and political divides regarding dual citizenship, we conducted in-depth interviews with experts on the issue and with MPs engaged in the legislative process. They represented an important source of information since Polish public and political deliberation on dual citizenship is rather limited and the issue is almost absent from the platforms of Polish political parties.

The political debate was examined through analyses of parliamentary discussions on several bills in 1999-2000 since in Poland this debate is virtually restricted to parliament. The parliament has two chambers – the lower (*Sejm*) and upper (*Senat*).

The latter has only a watchdog role,[3] whereas the *Sejm* legislates. Bills considered in the analysis include: the Bill on Renunciation of the Conventions on Avoidance of Dual Citizenship (1999), two bills on Polish Citizenship – the *Senat*'s (1999-2000) and the government's (1999-2000), as well as the Bill on a Polish Charter (1999-2001). We had to exclude, from this part of the analysis, the most recent version of the Bill on Polish Citizenship, presented in 2001, as it has never been discussed in the parliament. We used excerpts from debates held in the *Sejm*, both on the plenary sessions and in the Committees.[4] The debates held in the *Senat* were not considered, since it was the *Sejm*, not the *Senat*, that was the main forum for all of the discussed cases. The analysis covers debates held at each stage of the legislative process.

The scope and content of the public debate on dual citizenship was investigated through the pages of four national Polish newspapers: *Gazeta Wyborcza*, *Nasz Dziennik*, *Rzeczpospolita*, and *Trybuna*. Articles dating from the early 1990s through to 2002 (when the research was carried out) from the two main Polish newspapers (*Gazeta Wyborcza* and *Rzeczpospolita*), indexed according to such key-words as 'dual citizenship' and other possibly significant terms, were analyzed for their context (headlines, location within the papers, etc.) and content (for a list and description of the articles, see Figure 6.1).

On this basis, a sample was selected for in-depth analysis, derived from all four newspapers and covering two multiple-week periods (February-March 1998 and June-July 2000), when the concentration of articles of interest was the highest. For the February-March 1998 period, this concentration was linked to the thirtieth anniversary of March 1968 – anti-Semitic incidents involving forced emigration of Polish citizens of Jewish origin and their 'not fully voluntary' renunciation of Polish citizenship. The summer of 2000 was a period of parliamentary discussion of the Bill on Polish Citizenship. Both selected debates meet two criteria, namely: each provides a good example of discussions about dealing with the communist past and each is connected with a legislative process.

The Context

Ethnic Germans

Ethnic Germans are the largest group of dual citizens in Poland. Under the terms of the Yalta agreement, Poland acquired the so-called 'Regained Territories' that had been under German rule. After 1945, the Potsdam Treaty provided for the expulsion of 3.5 million German citizens from Poland (Matelski 1999). Emigration to Germany continued in later years of not only German citizens, but also of ethnic Germans (people claiming German origins). Emigration from Poland was promoted by the

---

3   It is responsible for ensuring that bills do not violate the Polish Constitution. The *Senat* can also propose drafts of legal acts.

4   The debate on the Bills was held in the following Committees: *Administration and Internal Affairs Committee* (AIA) and the *Committee on Liaison with Poles Abroad* (LPA).

Figure 6.1   Articles on Dual Citizenship in the Polish Press: Topics and Frequency

Types of Articles	*Gazeta Wyborcza*		*Rzeczpospolita*	
	Number of Articles	Per Cent	Number of Articles	Per Cent
Legislation in Poland				
Major themes:				
• Citizenship Act;				
• Polish emigrants;				
• Repatriation;	30	14	61	26
• Forced emigration of Jewish population in 1968.				
Minor themes:				
• Reprivatization.				
Polish minorities in the context of international relations and ethnic minorities in Poland				
Major themes:				
• German minority in Poland;				
• Polish-German relationship;	17	8	25	10
• Polish minority in Lithuania.				
Minor themes:				
• Polish minority in Ukraine;				
• Bilateral agreements between Poland and post-Soviet countries.				
Individual biographies				
Major themes:				
• Sportsmen.				
Minor themes:	55	25	59	24
• Businessmen;				
• Criminals and commercial offenders;				
• Politicians;				
• Artists.				
German debate				
Major themes:				
• Immigrants from non-European countries;	46	21	43	18
• Elections.				
Minor themes:				
• Racism.				
Citizenship in the former USSR	43	20	30	12
Others				
Major themes:				
• Ethnic minorities in other post-communist countries (e.g. former Yugoslavia, Czech Rep., Slovakia, Hungary).	27	12	23	10
Minor themes:				
• Immigrants in other Western countries (e.g. France, Holland, Sweden).				
Total	218	100	241	100

Source: Author's data analysis.

German *Aussiedler* policy of accepting and supporting the immigration of people who were able to prove their German roots. Immigrants could count on the help of the German state and had the right to German citizenship. In the 1980s, this type of emigration turned into mass migration – between 1981 and 1990, 740,000 registered ethnic Germans left Poland (Iglicka 2001).

In the Third Republic of Poland, *Aussiedler* emigration has diminished. Changes in German immigration policy of the early 1990s influenced the *Aussiedler* policy towards people from Poland: the policy became virtually limited to the granting of German citizenship instead of the promoting of emigration of ethnic Germans from Poland to Germany. Consequently, citizenship matters were moved to newly opened German consulates in Poland, where the procedure of granting German citizenship became faster and more efficient. The opening of these consulates was agreed upon at inter-ministerial talks and was not a subject of political and public debates in Poland. Both Germany and Poland were interested in opening more consulates to look after the interests of their citizens (not only dual) living abroad.

As a consequence of the past and present generous policy of granting German citizenship, there are a number of people living in Poland who have both Polish and German citizenship. According to the National Census of 2002, there are 279,639 Polish citizens holding German citizenship, constituting as much as 63 per cent of all dual citizens in Poland (Central Statistical Office 2003). This number is, however, likely to be a low estimate. For example, Thomas Urban (1994) argues that the number of Polish-German citizens is somewhere between 300,000-700,000 people, living mainly in the Upper Silesia region. For Opole Silesia itself (part of the Upper Silesia), Krystian Heffner and Brygida Solga (1999) estimated the number to be between 120,000 and 130,000.

German citizenship opens the European labour market to inhabitants of Poland. The typical mobility pattern is one of maintaining a permanent residence in Poland while making repeated trips to take up work (legally) in Germany and other European countries. The local press publishes employment offers for jobs in Germany to persons who hold German citizenship and speak German. Labour migration to Germany became commonplace in some regions, especially in the Upper Silesia region (Heffner and Solga 2003). Ethnic Germans, however, do not constitute a lobby interested in broadening the existing tolerance of dual citizenship. It can be argued that the scope of tolerance for dual citizenship in Poland is satisfactory for members of this group since it allows them to take advantage of their German passports without breaking their ties with local communities in Poland. It can even be argued that, for this group, the problem of acceptance of dual citizenship in Poland has already been settled satisfactorily by transferring the procedure of granting German citizenship to consulates in Poland in the early 1990s.

Emigration and Relations with Polonia

Poland is a country of emigration; immigration to Poland has been marginal to date, even though the beginning of the 1990s brought about a sharp increase in the inflow of foreigners to Poland. A tradition of maintaining contacts with Polish people abroad had developed in the nineteenth century and was institutionalized in the Second Republic of Poland (1918-1939) (Kołodziej 1998). This tradition was, to a large extent, broken by the Polish People's Republic from the late 1940s onwards, when emigrants were treated as traitors by the Polish government. At the same time, most *Polonia* members declared themselves to be anti-communist; the Polish Government in Exile, composed of *Polonia* representatives, operated in London between 1939-1990. All this made good relations between the Polish State and *Polonia* difficult if not impossible.

In the Third Republic of Poland, maintaining good relations with Polish emigrants and their descendants returned to the political agenda and became official governmental policy in 1991. Following the tradition of the Second Republic of Poland, the *Senat* became the institution responsible for contacts with Poles abroad. At present, however, there are several official institutions dealing with relations with *Polonia* and Polish emigrants.[5] The official policy towards emigrants has focused on organized *Polonia* in the West and in the East (comprising mainly territories of the former Soviet Union).

There are about 20 million Poles and Polish descendants living outside Poland, of whom 10 million reside in the United States alone,[6] whereas the total population of Poland is less than 40 million. The importance of *Polonia* for the Polish State should not, however, be ascribed only to the size of the group. *Polonia* includes hundreds of organizations all over the world aiming to preserve and promote Polish culture with the help of numerous media established and run by *Polonia* members. During the communist era, *Polonia* played an active role in opposition to the communist regime and supported anti-communist movements financially and in other ways. *Polonia*'s activities in the current period go beyond promoting Poland and Polish culture; it now also has organizational structures that lobby Polish political actors. The main channels of its influence are its members' personal contacts with Polish political figures (originating mainly from the former anti-communist opposition), the *Senat* as an official institution representing its interests, and the Polish media, where some of the most active *Polonia* representatives regularly publish their opinions.

It should be noted, however, that there is an important general division in the *Polonia* group between Western and Eastern *Polonia*. Western *Polonia* is well-organized and comprises mainly Polish emigrants and their descendants. Eastern *Polonia* has weaker institutional structures because of the limited opportunities for self-organization under communist rule. Eastern *Polonia* consists of Poles and their descendants who found themselves living in non-Polish territory because of post-war shifts of the Polish border or deportations. Consequently, members of Western Polonia are the most active with respect to contacts with Polish political actors. On the other hand,

---

5   These include: *Senat*, *Sejm*, the Ministry of Foreign Affairs, the Ministry of Education, the Ministry of Labour and Social Policy, government and the 'Assistance for Poles in the East' and 'Polish Community' foundations.

6   Data provided on the *Polonia*'s website (see www.polonia.org).

Eastern *Polonia* – less prosperous and poorly organized – is considered to need help from the Polish government to preserve its Polishness and to compensate for harms suffered during the communist era.

The issue of dual citizenship is pivotal in contacts with *Polonia*, as the end of the communist regime in Poland changed positions and attitudes towards the Polish state. *Polonia* members are frequently either dual citizens with Polish passports, foreign citizens considering restoration of their Polish citizenship, or individuals who demand some kind of recognition of their Polish origins by the Polish state. In fact, of all dual citizens in Poland, apart from German co-citizens, those possessing the citizenship of Poles' traditional countries of emigration are the most numerous, with American nationals in the forefront (7 per cent of the total) (Central Statistical Office 2003). Therefore, taking into account its relatively active role in past and contemporary Polish matters, *Polonia* should be considered as an important participant in debates on dual citizenship.

Political and Institutional Actors

The formation of the Third Republic of Poland initiated radical changes in the political and economic system of the country. It also gave rise to new political parties, made up of people from the *Solidarność* underground opposition during the last decades of the Polish People's Republic. The composition of political parties operating in Poland changed several times in the 1990s; nevertheless, historical differences between the post-*Solidarność* and the post-communist parties marked the major lines of division on the political scene of the Third Republic of Poland in the 1990s. Only at the beginning of the twenty-first century did this division start to diminish in importance in favour of a pro-EU and anti-EU division (Solarz 2001; Wnuk-Lipiński 1996).

Post-*Solidarność* parties were more active than post-communist parties in promoting the necessity of 'dealing with the past', but other dividing lines including ideological and ethical standpoints (such as attitudes to abortion and teaching religion in public schools) have not significantly influenced the Polish party system. Divisions concerning views on such issues usually cross party divisions and are of a temporary character. Likewise, no Polish political party has made its position on dual citizenship, Polish citizenship, or nationhood central to its platform; it can even be argued that Polish parties have not yet determined their own positions on these issues. MPs' opinions about the issues seem to represent their personal points of view and do not have to correspond with the orientation of their parties.[7]

At the same time, political actors can be divided into those actively supporting *Polonia* and others. The division does not correspond directly with inter-party divisions even though a claim could be made that pro-*Polonia* MPs tend to be found among post-*Solidarność* groups and in the *Senat*. It was no coincidence that work on the Bill on Polish Citizenship and other bills associated with *Polonia*'s interests occurred in 1999-2000, when post-*Solidarność* parties held the majority in the Polish parliament.

---

7   Information derived from interviews with politicians and experts.

In Poland, not only political but also institutional actors are important to the debate on dual citizenship. The *Senat*, despite the senators' varied affiliations with assorted political parties and coalitions, is unified in its support of *Polonia*'s interests and is an important actor in the field of dual citizenship. Another pivotal actor is the presidential chancellery. The president can grant and restore Polish citizenship rights and he also has the virtually unrestricted power to decide if a would-be Polish citizen may retain or must relinquish her foreign citizenship. His decisions in this field cannot be challenged by any Polish court. Therefore, the chancellery may run its own policies on dual citizenship. Its policy may also stimulate the debate on citizenship, even though the president does not involve himself in the parliamentary discussions. These powers notwithstanding, the presidential chancellery has never formulated its official position on dual citizenship, preferring not to run its policy transparently.

Legislative Framework and Politics

Law and the Politics of Dual Citizenship

Historically, dual citizenship was not accepted under Polish law. The 1920 and 1951 Acts on Polish Citizenship stated that 'a Polish citizen cannot be a citizen of another country at the same time'. Even though, under both acts, Polish citizens breaking the rule of loyalty to the state were deprived of Polish citizenship, the act of 1920 was stricter with regard to avoidance of dual citizenship. It foresaw automatic loss of Polish citizenship upon acquisition of a foreign citizenship, whereas the act of 1951 included only the rule that 'a Polish citizen can obtain a foreign citizenship only upon permission of Polish authorities for the relinquishment of the Polish citizenship'.

The act on Polish Citizenship of 1962, which remains in force, brought about a crucial change regarding dual citizenship. Its Article 2 states that 'a Polish citizen, according to the Polish law, cannot be recognized as a citizen of another country at the same time'.[8] This rule created many controversies and gave rise to various interpretations. The supporters of one interpretation argued that 'the Act does not allow for a combination of the Polish and a foreign citizenship' (Jagielski 2001, 81-2).[9] Others advocated that dual citizenship:

> is silently accepted [and] that there are situations when Polish citizens hold foreign nationalities and this fact does not have any negative (a requirement to give up a foreign citizenship) nor positive (special rights in Poland) consequences. (Borkowski 1988 quoted in Zdanowicz 2001, 173-4)

In fact, as the act of 1962 allows for discretionary decisions, tolerance of dual citizenship depends on how the law is applied, which has been liberalized gradually since the mid-1980s (Zdanowicz 2001).

---

8   Article 2, the Act of 1962, *Journal of Law* (1962), no. 10, item 49.
9   Pronouncement of the Supreme Administration Court on 1994-12-28.

The naturalization procedure is regulated by three articles of the 1962 act (Articles 8, 9, and 10). Whereas Article 9 is devoted to stateless people and persons whose citizenship is unknown, the two remaining articles state that 'the acquisition of Polish citizenship can be conditioned by the relinquishment of the previous citizenship'. In practice, the requirement that a naturalized Polish citizen gives up her previous citizenship has been implemented inconsistently, seemingly according to the current policy towards a given citizenship group (see for example Górny 2001). In particular, the requirement of relinquishment depends on the policy of the presidential chancellery in cases whereby naturalization takes place according to Article 8.

Bilateral conventions played a pivotal role in the field of dual citizenship in the Polish People's Republic, as Poland was a signatory to several such agreements on avoidance of dual citizenship with the countries of the Soviet Bloc. They included conventions signed with: the Soviet Union (1965), Czechoslovakia (1965), Bulgaria (1972), Mongolia (1975), and the German Democratic Republic (1975), (Albiniak and Czajkowska 1996). In practice, the conventions created inequality in the treatment of applicants for Polish citizenship. Most citizens of the Soviet Bloc were not allowed to keep their previous citizenship whereas for other foreigners it was subject to a discretionary decision.

As a consequence of the political and economic transition in Central and Eastern Europe, some signatories to the above agreements ceased to exist. Moreover, by 2002, Poland expressed its desire to withdraw from those remaining agreements with several of the signatories' successors.[10] In this way, international mechanisms calling for the relinquishment of the previous citizenship upon naturalization in the Third Republic of Poland disappeared.

As described earlier, the fall of communism, in practice, raised tolerance of dual citizenship. Because the Act of 1962 left considerable room for discretionary decisions in the field of granting citizenship, changes have been allowed with respect to how legislation relating to citizenship is interpreted and applied. In general, the present state of affairs is that dual citizenship is usually *de facto* tolerated in Poland, even though the exclusiveness of Polish citizenship holds.

The Proposed New Legislation on Citizenship

The Act on Citizenship was designed in the 1960s and, even after necessary amendments in the 1990s, no longer meets the reality of the Third Republic of Poland. This is due not only to a change in the understanding of the right to obtain Polish citizenship after 1989 and Polish accession to the European Union, but also to new social phenomena that occurred along with the democratization process in Central and East European countries. First and foremost, there is a need to define a procedure to restore Polish citizenship to people who were unlawfully deprived of it in the past. As well, the problem of repatriation of people of Polish descent

---

10 To date, only the Ukrainian government has not ratified the termination of such a convention.

from the territory of the ex-USSR regained its importance in the 1990s. Finally, the rapid growth of immigration at the beginning of the 1990s and the continuing influx of foreigners into Poland have made necessary a reconsideration of the rules of naturalization in Poland. At the moment, this problem is not a major concern but it will most likely gain in importance in the near future. All these 'new' aspects intersect with the problem of dual citizenship despite their different contexts.

Work on the Act on Citizenship began in the late 1990s and comprises three bills[11] proposed between 1999 and 2001. Originally, the above three components – restoration of Polish citizenship, repatriation and immigration – were to be tackled by a comprehensive new Act on Citizenship. However, while the bills were being drawn up, a separate Act on Repatriation was introduced in 2000. The final form of a new Act on Citizenship is still unknown, as none of the three bills was enacted. Nevertheless, some elements of these bills are worth mentioning for the insight they provide regarding the atmosphere around dual citizenship issues in Poland.

All three bills assumed, like the previous Acts on Citizenship, the blood principle as the basis of Polish citizenship. Moreover, as it was stated in the preamble to the most recent bill, 'returning Polish citizenship to all those who have the right to it' was a key matter to be addressed by a new Act on Citizenship. The extent of restoration proposed in the different bills varied, but emphasis was laid on returning Polish citizenship to those who had lost it on the basis of previous acts (1920, 1951, and 1962). With respect to the naturalization of foreigners, the bills featured different proposals but none of them would have necessitated the relinquishment of foreign citizenship upon naturalization in Poland.

On the whole, then, all three bills demonstrated a rather liberal treatment of dual citizenship. The strictest one, the governmental bill, proposed to retain the existing status quo by mandating the exclusiveness of Polish citizenship. The *Senat*'s bill presented the most liberal attitude in this field in stating that 'a Polish citizen holding, at the same time, the citizenship of another country has the same rights and duties as a person who holds only Polish citizenship'.[12] This approach was retained in the most recent versions of the bill. According to Zdanowicz (2001) such treatment of dual citizenship would represent higher tolerance of this phenomenon than is observed either in most West European countries' legislation and or as recommended in the European Convention on Citizenship from 1997.

Beyond the Law on Citizenship

Understanding tolerance of dual citizenship in the Polish context requires a look beyond the law on citizenship. In particular, two proposed legal solutions recognizing

---

11 They include: (1) the *Senat*'s Bill on Polish Citizenship submitted to the *Sejm* on 1999-04-28 (*Sejm* document [1999], no. 1222); (2) the Government's Bill on Polish Citizenship submitted to the *Sejm* on 1999-10-05 (*Sejm* document [1999], no. 1408); (3) the Deputies' Bill on Polish Citizenship submitted to the *Sejm* on 2001-04-11 (*Sejm* document [2001], no. 2842).

12 Article 4 of the Deputies' Bill on Polish Citizenship (*Sejm* document [2001], no. 1408).

the rights of *Polonia* members with respect to Polish citizenship should be mentioned: the Repatriation Act and the Polish Charter Bill.

The Repatriation Act, introduced in 2000, aims at solving the problem of people of Polish origin wishing to return to their homeland from the territory of the ex-USSR. According to the Repatriation Act, people qualify for repatriation exclusively according to an ethnicity criterion.[13] Repatriates are entitled to Polish citizenship without any restriction and become Polish citizens when crossing the Polish border with a repatriation visa. At the same time, they do not need to relinquish their foreign citizenship: thus, in fact they automatically become dual citizens.

The Bill on the Polish Charter was submitted by the *Senat* in 1999. It set out methods to determine the ethnic affiliation of persons of Polish origin or of Polish ethnicity and thus was designed not only to accommodate former Polish citizens, but also their descendants. The charter would have given such people freedom of entry and extended social rights in Poland while not imposing on them any duties or burdens, going so far as to make the application procedure free of charge. The bill was controversial apparently because of the perceived danger of creating a privileged group of foreigners with dual sets of rights in Poland, and it therefore never became law. However, work on a similar document – the Procedure of Recognition of Membership in the Polish Nation or of Polish Origin – is underway. Work on this document was restarted earlier than work on the Act on Polish Citizenship (early 2002), but none of the bills entered the parliamentary platform before the end of 2005.

Political and Public Debate

The Political Debate: Arguments of MPs

The main forum for political debates on dual citizenship was the parliament during the period when the post-*Solidarność* parties held the majority. The issue came up during discussions on terminating bilateral agreements that ensured avoidance of dual citizenship (1999) and on creating a 'new' Act on Polish Citizenship (1999-2000). The first debate was rather low-key and featured mainly arguments favouring tolerance of dual citizenship. The spirit of 'dealing with the past' overwhelmed any opposing arguments. The post-communist parties could not oppose the termination of the agreements too openly, because their position would have been immediately stigmatized as pro-communist. Thus, motions to withdraw from the agreements were easily passed.

Debates on the Bill on Polish Citizenship were more complex and heated. Debates peaked during discussions on the *Senat*'s proposed new approach to dual

---

13 A person is considered as being of Polish citizenship when she declares her Polish citizenship, proves her attachment to the Polish culture by cultivating the Polish language and traditions and when one of her parents, grandparents, or two great grandparents are either of Polish citizenship or held Polish citizenship in the past (*cf.* the Repatriation Act, *Journal of Law* [2000], no. 106, item 1118).

citizenship – that the Polish state recognized the right of any Polish citizen to hold dual nationalities. What was at stake in the debate over that amendment was the official acceptance of dual citizenship instead of the practice of unofficial tolerance. The debate focused on the issue of dual citizenship for people of Polish origin, both Polish and foreign residents, whereas the issue of foreigners with dual citizenship was tackled only very briefly.

The arguments in favour of official acceptance of dual citizenship were mostly of principled character – expressive and moral. They advocated continuation of the Polish tradition of tolerating dual citizenship and a need to compensate for injustices inflicted during the communist past. Principled argumentation also included the perceived obligation to take into account the rights and interests of Polish emigrants. Principle-based arguments were supported by pragmatic argumentation. In this way, the notion of the greater nation beyond the population of the Polish territory and the importance of the interests of those living abroad were stressed.

Opponents focused on the in-border group. Principled – expressive – arguments revealed worries about endangering the integrity and homogeneity of the nation. Concerns were raised about the potential misuse of the privileged dual status, especially by Polish citizens holding German citizenship, as well as about breaking the logic behind the institution of citizenship (loyalty towards one country). In this principled reasoning moral argumentation was less common, but there was regular mention of inequality of rights and duties of different types (dual- and mono-citizens) of Polish citizens.

Arguments against official acceptance of dual citizenship also had a pragmatic side, focusing on the interests of the in-border nation. It was openly asserted that the interests of *Polonia* should be treated as secondary to national security and the rights of Polish citizens living in Poland. The point was supported by another pragmatic argument, namely, that given the Polish tradition of tolerating dual citizenship, it should suffice to ensure dual nationals' proper treatment and no special provisions were necessary.

Evidently, principle-based arguments prevailed in the discussion on formal acceptance of dual citizenship in Poland. Interestingly enough, those favouring dual citizenship advocated the rights of *Polonia*, whereas the argumentation against the formal acceptance defended the interests of the in-border nation. These arguments of principle were supported by pragmatic reasons. They were particularly common in the argumentation against formal acceptance of dual citizenship, but occurred also in reasoning in favour of it.

Similar tendencies appeared in discussions concerning the Polish Charter. Principled pros advocated the right of *Polonia* members to be recognized as part of the Polish nation, the need to make up for the injustices of the Communist past, and so on. The main reasoning against the charter included pragmatic arguments pointing out the infeasibility of implementing this legal solution due to its organizational and financial burden. Thus, the argumentation against the Polish Charter was more pragmatic than the reasoning against formal acceptance of dual citizenship. However, they both focused on the interests of the in-border nation and the state.

It can be argued that the crucial point of the above discussions was who should constitute the Polish political community. An ethno-cultural understanding of nationhood prevailed, but some republican aspects, for example equality of rights and duties of all citizens, also played an important role. The latter issue was related to another important element of the discussions – the problem of 'dealing with the past'. Other aspects intersecting with the problem of dual citizenship were barely addressed. It is noteworthy that there was virtually no mention in the political debate of the largest group of dual citizens living in Poland – ethnic Germans. The only attempt to deal with this issue concerned the threat that ethnic Germans might abuse their dual rights – and this was a reason to oppose any broadening of tolerance of dual citizenship in Poland. It referred, however, to people living in Germany and not in Poland. The debates reflected the division into *Polonia* supporters (mainly the *Senat* and some right-wing politicians) and those who focused on interests of the in-border nation (all the other political actors). Clearly, party divisions were of secondary importance in these discussions.

Public Debate: Media Discussions

Public debate on dual citizenship is marginal, barely present and rarely verbalized in the Polish press, or in the context of Polish legislation. That makes the subject of argumentative structures and belief systems related to dual citizenship in Poland particularly difficult to research. The public debate differs, however, from the political debate in terms of actors involved and arguments verbalized. Thus, it is worthwhile to present some major themes and findings from the analysis.

The media debate on dual citizenship should be considered in the context of the following four major dimensions: emigration, dealing with the communist past, Polishness, and equality. Dual citizenship was first and foremost discussed with respect to the rights of Polish emigrants to regain the Polish citizenship they lost during the communist rule. The issue of dual citizenship virtually did not occur in the context of immigration, except for the case of self-repatriation.

The issue of citizenship was immersed in the debate on nationhood, in which the value of national membership, the criteria of belonging to the Polish nation, the level of Polishness of different groups, and their rights and duties resulting from national membership were debated. The idea of the greater nation seemed to resonate in Poland. The consensus was that members of the Polish nation were entitled to Polish citizenship. It was believed that Polish citizenship should be granted or restored to individuals of Polish origin by virtue of their ethnicity, their services to the Polish state, and as a compensation for their previous losses. In the debate on the anniversary of March 1968, the president made a promise publicly to return Polish citizenship to emigrants of Jewish and German origin. The debate nevertheless revealed controversies on granting Polish citizenship to people of non-Polish ethnicity.

The principle of equality appeared in the discussion on Polish citizenship in two forms. First, the principle was linked to entitlements to restoration of Polish citizenship and manifested itself in two general questions: a) who was truly entitled to Polish citizenship and b) if there were groups entitled to Polish citizenship how should they be prioritized? Second, the issue of equality was raised in relation to the rights and duties of foreign citizens holding Polish citizenship. The main argument supporting the idea of the exclusiveness of Polish citizenship on Polish territory referred to the equality of all Polish citizens regardless of their country of residence.

An analysis of the press indicates that the category of nationhood is more important in Poland than the category of citizenship. The right of former Polish citizens of Jewish and German origin to restored Polish citizenship was questioned, while the problem of foreign immigrants was virtually ignored. Therefore, the prevailing belief system might be described as a combination of an ethno-cultural vision of nationhood and a tendency towards ethno-cultural homogeneity.

Arguments used in the media indicate that, in Poland, two different discourses on citizenship coexist, or even clash – principled and pragmatic. The first discourse largely refers to expressive and moral arguments opting for the rapid and radical restoration of Polish citizenship to ethnic Poles deprived of their citizenship under communism, regardless of their current status. This standpoint was most apparent in the rhetoric of post-*Solidarność* parties and *Polonia* representatives. The tone of the principle-based reasoning favoured dual citizenship, although this was seldom explicitly formulated and openly expressed. Moreover, since the rhetoric was moral and expressive, the argumentation did not touch upon the practical and legal consequences of a far-reaching acceptance of dual citizenship. In this way, *de facto* and *de jure* states of affairs were somehow combined in this type of reasoning.

Within the second discourse, pragmatic arguments predominated. Support for limited tolerance of dual citizenship went only so far as it was compatible with the current abilities and interests of the Polish state (in terms of both numbers of potential individuals interested and the scope of their rights). In fact, within this discourse the arguments against dual citizenship, or more precisely against abolishing the exclusiveness of Polish citizenship, were the most common and most clearly articulated, and, by their very nature, were more extensively elaborated than principled arguments. This discourse was heard largely among Polish officials and governmental experts who concentrated on strategic and technical issues pertaining to *de jure* acceptance of dual citizenship.

To sum up, the two types of reasoning – principle-based and pragmatic – observed in the Polish media differ not only in the types of arguments but also in terms of issues tackled and actors involved. Therefore, there is only marginal, if any, interaction between them. Advocates in the 'principle-oriented group' seldom deal with practical obstacles and consequences and do not anticipate or counter the sophisticated legal and instrumental arguments of the 'pragmatic group'. The same has been observed in media discussions on the Polish Charter, enthusiastically received by *Polonia* but criticized by governmental experts due to its legal deficiencies and the burden it would put on the Polish state. It seems that it is a general feature of discussions regarding dual citizenship in Poland, since a similar dichotomy of discussion has taken place in the political debate.

The Importance of the Debates and their Outputs

A Political or a Public Concern?

Looking back at the short history of the Third Republic of Poland, there has been no visible shift in political orientations on citizenship matters. The process of 'dealing with the past' and of firming up relations with *Polonia* is not over. Settlement immigration to Poland is still a marginal phenomenon and issue. Thus, the context for debate on dual citizenship has remained unchanged since the beginning of the 1990s. At the same time, this issue appears to be of rather secondary importance to Polish political parties and coalitions. In fact, it has never become politicized in Poland.

The main reason such issues are politically relegated to the back burner is that most political actors consent to dual citizenship to some degree. The political and public discussion on the issue is framed by an ethno-cultural understanding of the Polish nation, an understanding that includes both in-border and out-border populations. This understanding favours tolerance of dual citizenship for Polish people. It can be argued that this belief system has remained uncontested through the formation of the democratic Third Republic of Poland and has even been strengthened during the process of redefining Polish citizenship, which took place during the Polish state's democratization (Staniszkis 1999; 2001).

Disagreements occur over the issue of the exclusiveness of Polish citizenship. This aspect involves legal intricacies of formal recognition of dual citizenship. Our research showed that there were very few MPs aware of these complex details and that most of them were not likely to pursue the subject. Their standpoint appeared to be that, since dual citizenship is tolerated in Poland, there is no point in bothering with the issue. Such thinking was also revealed in the analysis of the parliamentary debate and can be paralleled with the broader issue of the difference between law and its implementation in post-communist Poland (Staniszkis 1999; 2001).

The highly discretionary powers allowed under Polish law are not limited to the field of citizenship. This is arguably the heritage of the communist era at work, where unrealistic and sometimes even absurd laws were frequently subject to 'reasonable interpretation'. Post-communist state institutions in Poland that are charged with control of the execution of law are weak (Kamiński and Kurczewska 1994), thus reinforcing this legacy even further. This only widens the scope for civil servants' discretionary decisions.

There are also no strong interest groups to fight for broader tolerance of dual citizenship in Poland, apart from *Polonia* and the *Senat*. Immigrant groups are not well-established in Poland due to the relatively short period of immigration to Poland (*cf.* for example Hamilton and Iglicka 2000). Also ethnic Germans, who constitute the largest group of dual citizens living in Poland, have not formed an appropriate lobby interested in the topic. For them the problem seems to have been satisfactorily settled, as they enjoy the right to work in countries of the European Union without any limitation.

At the same time, according to one of the government representatives interviewed in this study, a shift of opinion on the part of leaders of Western *Polonia* has been observed. In the course of discussions on dual citizenship and the Polish Charter, they started to show more interest in the introduction of the Special Status Law than in achieving higher formal acceptance for dual citizenship. In this way, the most vigorous actors in the debates on dual citizenship became less involved in the issue at the beginning of the 2000s.

Finally, the media show no interest in the topic because of its complexity and its limited appeal to a wider number of readers. This lack of interest of course limits the opportunities for a public debate. And since no one can use the issue of dual citizenship to further its visibility, politicians have no reason to stimulate the political debate. Thus, discussions on the topic have been left up to legal and governmental experts and *Polonia* advocates. Political interest in the issue is extremely low, and consequently, dual citizenship has never become politicized in Poland. However, the restoration of Polish citizenship became part of a policy of 'dealing with the past', which supports *de facto* tolerance of dual citizenship for some categories of Polish people.

Legal Outputs

The legislation of the Third Republic of Poland is largely unproductive with respect to dual citizenship for repatriates. The exception is the Act on Repatriation of 2000, which did not expressly forbid repatriates' dual citizenship. None of the three bills on citizenship, proposed in 1999-2000, was enacted. In fact, the lack of consensus on dual citizenship (or more precisely on the exclusiveness of Polish citizenship) is an important reason why a new act on citizenship has not been introduced. The most recent bill that proposed formal recognition of dual citizenship was abandoned in the late stages of its preparation and never made it to parliamentary discussion. Explaining the abandonment of this legislation would require speculating about the influence of lobbies on decisions at the ministerial level. It should be noted, however, that such abandonment was unprecedented in Polish legislative practice. As of December 2005, a new bill on Polish citizenship has been already prepared, but parliamentary works are still to be restarted.

In parliament, lines of division fall between advocates for *Polonia*'s interests (mainly the *Senat*) who seek to remove the rule of exclusiveness of Polish citizenship, and more pragmatically-oriented MPs who stand up for the interests of the in-border nation and the Polish state, and who are against the abolishment of this rule. In fact, this disagreement revealed the complexity of belief systems regarding nationhood in Poland. The ethno-cultural concept of nationhood, dominant in the debates, includes in the nation ethnic Poles living within and outside the Republic's borders and consequently tends to support the tolerance of dual citizenship. At the same time, the republican ethos of equal rights and duties of all citizens (abroad and in Poland) is present and works against the creation of two groups of Polish citizens – with one and two or more nationalities.

Moreover, even though arguments referring to types of would-be dual citizens other than *Polonia* members – immigrants and ethnic Germans – were rare in the political debates, when they were brought up they featured mainly reasons not to abolish the rule of exclusiveness of Polish citizenship. The same picture emerges from interviews conducted with experts and MPs. This may be another reason the formal acceptance of dual citizenship, which would apply not only to Polish people, but to all dual citizens, did not find enough supporters on the Polish political scene.

The impact of the political debate on legal outputs is difficult to assess since the debate was cut off by removing the bill from the parliamentary agenda. However, if one takes into account the prevailing opinion with regard to nationhood (mainly an ethno-cultural concept with some republican aspects) and the nature of discussions in Poland, the existing status quo appears to be an acceptable solution for most Polish political actors. It can be also argued that the debate ended with an agreement that *Polonia*'s requirements should be satisfied somehow by an appropriate legal solution. As a result, work has begun anew on the Special Status Law in 2002.[14]

The public debate, dominated by the voices of *Polonia* advocating *de jure* acceptance of dual citizenship, had a limited impact on legal outputs. The intricacies of introducing *de jure* acceptance of dual citizenship were difficult to capture in the media. We can assume that *Polonia* helped to shape the *Senat*'s stand, although that point of view was not adopted by either a wider parliamentary audience or by experts.

Implementation of Law

The way the law has been implemented in Poland has given rise to a *de facto* policy concerning dual citizenship. In this respect, public debate seems to have played an important role. For example, media discussion on one practical aspect of the lack of *de jure* acceptance of dual citizenship, the so-called 'passport trap', appears to have influenced the *de facto* policy. The 'passport trap' refers to the bureaucratic difficulties encountered by *Polonia* members upon arrival in Poland due to the requirement that no Polish citizen may use a foreign passport when in Poland. Protests from *Polonia* in the media concerning the 'unacceptable' treatment of its members at the Polish borders stimulated government representatives to take part in a public discussion on this problem. Although this discussion did not effect changes in Polish law, it did influence *de facto* policies towards dual citizens. The scope of change is difficult to judge, but as a consequence of the media discussion, border guards received instructions recommending 'very careful' treatment of people with several passports.[15]

Public debate seems to be particularly influential concerning the restoration of Polish citizenship. In fact, we argue that the issue of restoration became incorporated

---

14 In fact, this work was interrupted in 2002 but was rescheduled for the beginning of 2004.

15 It should be noted, however, that the Polish border guard had not punished Polish citizens using foreign documents before the described discussion took place.

into the policy of 'dealing with the past'. Polish media reported that policy-makers were seeking automatic restoration procedures. Such procedures have not been introduced into Polish law, but the president has declared in the media that he would use his virtually unrestricted power to grant citizenship to restore Polish citizenship to people of Jewish and German origin who had been deprived of it in the communist era. This part of the public discussion, deeply embedded in the symbolism of 'dealing with the past', paved the way for greater *de facto* tolerance of dual citizenship.

The examples presented above show that, even though public debate on dual citizenship is limited in Poland, it influences the practical work of civil servants and policy makers. It should be noted, however, that public and *de facto* acceptance apply mainly (if not only) to dual citizenship for *Polonia* members and that this is what has been spotlighted by the media in Poland. Nevertheless, tacit tolerance of dual citizenship is pivotal in Poland. Therefore, the importance of public discussion in this field, although limited, cannot be doubted.

Conclusions

In Poland, *de facto* tolerance of dual citizenship is by and large uncontroversial, as revealed in the analyses of political and public debates. The aim of maintaining good contacts and transnational links with the numerous *Polonia* seems to be an important factor. A similar conclusion has been put forward in the case of another emigration country – Turkey (*cf.* Kadirbeyoglu this volume, chapter 5). In terms of the nature of the relationship with emigrants, however, the Polish case is considerably different from the Turkish one. Briefly put, the Turkish state is actively involved in the problems of Turkish emigrants' integration in Germany. Its involvement constitutes an important element of Turkey's policy on dual citizenship. Acceptance of it is regarded as a support for emigrants' integration and political participation in Germany. These aspects are absent in the Polish case, even though *Polonia* is active and willing to participate in 'Polish matters' abroad. The focus of contacts between Polish authorities and *Polonia* is domestic policies in Poland rather than what is going on in the countries of emigrants' residence. Evidently, in the realm of tolerance for dual citizenship, maintaining transnational links between the sending country and its emigrants is of primary importance, whereas the nature of those links is secondary.

The lobbying power of *Polonia* should not, however, be overlooked in explaining the tolerance of dual citizenship in Poland. Polonia's interest in this issue and its participation in the discussions in Poland have already resulted in some liberalization of practices regarding dual citizenship. If one posits the model of path-dependence in citizenship matters, as advocated by Thomas Faist, Jürgen Gerdes, and Beate Rieple (2004), one can see how Poland has charted a rather liberal path since the 1990s. That path in citizenship matters may lead to further liberalization in this field, such as the proposals for a new law on citizenship discussed in Poland in 1999-2000.

It is of more than passing interest that the problem of Polish-German citizenship for ethnic Germans in Poland (the largest group of dual citizens living in Poland) did not appear in public and political discussions on the national level. At least two reasons can be mentioned. The scope of the problem might be regarded as local, as it applies to a group that is large but also highly concentrated in a few western regions of Poland. Thus, only the local press published some articles on the issue. Second, German citizenship was being granted by the German state to inhabitants of Poland. Consequently, no special provisions were necessary, on the part of the Polish state, to tackle the issue of dual citizenship of members of this group, since their status is regulated by Polish citizenship law.

On the whole, discussions concerning dual citizenship are for all practical purposes limited to the problem of Polish emigrants holding foreign passports. Restoration of Polish citizenship to those who were unlawfully deprived of it in the communist era is a major part of political and public debates on dual citizenship. Such restoration is now a component of the symbolically important undertakings and intentions of the Third Republic of Poland to deal with the country's recent communist past. Putting the problem of restoration of Polish citizenship in such a context supports acceptance of dual citizenship in Poland.

The numerous factors supporting tolerance of dual citizenship in Poland notwithstanding, the official position of the Polish state on this issue has never been formulated. At the same time, efforts to introduce wider acceptance of dual citizenship by making it independent of Polish authorities' discretionary decisions have been unsuccessful. Origins of the virtual consensus on *de facto* tolerance of dual citizenship and the controversies surrounding its possible *de jure* acceptance can be traced to the argumentative structures of political and public discussions on dual citizenship.

The debates were framed mainly by a predominant belief system at the centre of which is an ethno-cultural concept of nationhood and citizenship, which tends to support tolerance of emigrants' dual citizenship. Yet, some arguments revealed elements of a republican inclination, emphasizing equality of rights and duties between Poles living in Poland and those living abroad. Arguments of this type were proffered to oppose official acceptance of dual citizenship. Ironically, similar reasoning – advocating equality of rights between immigrants and the native population – was used to argue in favour of tolerance of dual citizenship in immigration countries like Sweden and Germany (*cf.* Gerdes, Rieple and Faist this volume, chapter 2; Spång this volume, chapter 4). It is an interesting example of how similar arguments can be used in a different manner depending on the group of dual citizens involved.

Issues of immigration and multicultural policy were practically absent from the Polish debates on the issue. Consequently, the tacit acceptance of dual citizenship in Poland applies, in fact, only to selected groups of people (not including immigrants) and does not represent a broad acceptance of dual citizenship as such. This type of tolerance can be effectively manifested in the discretionary implementation of the law and does not require specific legal solutions. Therefore, political and public debates on dual citizenship do not flourish in Poland at the moment. Moreover, the

Figure 6.2   Poland: Chronological List of Dual Citizenship-Related Legislation

Date Legislation	Insitutional and Discursive Opportunity Structures
1920 First Citizenship Law	Established a rule that 'a Polish citizen cannot be a citizen of another country'.
	Introduced an automatic loss of Polish citizenship upon naturalization in the other country.
1951 Citizenship Law	Upheld the rule from the 1920 Act forbidding a Polish citizen to be a citizen of another country.
	Introduced a renunciation requirement instead of automatic loss upon naturalization in the other country.
1962 Citizenship Law	Introduced the rule that 'a Polish citizen cannot be recognized as a foreign citizen at the same time'. In this way it left the space for tolerance of dual citizenship.
	Upheld the renunciation requirement.
	Introduced the possibility of taking away Polish citizenship without agreement of its holder.
1997 Polish Constitution (for the Third Republic of Poland)	Introduced the rule that taking away Polish citizenship without agreement of its holder is impossible.
1999 Amendment of **Citizenship Act**	Extended marriage procedure to men.
	Made loss of Polish citizenship impossible without agreement of its holder.
	Introduced more precise rules of naturalization.
2000 Repatriation Act	Established a procedure of repatriation.
	Upheld the earlier practice regarding automatic acquisition of Polish citizenship by repatriates without a requirement to relinquish a foreign citizenship.
2001 Termination of the conventions regarding avoidance of dual citizenship	In 2001, the last convention on avoidance of dual citizenship (with Russia) was terminated although the position of Ukraine on this issue remains unclear.

complexity of the problem (the discrepancy between *de facto* and *de jure* tolerance in Poland) makes it relatively unattractive to political actors and the media. In the future, it may become a political and/or public concern by reason of increased immigration to Poland and the establishment of immigrant minorities, a likely scenario in view of Poland's accession to the European Union.

References

Albiniak, M. and Czajkowska, A. (1996), *Przepisy o obywatelstwie polskim 1919-1995* (Toruń: Wydawnictwo Dom Organizatora).

Alestalo, M., Allardt, E., Rychard, A. and Wesołowki, W. (eds) (1994), *The Transformation of Europe* (Warsaw: IFiS Publishers).

Borkowski, J. (1988), *Opinia w sprawie polskiego obywatelstwa w polskich przepisach* (Łódź: unpublished).

Brubaker, R. (1996), *Nationalism Reframed. Nationhood and the National Question in the New Europe* (Cambridge/New York: University of Cambridge Press).

Central Statistical Office (2003), *Migracje zagraniczne ludności* (Warsaw: Central Statistical Office).

Dacyl, J. W. (ed.) (2001), *Challenges of Cultural Diversity in Europe* (Stockholm: Centre for Research in International Migration and Ethnic Relations).

Faist, T., Gerdes, J. and Rieple, B. (2004), 'Dual Citizenship as a Path-Dependent Process', *International Migration Review* 38:3, 913-44.

Fowler, B. (2002), *Fuzzing Citizenship, Nationalizing Political Space: A Framework for Interpreting the Hungarian 'Status Law' as a New Form oOf Kin-State Policy in Central and Eastern Europe* (Birmingham: Centre for Russian and East European Studies, University of Birmingham), available at: http://www.one-europe.ac.uk/pdf/w40fowler.pdf, accessed at: 2006-04-25.

Górny, A. (2001), 'Polish Citizenship in Relation to Concepts of Integration and Transnationalism', in Dacyl, J. W. (ed.), 217-53.

Górny, A., Grzymała-Kazłowska, A., Koryś, P. and Weinar, A. (2002), *Dual Citizenship in a Globalising World. Germany of the Comparative Perspective. The Case of Poland – Issue Areas 2 and 3* (Warsaw: Institute for Social Studies, Warsaw University, unpublished).

Górny, A., Grzymała-Kazłowska, A., Koryś, P. and Weinar, A. (2003), 'Multiple citizenship in Poland', *ISS UW Working Papers Migration Series* No. 53 (Warsaw: Institute for Social Studies, Warsaw University).

Hamilton, I. and Iglicka, K. (2000), 'Introduction', in Hamilton, I. and Iglicka, K. (eds), 1-14.

Hamilton, I. and Iglicka, K. (eds) (2000), 'From Homogeneity to Multiculturalism. Minorities Old and New in Poland', *SSEES Occasional Papers* 45 (London: School of Slavonic and East European Studies).

Heffner, K. and Solga, B. (1999), *Praca w RFN i migracje polsko-niemieckie a rozwój regionalny Śląska Opolskiego* (Opole: Stowarzyszenie Instytut Śląski w Opolu).

Heffner, K. and Solga, B. (2003), *Social Situation on the Opole region of Silesia. Silesian Identity, German Minority, Foreign Migrations, Double Citizenship* (Opole: Silesian Institute in Opole, unpublished).

Iglicka, K. (2001), *Poland's Post-War Dynamic of Migration* (Aldershot: Ashgate).

Jagielski, J. (2001), *Status obywatela i cudzoziemca w orzecznictwie* (Warsaw: Dom wydawniczy ABC).

Kamiński, A. and Kurczewska, J. (1994), 'Institutional Transformations in Poland: The Rise of Nomadic Political Elites', in Alestalo, M., Allardt, E., Rychard, A. and Wesołowki, W. (eds).

Karpus, Z., Kasparek, N., Kuk, L. and Sobczak, J. (eds) (2001), *W kraju i na wychodźstwie* (Toruń: Wydawnictwo Uniwersytetu M. Kopernika).

Kołodziej, E. (1998), 'Emigracja z ziem polskich od końca XIX wieku do czasów współczesnych i tworzenie się skupisk polonijnych', in Koseski, A. (ed.), 11-24.

Koseski, A. (ed.) (1998), *Emigracja z ziem polskich w XX wieku* (Pułtusk: WSH).

Leoussi, A. S. (ed.) (2001), *Encyclopedia of Nationalism* (New Brunswick, NJ: Transaction Publishers).

Matelski, D. (1999), *Niemcy w Polsce w XX wieku* (Poznań: PWN).

Solarz R. (2001), *Kulturowe uwarunkowania procesu przekształceń polskiego systemu politycznego w latach 90* (Toruń: Adam Marszałek).

Staniszkis, J. (1999), *Post-Communism. The Emerging Enigma* (Warsaw: ISP PAN).

Staniszkis, J. (2001), *Postkomunizm. Próba opisu* (Gdańsk: słowo/obraz terytoria).
Urban, T. (1994), *Niemcy w Polsce. Historia mniejszości w XX w* (Opole: PIN-Instytut Śląski).
Wnuk-Lipiński E. (1996), *Demokratyczna rekonstrukcja. Z socjologii radykalnej zmiany społecznej* (Warsaw: PWN).
Zdanowicz, E. (2001), *Wielokrotne obywatelstwo w prawie międzynarodowym i krajowym* (Warsaw: Dom wydawniczy ABC).
Żukrowski, A. (2001), 'Dyskurs metodologiczny nad terminem Polonia', in Karpus, Z., Kasparek, N., Kuk L. and Sobczak, J. (eds), 681-89.

Interviews

Figure 6.3   Politicians and Experts Interviewed

Item*	Interviewee	Interview date	Interview duration
1E	Civil servant in the Office for Repatriation and Aliens	14 March 2003	2 h.
2E	Representative of 'Polish Community'	17 March 2003	45 min.
3P	Senator, right-wing	20 March 2003	1 h. 40 min.
4E	Lawyer, independent expert	26 March 2003	0.5 h.
5E	Civil servant in Ministry for Foreign Affairs	28 March 2003	1.5 h.
6P	Senator, UW (centre),	02 April 2003	50 min.
7P	MP, PO (centre-right)	03 April 2003	25 min.
8P	MP, SLD (centre-left)	07 April 2003	0.5 h.
9P	MP, German minority	09 April 2003	40 min.
10E	High-ranking official, Office for Repatriation and Aliens	17 April 2003	1 h.
11P	MP, PiS (right)	25 April 2003	40 min.
12P	Representative of the Prime Minister's Chancellery (SLD – centre-left)	09 May 2003	0.5 h.

* Interviews are presented in a chronological order. The symbol 'E' denotes an interview with an expert whereas 'P' stands for an interview with a politician.

Chapter 7

Dual Citizenship: Change, Prospects, and Limits

Thomas Faist

Abstract

The increasing tolerance of dual citizenship and the proliferation of new terminologies and concepts to describe it are certain signs that the boundaries of citizenship are changing. The contributors to this volume analyze these shifting boundaries by focusing on the similarities between as well as the significant differences in the approaches to dual citizenship in immigration and emigration states. Through the case studies presented here, it is clear that the concept of nationhood alone does not account for the current divisions over tolerance of dual citizenship. The primary factor is, rather, the complex belief system around the issues of 'societal integration', which refers to both the integration of society as a whole and the integration of immigrants. The analysis of dual citizenship has thus yielded rich insights into important political-cultural cleavages in immigration and emigration contexts. Above all, the empirical analyses of dual citizenship legislation contribute to the understanding of the very construction of boundaries between citizens and non-citizens and the broader aspects of societal integration.

Exploring the boundaries of citizenship provides insights into the changing relationship between individual rights and state sovereignty. The national case studies in this volume, on Germany, the Netherlands, Sweden, Turkey and Poland, serve to illustrate the negotiated character of citizenship, and to show what the boundaries between citizens and non-citizens look like in different democratic systems. Variations in the nexus between individual and equal rights of residents and state sovereignty are also highlighted in the case studies. While important factors in support of individual rights can be found beyond the level of the nation-state – for example, in conditions fostering gender equity in law – the political debates need to be analyzed at the respective national levels. All the case studies thus also uncover the process of democratizing state sovereignty (Balibar 2004). In doing so, they raise the interesting dilemma of the extent to which, in varying national contexts, considerations of equal rights for all permanent residents have changed the balance between individual rights and state sovereignty.

Despite the rich yield of these case studies, it is nevertheless useful to question the limits of the contested concept of citizenship in capturing societal integration and immigrant integration processes. To encompass the many recent developments associated with this contested term, new academic conceptualizations have mushroomed: Transnational citizenship (Bauböck 1994), partial citizenship (Parreñas 2001), nested citizenship (Faist 2001), global citizenship divide (Stasiulis and Bakan 2003), flexible citizenship (Ong 1999), citizenship gap (Brysk and Shafir 2004), postnational citizenship (Soysal 1994), cosmopolitan citizenship (Linklater 1999), extra-territorial citizenship (Fitzgerald 2000), global citizenship (Falk 1994), and overlapping citizenship systems (Johnston 2003). These conceptual innovations try to capture new constellations of membership, such as overlapping ties citizens may have, or the increasing role of human rights for citizenship, as in the case of dual citizenship. At the same time, there are also continuing inequalities in access to membership and citizenship. For example, access to formal citizenship may not be the most important expression of individual rights for certain categories of persons, such as undocumented migrants and highly skilled labourers. These examples point to the limits of the concept of citizenship when associated with a liberal interpretation of political citizenship while foregrounding the social and economic dimensions of citizenship.

In this concluding chapter the main empirical findings are summarized and interpreted in light of theories of citizenship. An analysis of global conditions favouring the tolerance or even acceptance of dual citizenship is followed by an overview of factors specific to various nation-states. Finally, the utility of the citizenship concept is questioned with regard to issues that go beyond political and cultural inclusion.

Global Changes Conductive to Growing Tolerance

On balance, tolerance of dual citizenship has increased steadily over the past few decades, albeit at a very uneven pace. This 'bumpy-line' trend towards increasing tolerance constitutes a path-dependant development. There is no reason to suppose that the development of dual citizenship has to unravel as if ushered along by some historical teleology, a charge often advanced against T. H. Marshall's triadic stages of the sequential development of civil, political, and social rights. Nonetheless, there is evidence that the transformation of citizenship has been shaped by significant developmental pressures.

The basic idea in a path-dependant process is that once collective actors such as states and state organizations have started down a track in a particular direction, the costs of reversal are high. There will be other choice points, however, at which decisions have to be taken. A path-dependant effect occurs when a previous decision, norm, or rule reinforces itself, when that decision determines in part the subsequent course of events. Decisions taken by nation-states and international organizations, over time, limit the range of available options at subsequent points, and thus may encourage continuity in the form of retention of the original choice. The path-dependence mechanism can help uncover both the main factors contributing to the overall global trend of growing tolerance of dual citizenship in the postnational perspective as well as the factors that explain the divergent paths taken by selected immigration states. In understanding the growth of tolerance of dual citizenship as a path-dependant process we can identify the 'positive' feedback effects – what in economics is called 'increasing returns' – driving this development (Pierson 2000).

One of the contextual conditions fostering the growth of tolerance of dual citizenship is the fact that sovereign states have tolerated multiple ties at the state level. Emigration states have demonstrated an increased interest in their citizens abroad, while immigration states have, in some cases, begun to soften the demand for unilateral allegiance, placing more weight upon principles of equal rights, such as the congruence principle. In the international realm, multi-lateral conventions have been increasingly tolerant of citizens' ties to multiple states. Moreover, the 'absence of war' between democratic states – with all its qualifications – may have led state authorities to view citizens' loyalties as less of a security problem. While there may be possible spill-over from the events of September 11, 2001, their primary impact appears to have been on the civil rights of citizens and non-citizens and on migration control measures, but no direct discernible impact as of yet on the readiness to tolerate or even accept dual citizenship. An exception may have been the Netherlands, where debates on security merged with contentious discussions on immigrant integration.

It is widely claimed that the increase in the importance of individual human rights vis-à-vis state sovereignty has its source primarily in either nation-state constitutions (Joppke 1998) or global human rights discourses (Soysal 1994). We argue that it is in fact the interplay of the two that has contributed significantly to the growing tolerance of dual citizenship worldwide. Norms and principles of human rights have moved from national constitutions into international conventions and back to national debates and policies. While it should come as no surprise that sovereign states still unilaterally decide on the attribution of citizenship, it must be recognized that they do so under conditions influenced by norms that are often codified both nationally and internationally. Changes in tolerance of dual citizenship have been driven by the slow transformation in the relationship between states and individual citizens in immigration states in four main areas – statelessness, gender equity, denizenship and democracy, and supranationalization (see Figure 7.1). Emigration states have responded to these changes mainly in an instrumental fashion. Generally, statelessness and gender equity, by now well entrenched in both national and international law, have been lock-in mechanisms since the 1950s (*cf.* Faist, Gerdes and Rieple 2004), leading to more and more exemptions regarding dual citizenship. Virtually every liberal democracy grants exemptions on these two grounds. The two other factors, denizenship and supranationalization, have not been present across the globe to the same extent and certainly have been absent in most emigration states, yet they have played a role in European nation-states. Increasing tolerance of dual

Figure 7.1   Global Conditions and the Growth of Tolerance of Dual Citizenship

Areas and Key Factors	Examples of Regulations	Mechanism of Path-Dependence
Statelessness	• Convention on the Reduction of Statelessness in 1961; • national regulations.	Lock-in
Gender Equality	• Convention on the Nationality of Married Women in 1957; • UN Convention against the Discrimination of Women in 1985; • European Convention on Nationality in 1997; • national regulations.	Lock-in
Denizenship and Democratic Congruence Two options: extend political rights to non-citizens or ease naturalization.	• National courts strengthening the rights of non-citizen residents (1960s ff.).	Disincentive
Supranationalization (EU)	• Principle of reciprocity among member states.	Disincentive

citizenship located in these two factors is probably easier to reverse than the lock-in effects. Therefore, they are best seen as disincentive effects.

If pressed to single out one key factor influencing the increase in tolerance of dual citizenship, it is perhaps the growing importance of human rights in international and national law. Viewed from a postnational perspective, citizenship has gradually emerged as a quasi-human right over the past decades, a trend that has been accelerated by supranational integration within the EU. For example, dual citizenship has become one of the means to combat statelessness for categories such as refugees. Similarly, the legal norm of gender equity has facilitated the acceptance of dual citizenship, reflected specifically in the right to independent citizenship for married women and the opportunity for either parent to pass on citizenship to their children.

Supranational developments further show how postnational and national levels are interlinked, as in, for example, the mutual recognition of nationalities within member states of the European Union. Such measures also make it increasingly difficult to exclude from dual citizenship within national-states immigrants coming from so-called third countries. As several cases suggest, such as Sweden, Switzerland and the Netherlands, granting dual citizenship to nationals abroad makes it harder to exclude immigrants from the same benefits since fairness considerations apply.

While the conventional postnational perspective suggests a decoupling of rights and identities linked to citizenship status and asserts the increasing salience of rights attached to personhood, the empirical study of dual citizenship provides an additional interpretation. Whereas half a century ago the judiciary prioritized the state's perspective when passing judgment on individuals' claimed links with states (for example the famous *Nottebohm* case in 1955), international courts have begun increasingly to shift attention to the rights of persons.

On the face of it, citizenship as a human right seems to challenge the traditional notion of state sovereignty, as expressed in the notion of *domaine réservé*. According to this principle, every state has the sovereign right to determine the criteria for acquiring the citizenship of that state. A few decades ago, most states agreed that multiple citizenships should be avoided as far as possible. The rights and duties of states versus citizens were constructed on the assumed congruence of an almost holy trinity of territory, people, and political regime, as expressed most prominently in the *Montevideo Convention* of 1933. Since then, there has been a shift from exclusive state sovereignty to the increasing recognition of the legitimate claims and rights of individuals. In particular, the human rights norms in international law since the Second World War have significantly constrained the states' 'sovereign prerogative paradigm' in citizenship law (Kimminich and Hobe 2000). This is clearly expressed in Article 15 of the *Universal Declaration of Human Rights* (1948) according to which '[e]veryone has the right to citizenship'. That article recognized citizenship as the precondition for effective individual rights, and, at least initially, implied only a minimal constraint of state sovereignty, because no particular state was thereby required to grant the right to citizenship. Like the right to emigration, the individual right to change one's citizenship is essentially of a negative kind. Furthermore, citizenship as a human right has found its way into only one of the major human rights treaties adopted in the post-World War Two era, namely the *American Convention on Human Rights* (1969), upheld by the Inter-American Court of Human Rights (1988). Because states have been reluctant to relinquish their right to determine the conditions of their citizenship, in the *International Covenant on Civil and Political Rights* (1966) Article 24, Paragraph 3 gives the right to acquire a citizenship only to children.

Nevertheless, the individual's right to citizenship against the claims of states to define citizenship rules exclusively has been strengthened in several respects by international conventions and treaties, judgments of international courts, and evaluations of citizenship laws by inter-governmental organizations. That right has been reinforced especially in relation to statelessness and gender equality. Examples include:

1. the Convention on the Reduction of Statelessness in 1961;
2. the Conventions on Dual Nationality by the Council of Europe in 1963, 1977, and 1997;
3. the Convention on the Nationality of Married Women in 1957; and
4. the Convention on the Elimination of All Forms of Discrimination against Women in 1979.

In sum, states' regulations bearing on citizenship can no longer be deemed to lie solely within their own jurisdictions but are in fact circumscribed by obligations to ensure the full protection of human rights (Chan 1991).

On the national level these processes intersect with processes of democratic proliferation in a path-dependant manner: liberal democracies tend to face this dilemma when adhering to the principle of avoiding dual citizenship as far as possible. Because of the importance of individual rights, liberal democracies are compelled to accept dual citizenship upon naturalization if the respective other state makes renouncing citizenship impossible, or imposes unreasonable demands. Liberal democracies also tend to accept dual citizenship in the name of gender equity when citizenship is acquired by birth. Furthermore, such states may be inclined to grant dual citizenship based upon reciprocity within regional governance systems such as the EU. Once certain exceptions have been granted, new interpretations of individual rights and new claims of other categories of persons combined with court cases could easily follow, and lead to yet more exceptions, a process best described as a proliferation of 'exception groups'. The more exceptions and thus potential claimant groups, the greater the likelihood that questions of legitimating different treatments for different citizen categories arise because each exemption has to be justified on reasonable grounds. Problems of justification and rising costs of administrative procedures have had the effect of increasing tolerance of dual citizenship. In the rather restrictive German case, for example, it is not unlikely that unequal treatment as a consequence of the so-called 'option model' could result in increased tolerance.

Overall, the empirical evidence suggests that dual citizenship is not simply a foreboding of global citizenship. Rather, the increase in tolerance of dual citizenship has resulted from an emerging trend of legal citizenship as a human right. Indeed, the very principles national states have enshrined in their constitutions and agreed upon in international conventions, regimes, and institutions have found their way back to shape legislation on citizenship and the practices of citizenship.

The growing tolerance of dual citizenship suggests that there has been a long and clearly discernible route from insoluble allegiance in the latter part of the nineteenth century and the first half of the twentieth century to exclusive but transmutable allegiance across most of the twentieth century – to multiple allegiances of citizens as a main trend leading into the twenty-first century. People tend to have multiple memberships in many dimensions within states, leading to an inclusion of citizens into civil society and to a multiplication of loyalties. Such processes, in turn, strengthen what has been called 'institutionalized individualism' (Parsons and White 1964). Ties to states still differ, of course, from ties to non-state organizations and communities, yet the nature and extent of these ties are no longer determined simply by state prerogative. The multiple aspects of ties to manifold collectives within and beyond states ultimately raise important questions regarding the understanding of politics beyond the state.

This increase in *de jure* and *de facto* tolerance should not diminish the importance of significant national variations in tolerance, ranging from basic exceptions, such as dual citizenship as an instrument to avoid statelessness, to outright acceptance and a general withdrawal of the renunciation requirement. In the various case studies presented in this volume we have traced this development with respect to changes in the institutional and discursive contexts of dual citizenship policy.

Figure 7.2 Institutional Structures

	Sweden	The Netherlands	Germany	Poland	Turkey
Voting Rights for Denizens vs. Dual Nationality	Proponents saw dual citizenship as a means to extend political rights of immigrants; in addition to local voting rights for permanent residents.	Proponents saw dual citizenship as an alternative to extending voting rights for immigrants.	Same as in NL; Federal Constitutional Court rejected voting rights for non-citizen immigrants.	(No debates on voting rights for non-citizens).	(No debates on voting rights for non-citizens).
Party System	Mix of bloc politics (Social Democrats vs. Centre-Right) and consensus politics (Social Democrats forming minority governments).	Orientation towards pragmatic consensus politics: elite consensus broke down in late 1980s.	Permanent conflict between the two major parties in a federal system.	Most parties in favour of selective tolerance of dual citizenship (*de facto* tolerance without *de jure* acceptance).	All political parties supported toleration of dual citizenship for emigrant citizens.
Other Institutions	Deliberation in expert commissions (1985, 1997).	Expert commissions (WRR 1989; SCP 1996).	Legal institutions (courts; politicized legal scholars with strong political party affiliations).	Discretionary power of the president; Senate in favour of *Polonia*.	Military rulers enacted dual citizenship legislation prepared previously under civilian rule.
'De facto'-Existence of Dual Nationality	*De facto* tolerance (increasing exceptions), combined with aspects of gender equity, has been a decisive argument in general acceptance of dual citizenship.	Increasing rates of naturalization, combined with high tolerance of dual citizenship, led to doubts about connection between naturalization and integration.	*De facto* tolerance played only minor role; more important: equality regarding ethnic Germans.	Tacit *de facto* tolerance has been the hallmark; more explicit legislation failed (Polish Charter).	Increased tolerance as an instrument to maintain links to emigrant citizens abroad.
Politicization of Debates	No politicization of debate.	Increasing political conflict in the 1990s; focus on non-western *allochtones*, referred to as 'Muslims'.	Citizenship (like immigration) as a 'meta-issue', characterized by symbolic politics.	(No legislation and no debates on dual citizenship for immigrants).	(No legislation and no debates on dual citizenship for immigrants).

Institutional Structures

The conditions and factors discussed so far have been located both on the supra- and international level on the one hand and the national level on the other. We turn now to the major factors that account for specific variations of *de jure* tolerance of dual citizenship at the level of the nation-state. Some apply in principle to both immigration and emigration countries, but most to the former only: voting rights for denizens, party systems and political debates, other institutions such as courts or advisory bodies, selective tolerance by discretionary measures, and the *de facto* existence of dual citizenship. Other factors have been clearly more specific to either immigration or emigration countries, such as differentialist transnationalism in emigration countries and multicultural transnationalism in immigration countries (see Figure 7.2).

Voting Rights for Denizens vs. Dual Citizenship

In all three immigration countries considered in this volume, dual citizenship figured in debates on the validity and extension of democratic principles. Interestingly, in Sweden and the Netherlands dual citizenship emerged as an alternative to expanding voting rights to non-citizens, which would have led to even more porous boundaries between established residents and citizens. In Sweden, the Social Democrats proposed in the early 1980s extending the franchise to denizens at the regional and national level, thus going one step beyond local voting rights for permanent residents, which had been introduced in 1975. Strong opposition immediately arose from the centre-right parties, who considered the franchise inextricably tied to citizenship. The Social Democrats then moved to dual citizenship as an alternative, and institutionalized the first commission on the subject in 1985, leading, in a process that took 15 years, to the eventual acceptance of dual citizenship.

The origin of increased tolerance in the Netherlands bears a great similarity to the Swedish case in the early stages. Equal rights proponents also pushed for permanent residents' voting rights, and here also dual citizenship was developed as an alternative. The Social Democratic (*PdvA*) and Christian Democratic (*CDA*) coalition then reached a compromise in 1991 to scrap renunciation as a prerequisite for naturalization. Subsequently, the *PdvA* withdrew its plans for voting rights for non-citizen residents on the national level. At around the same time the *PdvA* also dropped its plans for specific anti-discrimination laws. In return, the *CDA* gave up its opposition to dual citizenship. Yet, the political consensus backing increased tolerance held only until 1997. *De jure*, the renunciation agreement was reinstitutionalized for three reasons, though many exceptions prevailed. First, the *CDA*, an opposition party since 1994, no longer felt bound to the compromise. Second, in public debates and in opinion polls, the increase in the number of naturalized immigrants was viewed not as the result of successful political integration but as clever benefit-calculations on the part of applicants for citizenship. Third, the breakdown of the political consensus meant that discussion of immigration and membership issues during the election campaigns was no longer taboo, and dual citizenship became a contentious subject in public debate.

In Germany, local voting rights likewise served as a stepping stone in the debates on dual citizenship. Equal rights proponents suggested extending local voting rights for non-citizen permanent residents in 1989, following the Swedish and Dutch examples. Yet, when the states of Hamburg and Schleswig-Holstein tried to institutionalize local voting rights, the Federal Constitutional Court rejected the move, arguing that only members of the *demos* have the franchise. Nonetheless, and this furthered the cause of citizenship law reform in Germany, the highest court also affirmed that political integration of immigrants could be enhanced by changing the citizenship law, that is, easing naturalization requirements for permanent resident immigrants. Throughout the 1990s, proponents of dual citizenship tied the issue to political equality and argued that all immigrants should enjoy access to dual citizenship, not just ethnic Germans and EU-citizens.

Political Party Systems

Swedish politics has been characterized on the one hand by an even mix of bloc politics which has pitted above all the Social Democrats vs. the centre-right parties, and on the other hand, consensus politics. In the left bloc, the Social Democrats have managed to attract about 40 per cent of the vote, which has led them to form mostly minority governments. As a result, these governments are engaged in a constant search for a general and broad consensus going beyond the blocs, a factor that influences debates on constitutional principles, defense, and foreign policy. This characteristic mix of bloc and consensus politics accounts for the fact that the Social Democrats ceased pursuing the further liberalization of dual citizenship rules in the 1980s after they encountered strong opposition from parties of the centre and the right. It also explains why the centre-right parties did not turn dual citizenship into a contentious political issue, nor have they engaged in populist politics around it, an outcome that was certainly helped by the fact that there was no significant right-wing populist party on the national level. On the local level, populists focused on related but distinct issues, such as asylum seekers and refugees.

In the Netherlands a significant shift took place in the understanding of immigrant integration and of nationhood. Throughout the 1970s and 1980s, pragmatic consensus politics ruled the day and a large number of small parties fostered pragmatic coalition building. Immigration, integration, and citizenship issues had been a matter for professional experts, at least until the early 1990s, when political elite consensus broke down. Dual citizenship did not emerge as a divisive election issue until the sudden and meteoric rise of the populist party of Pim Fortuyn (*LPF*), whose platform was focused on multiculturalism and immigrant integration: The rise and overwhelming initial success of *LPF* enticed other parties to capture these issues, and thus a 'new realism' (see de Hart, this volume, chapter 3) began to take hold.

The mainstay of German politics after World War Two has been permanent conflict between the two major parties in a federal system, the Christian Democrats

(*CDU/CSU*) and the Social Democrats (*SPD*). The dominant party constellation on the federal level is often mirrored in the *Länder* (regional states) – noteworthy because many decisions need co-ratification by the *Länder*-chamber (*Bundesrat*). There is a strong incentive to deal with political issues on both the federal and the state level, so as to influence majorities on the federal level. The debate on dual citizenship perfectly reflects these constellations, the latest citizenship reform of 1999 being a direct expression of the prevailing divisions. The populist use of the issue in a state election by the Christian Democrats for discursive and strategic advantages represents efforts to tap into the reservoir of right-wing voters – possible only because of the absence of a coherent and consistently successful right-wing populist party.

In Turkey, political parties have been rather weak because of a clientelist structure, in which personal loyalty to a party leader matters much more than party discipline. The most significant issue for the policy debate on dual citizenship is the position of Turkish emigrants abroad which, when threatened, has evoked great unity among Turkish party politicians. Prominent examples were the response to the arson attacks in Germany (Mölln 1993), and the introduction of the 'pink card' in 1995. Politicians of all parties in the Turkish parliament looked upon dual citizenship as an instrument to improve both the rights of Turkish emigrants and to maintain ties to them.

In Poland, the central ideological division has run between the post-communist parties on the one side and the post-*Solidarność* parties on the other. The latter parties have been devoted to politics aimed at rectifying injustices of the past, among them forced expatriations and loss of citizenship. Although the differences in support of Polish expatriates (*Polonia*) do not run strictly along party lines, there is a stronger tendency in the post-*Solidarność* parties to favour *Polonia*'s interests. Furthermore, the Senate, the second chamber of parliament, and various 'right-leaning' politicians have consistently supported the claims of the Polish diaspora. Accordingly, reform bills concerning (dual) citizenship were introduced in 1999-2000 when the post-*Solidarność* parties enjoyed a majority in parliament.

There has been virtually no politicization of the debates in emigration countries, where mainly instrumental and strategic concerns about ties with emigrants figured prominently. Immigration countries, on the other hand, experienced an interesting range. At one end of the spectrum, the Swedish debates were decidedly apolitical. In the Netherlands political conflict around integration and citizenship slowly evolved with a focus on non-western *allochtones*, referred to as 'Muslims'. Populist politicians such as Frits Bolkestein and Pim Fortuyn and intellectuals such as Paul Scheffer helped to articulate the discontent with minorities and citizenship policy. In Germany, citizenship – like immigration since the early 1980s – has emerged as a meta-issue, characterized by symbolic politics (*cf.* Faist 1994). Interestingly, a closer look reveals that symbolic politics is not necessarily synonymous with populist politics. Indeed, as the parliamentary discussions in countries like Germany suggest, the issues at stake may be more about notions of the 'good citizen' and the 'good society'. Citizenship policies seem to be a lightning rod for the expression of strong views on fundamental concepts of politics.

Other Institutions: Courts, Government Advisory Bodies, and Migrant Associations

Expert commissions have played a significant role in both Sweden and the Netherlands. In Sweden, deliberation in parliamentary commissions has certainly, *ceteris paribus*, contributed to a disciplined debate and has partly helped to prevent the politicization of dual citizenship, most prominently in 1985 and in 1997. In the Netherlands, expert commissions have been instrumental in pushing for liberalization in the early 1990s but also in adopting a more critical stance in the late 1990s. In 1991, the Scientific Council for Government Policy (*WRR*) recommended liberalized naturalization rules as a means to improve the legal position of immigrants and advance their social integration. Yet, in 1996, the Socio-Cultural Planning Office (*SCP*) interpreted rising naturalization figures not as a sign of successful integration, but as an outflow of individual cost-benefit calculations on the part of scheming and disloyal immigrants. In Germany, legal institutions, in particular the Federal Constitutional Court, played an important role in delaying the reform of citizenship law. First, in its interpretation of the Basic Law, the court rationalized the idea that the prospect of German unification should not be endangered by premature citizenship reform. Second, the court upheld the Basic Law's fairly restrictive rules concerning the loss of German citizenship, based on the experience of the Nazi Regime which disenfranchised many individuals and categories. This restrictive stance carried implications for acquiring German citizenship. Third, the Federal Constitutional Court interpreted dual citizenship as an 'evil' (1974) and argued for citizenship as the basis for voting rights (1990). It strictly adhered to the classic triadic congruence of state territory, state authority, and the people (*demos*). Nonetheless, the latter ruling provided a push for citizenship law reform. Finally, in the expert hearings in parliament we see that the experts not only leaned towards one or the other party position, but also that legal scholars were overrepresented compared to social scientists and professionals from other fields.

Not surprisingly, immigrant organizations in Europe and in Germany in particular, have strongly supported dual citizenship. Quite a few of these organizations have engaged in bi-directional lobby politics, as for example in the case of the debates on the 'pink card' (1995) in Turkey. The Turkish government devised the specific regulations after consultations by an expert on Turkish constitutional law with Turkish immigrant organizations in Germany. When the expected reform in dual citizenship legislation in Germany did not materialize in 1999, Turkish immigrant organizations in Germany commented critically on the decision. They also proposed to the Turkish government forbidding release from Turkish citizenship, so as to force the German authorities to grant dual citizenship to Turkish citizens naturalizing in Germany.

Transnational ties also figure importantly in the Polish case. The Senate, whose function is to check the constitutional validity of laws but which has no legislative power of its own, usually supports, independent of party affiliation, the demands of *Polonia*. And the tendency in the 'western' *Polonia* has been not to demand outright acceptance of dual citizenship but rather a special and privileged status for expatriates, very much akin to the Turkish 'pink card'.

Selective Tolerance by Discretionary Measures and the de facto Tolerance of Dual Citizenship

The tendency towards a confluence of selective tolerance and the desires of migrants has been reinforced by discretionary measures on the part of bureaucracies. In Turkey, selective tolerance seems to be the rule – those with Turkish citizenship are clearly preferred over immigrants in Turkey. In other words, dual citizenship is tolerated for Turkish citizens residing abroad but not for immigrants residing in Turkey. In general, the more discretionary the rules and the more latitude the authorities have, the more this trend prevails, a state of affairs that essentially signals weak development of the rule of law. In Poland, very clearly, the widespread *de facto* tolerance of dual citizenship rests upon the discretionary nature of governing, and thus also, as in the Turkish case, allows for differential treatment of categories – (former) Polish citizens abroad and ethnic Germans on the one hand, and immigrants in Poland, on the other. The discretionary aspect has been reinforced by the restoration of citizenship for persons of Jewish and German descent. Moreover, the president can decide on granting or restoring citizenship, as well as whether renunciation of another citizenship is required. Only after the restoration of citizenship was completed did discussions on dual citizenship come up. But at no point did citizenship turn into a major political issue. In Poland, the task of managing momentous political and economic transformations has been so overwhelming that citizenship issues have been considered to be in the realm of 'low politics'.

Given other propitious institutional and discursive conditions, a high level of *de facto* tolerance of dual citizenship has led to increased tolerance in a path-dependant fashion. The best case in point was Sweden. *De facto* tolerance, coupled with increasing exceptions, especially when connected to implementing principles of gender equity, proved to be decisive. Overall, the two most important types of exceptions were, first, that persons unable to nullify their existing citizenship could not be barred from acquiring Swedish citizenship, and, second, that a person willing to naturalize would experience significant disadvantages if forced to renounce existing citizenship. Combined with the principle of political equality, these arguments led to an acceptance of dual citizenship. The centre-right parties changed their view.

Yet existing rules could also work in a more restrictive direction. In the Netherlands, increasing rates of naturalization after 1991, along with high *de jure* tolerance of dual citizenship, gave rise to doubts about the link between naturalization and integration. In Germany, *de facto* tolerance has played only a minor role up until recently, with the debate focused more on equal rights considerations towards immigrants vis-à-vis ethnic Germans. However, opponents of dual citizenship chose to downplay this equal rights argument in favour of legal guarantees.

Differentialist and Multicultural Transnationalism

Transnationalism in the politics and policies of emigration countries can be seen as a 'top down' feature, namely a state-directed effort to control emigrant populations abroad. While the two emigration countries analyzed here have come to tolerate dual citizenship for emigrants abroad in a *de facto* (Poland) and *de jure* (Turkey) manner, they have not provided similar rules for immigrants. Therefore, these citizenship policies can be termed differentialist. Major emigration countries such as Turkey have engaged in a two-way transnationalism, directed both at domestic politics and at emigrants abroad. The export of labour served as an economic policy strategy in the 1960s to reduce the domestic unemployment rate, created a flow of remittances from emigrants abroad, and enticed the return of human capital with re-migrants. Well into the 1980s, for example, about a fourth of all foreign currency earnings still originated from emigrants. It is plausible to surmise, therefore, that sustaining economic ties has been one of the major factors favouring tolerance of dual citizenship. In the Turkish-German case this effort has been associated with a sort of 'citizenship light', the so-called 'pink card'.

Yet, dual citizenship cannot be reduced to economic self-interest. Long before accession to the European Union was on the agenda, the Turkish government at times referred to Turkish migrant 'communities' as a lobby group abroad. For example, one of the conservative-national parties in the 1990s, *ANAP* (Motherland Party), openly declared that voting rights for Turkish immigrants in Germany were important because (1) Turkish immigrants in Germany could then influence the two major parties which then (2) would be more interested in solving Turkish immigrants' issues and problems, and ultimately (3) help open the doors to Turkey's accession to the EU. The introduction of the so-called 'pink card' in 1995 certainly was not an outflow of the interests of the Turkish government but of its German counterpart, which aimed to undercut the spread of dual citizenship among Turkish citizens naturalizing in Germany. While the German government demanded release from Turkish citizenship as a requirement for inclusion into German citizenship, the Turkish authorities had seen no problem in re-granting Turkish citizenship to those it had released before. In sum, all changes in Turkish citizenship regulations after 1981 have to be understood in the context of relations to the main country of emigration, Germany.

It is noteworthy that these state-directed transnationalist influences run on ethno-national lines: neither Turkey nor Poland has lifted restrictions on citizenship for immigrants in their own countries. The liberalized rules have only been written for and applied to emigrant citizens living abroad. In the Polish case, successive governments, who for historical reasons can be assured of the loyalty of Polish diasporas abroad, have attempted since the late 1980s to rekindle and maintain ties to *Polonia*. At the same time, the Polish government does not support the extension of human rights in the immigration states. The contacts between *Polonia* associations and the Polish government are centred on domestic Polish matters. As in Germany, debates on dual citizenship in Poland have been part of wider discussions and reform projects since the opening of the Iron Curtain. Since that time the politics of citizenship in Poland has been characterized by both the problematic nature of the overlap of the nation and the state and dealing with the burden of the communist past. Reconstitution and restoration of citizenship to those who lost it in the past are key issues in the public debate. A wholesale reform of the 1962 Citizenship Act, explicit legislation on dual citizenship, and the regulation of the membership of the diaspora by means of the Polish Charter did not materialize. Nonetheless, the interpretation of the existing law has changed. During the communist era Poland had entered into bilateral agreements with most other Eastern bloc countries with the aim of avoiding dual citizenship. Virtually all of these accords were cancelled during the 1990s, opening the way to implicit tolerance (and indeed, *de facto* recognition) of dual citizenship in Poland without changing the letter of the law.

The explanation for *de facto* rather than the *de jure* regulation in Poland, and thus for selective tolerance, is historical. It is striking that discussion of citizenship emphasized the exclusiveness of citizenship as linked to Poland's territory, a focus that may be related to the history of divisions between state and nation in past centuries. There is no obvious legal explanation because it is a clear principle of international law that the country where the dual citizen is located at the moment takes no account of the individual's other citizenship (meaning that the person concerned does not enjoy diplomatic protection).

Poland and Turkey constitute two variants of a tolerant stance on dual citizenship. The Polish government made no legislative changes, but simply has turned a blind eye to dual citizenship, thus engaging in *de facto* tolerance. The Polish case is to date the clearest expression that governments have increasingly come to view dual citizenship neither as a value in itself – in contrast to national citizenship – nor as an evil. The Turkish authorities do officially allow dual citizenship, the only stipulation being that the person notifies the Turkish government when another citizenship is acquired. These differences raise questions about the impact of the respective diaspora communities on the *de facto* tolerance and the *de jure* regulations in the home countries. Certainly, group size would be a factor: the larger the diaspora, especially those well organized in wealthy countries, the more it might be perceived as a threat to the domestic politics in the country of emigration. It is worth comparing Poland and Turkey in this regard. With a total population of around 40 million living within the territory of the Polish state, the estimate is that the Polish diaspora, East and West, amounts to about 10 million persons. This is a much larger share than the Turkish population living abroad, about 4 to 5 million, held against a total population in Turkey of about 60 million.

Transnationalism has taken a very different form in the immigration countries. In two out of the three immigrant countries studied here, transnational issues have played a significant role in the debate on dual citizenship, and have been linked to a multiculturalist framework of understanding. Nonetheless, in Germany and increasingly in the Netherlands, a differentialist understanding is also visible. For Sweden, a comparison of the debates in the 1980s with those of the 1990s suggests a shift from a national to a transnational perspective: in the 1980s, the concern with denizens was paramount, and the acceptance of dual citizenship was discussed as an issue of integration of immigrants and the meaning of equality. By the 1990s, however, this aspect was complemented by questions about what globalization and migration meant for belonging and identity, that is, what transnational ties of citizens meant for one of the main principles of Swedish multicultural policy, freedom of choice. Thus, the national equal rights perspective was supplemented by multicultural transnationalism, implying equality of treatment for both Swedish emigrants abroad and immigrants in Sweden. In the Netherlands multicultural overtones became visible in the late 1980s. Yet, conservative parties have consistently championed the interests of emigrants, and have privileged dual citizenship for emigrants while opposing it for immigrants. This shift became more evident during the 1990s when these parties articulated a more explicit ethno-national and differentialist transnationalism, claiming a stronger focus on tolerance of dual citizenship for Dutch citizens abroad. Although the proponents of dual citizenship wanted to use dual citizenship for emigrants as an argument in favour of extending dual citizenship to immigrants, this strategy failed completely. Parties such as the *VVD* held that the state should prohibit dual citizenship for immigrants, and the Christian Democrats (*CDA*) insisted that Dutch emigrants do not cause problems of integration while immigrants clearly do.

In Germany, the transnational aspect is complex. The proponents' claims turned on the issue of 'dual identity', but not as an explicit transnational argument. Rather, in the tradition of dealing with immigration in 'social work' terms, some proponents felt that dual citizenship would address the problems of an immigrant deficiency, that is, it would compensate their psycho-social needs. As far as their own nationals are concerned, German authorities have long tolerated dual citizenship for ethnic Germans, living in Poland or returning to Germany from all over Eastern and Central Europe. But until 2000 the authorities have not as a rule tolerated dual citizenship for German citizens living abroad. There are few exemptions: if German citizens abroad have strong family ties to Germany, they may be allowed to maintain German citizenship upon naturalizing abroad, and also outside the EU. Moreover, there are additional exemption rules for German women married to men in the 'Muslim cultural circle'. Due to effective lobbying by German women married to Turkish men, organized in *'Die Brücke'*, the exemption was granted. But these are the only exemptions.

Discursive Structures: Towards Societal Integration

The analysis in this realm focused on belief systems, reconstructed through arguments of political actors in legislative processes concerning dual citizenship. Each country case was examined with respect to belief systems concerning the tradition of nationhood – republican vs. ethno-cultural – and immigrant integration – multiculturalism vs. assimilationism. Going beyond these well-known belief systems, the case studies provided material for the analysis of the construction of a 'societal

Figure 7.3   Discursive Structures

	Sweden	The Netherlands	Germany	Poland	Turkey
Nationhood	Social democratic and socio-political concept of 'people's home' (*folkhemmet*): integration of immigrants as a welfare state project.	No evidence of discussion of 'nation' in 1970s and 1980s; since the early 1990s: focus on the 'good citizen'.	Republicanism: proponents – congruence of demos and resident population vs. opponents – loyalty to the state; nations unlike clubs.	Restoration of Polish citizenship after the end of communist rule as an essential element to unite nation and state.	Republican ideology with strong ethno-national elements in practice.
Multiculturalism vs. Assimilation	'Multiculturalism' discourse receded in the 1990s without being contentious; the 'freedom of choice' principle was replaced by increased demands for immigrant adaptation.	1980s 'Ethnic minorities policy': multiculturalism, equality, and equal opportunity policies based on group-approach; in the early 1990s replaced by immigrant or *allochtonen* policies: focus on individual obligations.	'Multiculturalism': adherents pleaded to recognize Germany as a 'country of immigration'; for opponents it has been an expression of 'disintegration' and 'parallel societies'.	Absence of multiculturalist agenda for Polish citizens abroad.	Nationalist multiculturalism: government support primarily of human and cultural rights of Turkish citizens abroad.
Societal Integration	Socio-political (welfare state) and socio-cultural (cultural pluralism).	Since early 1990s neo-republican views (inburgering) and cultural integration views (shared Dutch values) have expanded.	Communitarian (e.g. subsidiarity) vs. political egalitarian: different understandings of the role of individual, society and state.	Diaspora as an essential element of the Polish polity for more than two hundred years.	Growing government interest in citizens, their organizations, and communities abroad.
Social Integration of Immigrants and Emigrants	Naturalization as an instrument of integration.	Same as in Sweden until late 1980s; fundamental change since then; liberal acquisition rules viewed negatively.	Naturalization as a means and prerequisite for integration vs. naturalization as an end result of integration.	Diaspora as lobby group abroad; no mention of immigrants	Emigrants as a lobby group abroad; no mention of immigrants.
Transnational Perspective	During 1990s subtle shift from national to *transnational* interests of Dutch emigrants abroad.	Conservatives represented interests of Dutch emigrants abroad.	Few transnational references; opponents rejected dual citizenship for German emigrants.	State-led and ethno-national transnationalism, directed towards emigrants abroad.	State-led and ethno-national transnationalism, directed towards emigrants abroad.
Principled vs. Pragmatic Arguments	Proponents first advanced ideas on moral and expressive lines; critics waged expressive citizenship prevailed; since the mid-1990s increasingly principled arguments.	Until early 1990s pragmatic perspective on dual citizenship prevailed; since the mid-1990s increasingly principled arguments.	Proponents of dual citizenship used moral and expressive arguments; opponents the expressive with legal and instrumental elements.	Principled arguments in restoration of citizenship; pragmatic arguments regarding Polish citizens abroad.	Preponderance of pragmatic arguments.

integration' belief system. This analysis examined the extent to which notions of equal rights conflicted with claims to the protection of particular (national) cultures, and how these substantive differences were reflected in the types of arguments (pragmatic vs. principled) used in public debates (see Figure 7.3).

The 'Nationhood' Belief System: Republicanism vs. Ethno-Nationalism

We began our research with the conventional hypothesis for immigration states, namely: The more the understanding of nationhood is oriented towards a republican concept, which gives newcomers a high amount of choice, the greater the likelihood that a favourable framework exists for political decisions concerning the tolerance or even acceptance of dual citizenship. Conversely, the more that national self-understanding is oriented towards an ethno-national concept, the smaller the chances for political actors to advance tolerance of dual citizenship for immigrants. By contrast, an ethno-national understanding favours dual citizenship for emigrants or expatriates. This hypothesis generated valuable insights. The German case shows the obvious yet underappreciated point that understandings of nationhood developed against a backdrop of concrete historical experiences at a certain time period. In the heyday of nationalism, Friedrich Meinecke (1909) justified the German and Eastern European version of *Kulturnation*, nationhood preceding statehood. Rogers Brubaker turned this typology on its head by indicating the enormous normative potential of this dichotomy (*cf.* Gosewinkel 2000). As we gradually came to realize in the research process, there are at least two fundamental problems with this dichotomy.

First, cases such as Sweden and the Netherlands do not fall neatly in this 'nationhood' divide, and conceptually the dichotomy simply does not capture their experiences. In Sweden, the socio-political concept of the 'people's home' (*folkhemmet*) has dominated understandings of full membership. Thus, it comes as no surprise that the integration of immigrants has been conceived mainly as a welfare state project. The 'people's home' has played a major role since the 1920s in underpinning political coalitions across classes mobilizing for the welfare state. Such an approach corresponds neither to a civic-republican nor to an ethno-national concept. Changing ideas about the 'people's home' have espoused both inclusive elements, such as workers as citizens, and excluding elements, for example, indigenous groups such as the Sami, who were not included until the mid-twentieth century. In the Netherlands, one would be hard pressed to muster evidence of a discussion of 'nation' or debates on nationhood in the 1970s and 1980s. Since the early 1990s, the focus has been on the 'good citizen', that is, a 'moral citizen'. On the one hand, this emphasis has referred to elements of republican, active, and 'good citizenship' but also to ethno-national elements: immigrants have been increasingly depicted in public debates by opponents of minorities policy as being incapable of developing the competence necessary for good citizenship.

Second, the hypothesis does not fit the German experience of the late 1990s, an experience that might be embodied in the phrase, 'we are all "Republican" now'. This raises the question of whether there are variants of republicanism that account for differing positions on dual citizenship, such as equal rights vs. duties and active engagement. While the republican proponents of increased tolerance referred to the lack of congruence between *demos* and resident population, republican sceptics and opponents privileged the principle of self-determination of the national political community over individual rights. According to the latter view, citizenship requires active readiness and competence of individuals to be self-reliant and participate in society. The opponents of increased tolerance also demanded loyalty to the state. It becomes clear that the sceptics' position cannot be reduced to an ethno-national concept despite or rather because of communitarian overtones in their arguments. In sum, fault lines other than the tradition of nationhood have become much more important.

The tradition of nationhood approach has greater purchase on the emigration cases under scrutiny, reflected in the clearly unequal treatment of emigrant citizens abroad versus immigrants. Yet even in these cases, we find a complex mixture of republican and ethno-cultural and ethno-national elements. In the Polish tradition, citizenship and belonging to the nation have been conceptually distinct. The partitioning of the Polish state between 1772 and 1918 brought about a dichotomy of the Polish nation and a non-Polish state. This dichotomy was replicated, to some extent, in the Polish People's Republic (1945-1989) in the form of the communist state and the non-communist civil society. An ethno-national understanding of nationhood in Poland is one of the main factors responsible for tolerance of dual citizenship for persons of Polish descent. The belief system around the concept of 'nation' has been strengthened in the process of democratization in the post-communist period, along with the idea of a greater Polish nation consisting of members of the Polish national community living inside and outside of Poland. All of these citizens can lay claim to Polish citizenship on three grounds: ethnicity; contribution to the Polish nation; and restoration of citizenship because of former expatriation during the communist era. Nonetheless, public discussions also addressed the question of whether the Polish citizenship of persons of German and Jewish origin should be restored. The ensuing political and public debates, in which the equality of rights for all citizens was upheld, clearly reflected republican elements. Thus, the president restored citizenship to persons of Jewish and German origin, and even opted against special *de jure* privileges for Poles abroad, the Polish Charter. In Poland it is striking that politicians engaged both ethno-cultural and republican arguments to argue for and against dual citizenship. Republican arguments for the reconstitution of the communist past intersected with what could be termed ethno-national considerations to tolerate dual citizenship selectively for members of *Polonia*.

The Turkish arguments have also been characterized by a vivid and sometimes confusing mix of both republican and ethno-national elements. While the proclaimed national self-image of Turkey has a civic-republican appearance, citizenship policies veered mostly in the direction of ethno-culturalism. The law of 1981, for example, disallowed dual citizenship for non-Muslim, that is, Christian and Jewish, minorities who left Turkey before that date. The law also does not apply to immigrants in Turkey. Second, earlier laws contained similar discriminatory rules, such as those governing access to Turkey for refugees in 1934. Muslim-Sunni groups were accorded refugee status but members of Christian-Orthodox and Muslim-Shiite groups were not. Third, non-Muslim minorities, such as Christian and Jewish minorities, have historically been burdened with heavy property taxes, amounting to many times those demanded from Turkish citizens. Certainly, one cannot conclude that republican ideology led to increased tolerance of dual citizenship. Yet, a *de facto* ethno-national understanding promoted the tolerance of dual citizenship for Turks living abroad. This outcome would be expected from our earlier hypothesis.

In sum, the original proposition relating to the 'nationhood' belief system has been helpful in understanding the cases of emigration countries, but less so in explaining the growing tolerance of dual citizenship in immigration countries. A partial exception is the Netherlands, where growing opposition in the course of the 1990s and early 2000s was accompanied by a partial surge of ethno-national discourse. But even in this case the republican-dominated discourse on the 'good citizen' seems to have prevailed.

The 'Immigrant Integration' Belief System: Multiculturalism vs. Assimilation

We set out with the widely accepted thesis that the more actively an immigration state pursues the integration of immigrants into a political community through multicultural policies, the more likely it is to tolerate dual citizenship. By contrast, the more state policies are geared towards assimilationism, that is, melting immigrants into the 'majority core', the fewer opportunities there are to advance the cause of dual citizenship. One fundamental problem emerged at once regarding this classification of immigrant integration regimes. In terms of discourse the differences between Sweden and the Netherlands on the one hand and Germany on the other hand are fairly obvious. However, in certain policy areas, such as religious tolerance, it is also evident that Germany falls into the multicultural camp.

Stark differences emerge in the discourses. In Sweden and the Netherlands we observe a meteoric rise in the use of terms such as 'multiculturalism' and 'minorities policy' during the 1980s. By contrast, in Germany, the term 'multiculturalism' was used in manifold and conflicting ways. Churches and social workers, along with the then general secretary of the Christian Democratic Union (*CDU*), introduced the concept, later taken up by the Green Party. Multiculturalism in the German context denoted diverse ideas such as Germany as a 'country of immigration', antidiscrimination policies, but also genuine multiculturalist policies such as religious exemption laws.

In Sweden, multicultural arguments played an important role in furthering the recognition of dual citizenship because cultural pluralism remained an accepted means of creating political equality even when the multiculturalism discourse receded in the 1990s. During that decade, the 'freedom of choice' principle, introduced in 1975, was replaced by an emphasis on immigrant adaptation and the recognition that all policies reflect pluralism. Two stages of multiculturalist ideas followed. In the 1980s multicultural arguments focused on the extension of voting rights to immigrants, making it easier for denizens to become citizens under the banner of assuring political equality for all residents. Although multiculturalism was ideologically less pronounced during the 1990s, it was tied to transnational aspects late in the decade. The general argument was that due to greater mobility of individuals and increasingly evident cultural diversity, more and more people feel attached to more than one state. Furthermore, according to official cultural pluralist discourse, such multiple attachments do not necessarily diminish allegiance and loyalty to Sweden. This argument on multiple attachments was applied to both 'Swedes' abroad as well as 'immigrants' in Sweden. This general line of argumentation was important for the emerging consensus because it allowed the centre-right parties to claim that Swedes abroad would also benefit. In short, multicultural discourse proved to be important because it struck a chord with the principle of political equality, supported by all political parties.

In the Netherlands the path of multiculturalist ideology led from a reformist agenda to a dystopian one. The Dutch 'ethnic minorities policy' devised in the 1980s rested on three pillars: multiculturalism, equal rights, and equal opportunity policies based on a group identity approach. Put simply, the socio-economic exclusion of immigrants was often seen as being connected to cultural differences, only this time with the claim that cultural factors would positively impact on educational and labour market integration. Nonetheless, as far as equal rights and equal opportunities were concerned, the primary idea was that naturalization was a prerequisite for integration. Dual citizenship also came to be seen as an instrument to advance the social integration of immigrants in the late 1980s. Yet, from the 1990s immigrant or *allochtonen* policies came to replace ethnic minorities policies, and the group- and cultural approach was blamed for unresolved issues of immigrant integration. In a nutshell, the promotion of culture was replaced by concerns about unemployment. In a radical shift, the former focus on culture was now all of a sudden interpreted as a barrier to integration. Moreover, the group-identity approach gave way to strengthening individual responsibility, especially when connected to welfare state policies. A discourse on obligations emerged, touting loyalty to the Dutch state and the adaptation to Dutch values and norms as essential for full political and social membership. In particular, it was alleged that immigrants who held dual citizenship, which was conceived to be part of multiculturalist policies, misused this status to travel freely. The conclusion was obvious: dual citizenship tolerance failed because it was an element of multicultural policy which had gone awry.

In the German context multiculturalism provided fertile ground for ideas and concepts about immigrant integration and its consequences. Among other proposals, adherents of multiculturalism pleaded for the recognition of Germany as a 'country of immigration' and for taking measures appropriate to this status, for example, easing naturalization procedures, changing citizenship law and controlling immigration. For opponents it has been an effort to treat immigrants akin to national minorities such as Sorbs and Danes with all the attendant rights, and the 'disintegration' of immigrants and the emergence of 'parallel societies'. Needless to say, in these readings multiculturalism came across as a dystopian vision.

In at least one of the two emigration states analyzed, multiculturalism could be characterized as ethno-national or ethno-cultural-ethnic in so far as it refers only to one's own citizens abroad, not to immigrants in one's own country, and multicultural in that multiculturalist demands in immigration countries were supported by the country of emigration's governments and associations. In Poland, regarding *Polonia*, the support of a multicultural agenda in countries of immigration has never been a matter of debate, perhaps because there was an implicit assumption that Polish emigrants would keep their ties to the Polish nation. For Turkey, in contrast, the goal of improving the human rights situation of Turkish emigrants abroad has been a staple policy since the mid-1980s. The analysis of the debates in the Turkish parliament and media coverage of dual citizenship and human rights indicates that the focus tended to be solely on Turkish citizens living abroad. The official line read that these emigrants would continue to practice elements of Turkish culture, such as language and customs – even when naturalized in countries such as Germany. Legislation liberalizing dual citizenship applied only to emigrants and not to the growing number of immigrants coming to Turkey from Asia and Africa. This observation and the perceptions of emigrants as voluntary labour migrants go a long way to explaining why there was no disagreement about the legislation passed.

The 'Societal Integration' Belief System

As shown in the German case study in particular, it is useful to go beyond the particular results derived from the analysis of the 'nationhood' and 'immigrant integration' belief systems and to connect them to even broader notions of societal integration and the respective functions and spheres of persons, civil society, and the state. In general, we can discern two ideological camps in all three immigration countries, and with lesser force in the two emigration countries. The central dividing line runs between, on the one hand, equal rights proponents who advocate universally applicable human rights and democratic principles mostly in the national sphere, and, on the other hand, those who uphold claims of particular political communities in a fashion reminiscent of communitarianism.

This general dividing line comes in various national guises. In Sweden, it has been above all a difference in the matter of degree and extent to which a socio-political understanding of collective identity, a cultural-pluralist understanding of civil society, and an equal rights interpretation of citizen rights should be fostered. In the Netherlands the official culturally pluralist and group-oriented approach of the late 1980s has been replaced since the early 1990s by neo-republican views of the 'good citizen' (*inburgering*) and a call for adaptation to Dutch norms, whatever these may be. In Germany, the opposing camps have perhaps emerged in the starkest manner because of contentious party politics, which regularly ends in displays of the ideological arsenal. We find both a communitarianist orientation, enriched by notions of subsidiarity and undivided loyalty of citizens to the state, and a political egalitarian view (see Figure 7.4).

Figure 7.4   Belief Systems: 'Societal Integration' of Political Parties in Germany, The Netherlands and Sweden

Dimensions of Integration / Important Political Parties	Immigrants	Society	State
Germany: Christian Democrats (and Free Democrats) *The Netherlands*: CDA *Sweden*: Conservative Party	• Loyalty (all countries); • Socio-economic- cultural integration: subsidiarity (Germany).	• Societal solidarity (all countries).	• Effective legitimacy (all countries).
Germany: Social Democrats/Greens/PDS (and Free Democrats) *The Netherlands*: PdvA, DC66 *Sweden*: Social Democrats	• Equal rights (all countries); • Political integration (all countries); • Freedom of choice (Sweden).	• Political solidarity (Germany); • Civic integration (*inburgering*) (The Netherlands); • Socio-political and multicultural solidarity (Sweden).	• Procedural legitimacy (all countries); • Effective legitimacy (all countries).

In order to capture the conflicting belief systems on societal integration in a more fine-grained way, a threefold distinction between the individual, civil society and the state is appropriate. With regard to the function and role of the individual, the opponents' notion of integration was guided by the Catholic social doctrine of subsidiarity in Germany, adaptation to Dutch norms and values in the Netherlands, and a smooth integration into the welfare state in Sweden. From these perspectives, individuals should prove that they have made efforts to integrate civically and socio-economically before naturalization 'crowns' the integration process. Moreover, renouncing the original citizenship constitutes a loyalty oath of sorts. The opposing camp focused in a social democratic manner on the enabling function of the state, which is supposed to provide equal rights to all permanents residents. On the civil society level, the opponents emphasized that trust and reciprocity among citizens are resources that cannot be created by the state. It is therefore of utmost importance that laws and rights do not interfere with social solidarity. Undermining principles such as 'one person, one vote', or, more correctly, infringing on the vital Aristotelian feedback loops between the governing and the governed, would ultimately result in decreasing levels of trust among citizens, and possibly in an undermining of welfare state solidarity and reciprocity. In essence, there is a belief that political communities are at heart socially and culturally defined. Quite to the contrary, the proponents of dual citizenship emphasized a concept of political solidarity, which does not place such a high premium on the right of a political community to defend its boundaries if equal rights are at stake. This belief relies more on the formative role of political institutions and less on the pre-constitutional requirements of political integration. The role of the state was also viewed differently. Opponents focused upon the state's core function of providing security, thus privileging law and order. The latter point has been especially important in the Dutch debates over the past years. In addition, proponents foregrounded effective legitimacy, that is, the empirical consent of the established citizenry for immigration and integration policies. The proponents, for their part, pointed to principles such as democratic congruence, constitutional patriotism, and equal political rights to participation as the very basis of legitimacy. They thus placed more emphasis on a procedural understanding of democracy. In sum, while the opponents to further boundary blurring referred to a more communitarian concept of the inter-relationship between individual, civil society, and the state, the proponents tended to take a liberal equal rights perspective.

The central dividing line ran, therefore, between equal rights vs. particular culture. In Sweden, the freedom of choice principle and equal rights for both emigrants and immigrants could be reconciled. In the end, dual citizenship could be accepted because, first, it does not imply specific cultural rights but an expression of citizen equality and second, dual citizenship does not entail collective rights but only individual ones. After all, the idea of citizens' equality was part of the old concept of a 'people's home'. In the Netherlands, dual citizenship was increasingly seen as an expression of cultural and ethnic identity during the 1990s, with culture viewed as a homogeneous whole and related to objective criteria of descent. Also, and this was crucial, politicians opposed to minorities policy referred to dual citizenship as part of the failure of such multicultural policies to address the fundamental problem of socio-economic exclusion. In sum, ethnic minorities policy came increasingly to be interpreted as a 'culturalist' fallacy.

In Turkey, the dichotomy of 'equal rights' vs. 'particular culture' was exactly mirrored in the distinction between the transnational and the domestic realms. The Turkish government has, at times, urged dual citizenship as a prerequisite for political equality in the country of immigration. At the same time, it proclaimed dual citizenship as an instrument for maintaining links with emigrants abroad, that is, for fostering economic, political, and cultural ties to Turkey. Domestically, the particular culture perspective clearly prevailed in three ways. First, the 1981 law clearly rejected restoration of citizenship to minorities who left Turkey before that time, namely Armenians, Jews and Greeks. Second, the 'pink card' has been available only for persons who acquired Turkish citizenship by birth and have given up their Turkish citizenship by consent of the Council of Ministers. And third, dual citizenship has also been used as a political weapon against politicians of Kurdish and Islamic parties whose political goals were perceived to be directed against the integrity of the Turkish state.

In Poland, the dominant notion that dual citizenship has been tolerated as an expression of particular culture cannot be overlooked. As in Turkey, there was no discussion on recognizing dual citizenship for immigrants, for example, from neighbouring Ukraine. However, the transnational dimension, that is, connecting arguments to the position and politics of immigrants in the countries of settlement, was absent. Instead, the justifications all referred to the selective, discretionary, and *de facto* tolerance of dual citizenship for Polish expatriates. The restoration of Polish citizenship can be interpreted as an expression of citizens' equality. Yet, parliament and bureaucracy initially interpreted the rules in an ethno-national fashion with respect to former nationals of non-Polish descent, that is, Jews and Germans. But the president openly declared that he would use his discretionary power to restore citizenship in those cases as well – and he did.

Belief Systems and Corresponding Arguments: Principled vs. Pragmatic

On the ground level, the types of arguments mirrored the contending belief systems and the respective institutional structures. In Sweden, the advocates of dual citizenship first advanced ideas along principled lines, and later shifted to pragmatic arguments, while the opponents waged principled arguments. Only in the beginning did the proponents argue along principled lines. Later, pragmatic arguments focusing on probable practical and immediate effects prevailed, effects which were all deemed minor in terms of negative consequences. Above all, the arguments focused on continuous border-crossing ties of immigrants and emigrants in a globalizing world. By contrast, the opponents gradually came to wage their arguments in principled ways, for example, along expressive lines: political communities should not be confounded with 'clubs'. In their view, a clear commitment to the new political community of choice was necessary. The institutional context proved decisive for the overall pragmatic tone, albeit coupled with principled arguments. The debate in the various government-appointed commissions enabled a pragmatic exchange of opinions and arguments. Dual citizenship was not discussed in the broader realm of all other immigration related issues, such as integration of newcomers into the welfare state, or crime, as was the case in the Netherlands and Germany. This propitious constellation shifted the burden of proof to the opponents who had to show that the costs of accepting dual citizenship would outweigh the benefits.

In the Netherlands we observe almost the reverse development. While pragmatic arguments characterized the early stage of debates until the passage of liberalized legislation in 1991, the arguments exchanged became ever more principled after that. During the 1980s naturalization was seen as a means to advance social integration, and thus the legislature successively liberalized the naturalization rules, for example, doing away with the renunciation requirement. In a way, however, this early pragmatic-instrumental perspective rested on the second pillar of ethnic minorities policy, i.e. the principled argument that social integration of immigrants required a secure legal position. During the 1990s dual citizenship increasingly turned into a principled question, when centre-right parties such as the *CDA* and *VVD* came to look upon citizenship as the crown of the integration process. In similar fashion, the 'culturalist' aspects of ethnic minorities policy were replaced by a demanding and duty-oriented republicanism with assimilationist tendencies. Only liberal-left parties, the *PvdA*, *D66*, and the Green Left, continued to view dual citizenship as a means of integration. The opposition against dual citizenship has mounted ever since. In 2004, for example, the *CDA*, *VVD*, and *LPF* proposed that only third-generation immigrants could acquire Dutch citizenship. And there have even been proposals to withdraw citizenship from naturalized citizens in case of crimes such as 'honour killings', or because of insufficient assimilation to Dutch standards.

The German debates on dual citizenship have been characterized by a preponderance of principled arguments throughout. Reflecting the persistent line of ideological conflict between the two camps on dual citizenship and *jus soli*, the proponents of dual citizenship used moral and expressive arguments while the opponents emphasized expressive arguments with legal and instrumental elements. The principled ideological nature of debate sharpened because the proponents advanced mainly moral arguments, while the opponents focused on expressive arguments, emphasizing the perspective of the state and thus loyalty of citizens to the state. Even the pragmatic arguments concerning the integration of immigrants, for example, predicting higher rates of naturalization if dual citizenship were tolerated, were always understood within the context of overall differences between the two camps on matters of societal integration. Even the academic experts heard in subcommittees of parliament advanced arguments along the party trench lines.

In public debates in Poland, those supporting dual citizenship were more likely to use principled arguments, emphasizing that the injustices of the past had to be rectified. Those in favour of maintaining the status quo of *de facto* dual citizenship and thus arguing against a *de jure* acceptance were more likely to advance pragmatic arguments, focusing on technical and strategic aspects. The parliamentary debate itself was above all of a principled nature, when issues of dealing with the communist past were at stake, such as ending bilateral agreements on avoiding dual citizenship. Different types of rationalizations emerged in different contexts. For example, tolerance vis-à-vis expatriates was justified in ethno-national terms as a question of descent, while those robbed of their citizenship under the communist regime in terms of a civic-republican concept of equality. Interestingly, as would be expected in an emigration country with civic-republican elements, participants in the debates waged both ethno-national and republican arguments against and in favour of tolerating dual citizenship. For example, opponents focused on the potential threat to national homogeneity in an ethno-national vein, but also on state integrity and the uneven distribution of rights and duties for mono-citizens and dual citizens in a rigid civic-republican way. As to the arguments involved, the debates on restoration were of a principled nature – both moral and expressive – while those on the Polish Charter turned out to be more legal and instrumental in nature and did not raise deeper questions. The question emerges as to why the discussions on the Polish Charter were based on pragmatic reasoning and did not give rise to principled arguments. It may be that members of the diaspora are widely considered to be an extra-territorial yet integral part of the Polish nation, on the one hand, while the discussion of the diasporic political influence could raise vexing questions as to the understanding of the relationship between nation and state, on the other. Thus, more principled discussions were avoided. And, as in Turkey, no open public debate on dual citizenship took place. The Turkish case is the most straightforward: Virtually all of the arguments ran along pragmatic considerations. It stands to reason that more principled arguments along expressive lines could have arisen if immigrants in Turkey had also been included in the debates and the legislation.

Outlook: The Prospects and Limits of (Dual) Citizenship

Dual citizenship is a crucial and strategic research site for understanding how fixed or permeable the boundaries of membership in democratic polities have become over the past few decades. The analysis of the 'societal integration' belief system, standing on the shoulders of earlier attempts such as 'tradition of nationhood' and 'immigrant integration', has allowed us to push the empirical research on the determinants of citizenship beyond conceptual and geographical borders without succumbing to misleading generalizations about the 'end' of national citizenship, or the opposite, its unsurprising continuing relevance. Conceptually, the 'societal integration' belief system as a political-cultural concept goes beyond one-dimensional understandings of citizenship which privilege notions of collective identity, as in the tradition of the nationhood approach, or rights, obligations, and their institutionalization, as in the immigrant integration approach. Instead, it combines the two and goes one step further in adding the element of democratic self-determination and equal rights. The 'societal integration' framework is thus congruent with the citizenship framework. Only in a multi-dimensional view, with a focus on important levels of social action – individuals, civil society, state – can we begin to understand the challenge presented by admitting and incorporating newcomers into polities in a mobile world. A focus on the democratic element in analyzing (dual) citizenship is critical because it helps us to raise the boundaries issue. In nuce, democracies have rather clearly demarcated external and even internal boundaries, while empires used to have frontiers. The commonly made comparison of European trends to medieval patterns and relations between majorities, minorities, and peoples resembling the *de facto* multiculturalism of an era prior to nationalism is quite misleading. Boundary building, boundary maintenance, but also boundary changes in democratic polities may be attributed to the privileges of full membership and the resources attached to citizenship. After all, a good deal of the legitimacy of ruling and rulers in a democratic system comes from the collective self-determination of citizens and the rights pertaining to it. Collective self-determination, associated citizens' rights, and the integration of society were interpreted somewhat differently by the opponents and proponents of dual citizenship. Some variation can be accounted for by ideological trench lines, associated with particular 'liberal' equal rights or 'communitarian' culture camps. Nonetheless, even given the trend that 'we are all "Republican" now' and thus more distant than ever from ethno-cultural and ethno-national ideologies and policies, there continues to be strong opposition against more porous boundaries.

There is a larger issue lurking in the background, namely the legitimation of democratic rule not only by a focus on citizens' rights and their effective implementation through policy, but also the growing importance of even more far-reaching human rights, which are enshrined in national constitutions and international conventions. In this volume, we have traced the importance of human rights and have confirmed their importance in the growing tolerance of dual citizenship – for example, principles applying to statelessness and gender equality. In this way, we have established once more the inextricable linkage between human rights and citizens' rights. Yet, it should not be forgotten that there is also an inherent tension between citizens' rights and human rights. Human rights point towards open borders and a pattern of membership which is not only overlapping and nested but also gradual, with no fixed but rather porous lines, furthering the inclusion of outsiders. In contrast, citizens' rights point towards the necessity of protecting social and political orders from over-inclusion.[1] The fields in which this tension has been played out concern not only citizenship issues in a more narrow sense but also membership issues, ranging from admission to bounded territories to full membership within bounded polities, and the manifold overlapping and nested ties of various social and political actors across borders.

The focus on the 'societal integration' belief system not only opens new conceptual opportunities but also widens the geographical or territorial horizons. The analyses collected in this volume have as their focus distinct nation-state political cultures. Yet, the normative horizon goes beyond national cultures. Concepts such as human rights or democratic governance are universal reference points, even though they may not be understood in the same way everywhere. Thus the concept of societal integration eliminates nationhood as the main predictor of citizenship by opening up conceptual avenues to theories of citizenship 'beyond' the nation-state, not simply as border-crossing citizenship but as an instance of the 'internal globalization' of citizenship within polities on all levels – regional, national, supranational.

The question is how liberal and communitarian concepts can be a meaningful guide for policies not only for granting full membership *de jure* and thus full political rights, but also for policies, which address social exclusion. Seen from the immigrant's point of view, a continuum of membership from few to full rights seems to be most appropriate. Citizenship in a mobile world is not a concept for navigating between the principles of universal justice and human rights on the one hand, and justice within bounded political communities such as nation-states on the other hand (*cf.* Jordan and Düvell 2001). Justice within the latter requires some sort of social closure and exclusion of outsiders. This becomes obvious in the case of unauthorized migrants. There is a fundamental tension between state control and efficiency in guarding citizens' rights on the one hand and the claims of individuals such as illegal migrants on the other. Both converge in the issue of legitimation of democratic states. While the protection of citizens' rights in bounded welfare states

---

1 These positions are ideal-typical, and may lead to similar policy conclusions. But the starting points differ. In political theory, liberal human rights positions which advocate free movement across borders and easy access to membership usually ask for reasons why democratic polities and welfare states need to be protected (e.g. Carens 1987). And communitarian positions which prioritize citizens' rights usually also consider inalienable individual rights which provide inroads for human rights.

is clearly connected to efficient state policies, the protection of illegal immigrants' rights is also – but with respect to human rights and not citizens' rights; hence the appropriateness of speaking about the 'paradox of democratic legitimacy' (Benhabib 2004). In principle, illegality undermines the effectiveness of immigration policies and the maintenance of established standards in labour markets and working conditions, threatens the legitimacy and financing of social insurance systems, and challenges the established system of collective bargaining between unions and employer associations. Nevertheless, democratic nation-states, which are essentially legitimized by respecting human rights, cannot completely ignore the individual claims of illegal immigrants to equal consideration according to rule of law, such as medical treatment in emergency cases and basic education for their children.

In a world of ever increasing and widening mobility not only of capital and goods but also of people, one may look back in time to see how political communities have dealt with such challenges. Liberal states in Europe and elsewhere are not only democratic states – they are also welfare states. Historically, welfare states in the currently constituted OECD have their origins in elite responses to the vagrant poor in Europe and elsewhere (de Swaan 1988). But the admission-membership dilemma of universal justice vs. social justice in welfare systems is not solved by creating ever larger collectivities dealing with social risks. As the process of incipient Europeanization of national migration policies and weak attempts at the collectivization of social policy and immigration policy at the Union level suggest, the tension has only been replicated at a higher level of aggregation, or more precisely, partly transferred to a multi-level governance system (*cf.* Faist 1997).

All of this leads to the preliminary conclusion that citizenship as a normative-political concept, especially in its civic-republican version, liberal or communitarian, is inadequate to understand the larger issues going beyond naturalization and involving both admission and social exclusion. Instead, when viewed in a global perspective, citizenship in western liberal democracies is more likely to stand for 'the modern equivalent of feudal privilege – an inherited status that greatly enhances one's life chances' (Carens 1987, 252), and thus constitutes one of the mechanisms reproducing social inequality on a global scale (Shachar 2003).

Despite all their shortcomings, theorists of postnational citizenship have rightfully pointed the way to a growing trend in which human rights discourse has a powerful impact on issues of immigrant integration. Following the arguably questionable approach of a decoupling of rights and identity, certain theorists cogently speak of 'membership' instead of 'citizenship' (Soysal 1994). One needs to go a step further. It might indeed make sense to speak of membership rights, obligations, identities, and practices as a sort of continuum. This does not mean following the usual path from alien, denizen (in social science parlance permanent residents with almost equivalent civil and social rights to citizens), and citizen, as if this were a natural progression in a mobile world. Republican concepts of citizenship still imply this path as a series of gates through which immigrants ideally pass. And this image evokes a powerful progression from admission to the territory and few rights to full inclusion into a national political community from the vantage point of nation-states.

Taking a more global perspective or even one that uses concepts such as world society to suggest that social actors at times refer to the normative and factual horizon of worldwide economic, political, and cultural configurations, citizenship still remains one crucial defining aspect of full inclusion at the nation-society or nation-state level. Nonetheless, as the brief reference to illegal migrants seems to indicate, various categories of geographically mobile persons may be in need of very different legal opportunities to participate meaningfully in societal life. Citizenship is one of them but certainly not the only one since this concept, especially in its republican incarnation, implies a sharp distinction between insiders and outsiders and not a continuous scale in tune with the needs of border-crossing migrants.

References

Balibar, E. (2004), *We, the People of Europe? Reflections on Transnational Citizenship* (Princeton: Princeton University Press).

Basok, T. (2004), 'Post-national Citizenship, Social Exclusion and Migrant Rights: Mexican Seasonal Workers in Canada', *Citizenship Studies* 8:1, 47-64.

Bauböck, R. (1994), *Transnational Citizenship: Membership and Rights in International Migration* (Aldershot: Edward Elgar).

Benhabib, S. (2004), *The Rights of Others: Aliens, Residents and Citizens* (New York: Cambridge University Press).

Brecher, J., Childs, J. B. and Cutler, J. (eds) (2003), *Global Visions: Beyond the New World Order* (Boston, MA: South End Press).

Brysk, A. and Shafir, G. (2004), 'Conclusion: Globalizing Citizenship?', in Brysk, A. and Shafir, G. (eds), 209-16.

Brysk, A. and Shafir, G. (eds) (2004), *People Out of Place: Globalization, Human Rights, and the Citizenship Gap* (New York: Routledge).

Carens, J. (1987), 'Aliens and Citizens: The Case for Open Borders', *Review of Politics* 49, 251-73.

Chan, J. M. M. (1991), 'The Right to a Citizenship as a Human Right: The Current Trend towards Recognition', *Human Rights Law Journal* 12:1/2, 1-14.

Delanty, G. (2000), *Citizenship in a Global Age* (Buckingham, UK: Open University Press).

de Swaan, Abram (1988), *In Care of the State: Health Care, Education and Welfare in Europe and the USA in the Modern Era* (Oxford: Oxford University Press).

Fahrmeier, A. (2000), *Citizens and Aliens: Foreigners and the Law in Britain and the German States 1789-1870* (Oxford: Berghahn).

Faist, T. (1994), 'How to Define a Foreigner? The Symbolic Politics of Immigration in German Partisan Discourse 1978-1993', *West European Politics* 17:2, 50-71.

Faist, T. (1997), 'Migration in Contemporary Europe: European Integration, Economic Liberalization, and Protection', in Klausen, J. and Tilly, L. (eds), 223-48.

Faist, T. (2001), 'Social Citizenship in the European Union: Nested Membership', *Journal of Common Market Studies* 39:1, 39-60.

Faist, T., Gerdes, J. and Rieple, B. (2004), 'Dual Citizenship as a Path-Dependent Process', *International Migration Review* 38:3, 913-44.

Falk, R. (2003), 'The Making of Global Citizenship', in Brecher, J., Childs, J. B. and Cutler, J. (eds), 39-50.

Goldring, L. (2002), 'The Mexican State and Transmigrant Organizations: Negotiating the Boundaries of Membership and Participation', *Latin American Research Review* 37:3, 55-99.

Gosewinkel, D. (2000), *Einbürgern und Ausschließen: Die Nationalisierung der Staatsangehörigkeit vom Deutschen Bund bis zur Bundesrepublik Deutschland* (Göttingen: Vandenhoeck & Ruprecht).

Hutchings, K. and Darneuther, R. (eds) (1999), *Cosmopolitan Citizenship* (Basingstoke: Macmillan).

Johnston, P. (2003), 'Transnational Citizenries: Reflections from the Field in California', *Citizenship Studies* 7:2, 199-217.

Joppke, C. (1999), *Immigration and the Nation-State: The United States, Germany, and Great Britain* (Oxford: Oxford University Press).

Jordan, B. and Düvell, F. (2001), *Irregular Migration: The Dilemmas of Transnational Mobility* (Cheltenham, UK: Edward Elgar).

Kimminich, O. and Hobe, S. (2000), *Einführung in das Völkerrecht*, 7th edition (Tübingen: Francke).

Klausen, J. and Tilly, L. (eds) (1997), *European Integration in Social and Historical Perspective 1850 to the Present* (Boulder, CO: Rowman & Littlefield).

Kymlicka, W. and Norman, W. (eds) (2000), *Citizenship in Diverse Societies* (Oxford: Oxford University Press).

Linklater, A. (1999), 'Cosmopolitan Citizenship', in Hutchings, K. and Darneuther, R. (eds).

Meinecke, Friedrich (1919), *Weltbürgertum und Nationalstaat: Studien zur Genesis des Deutschen Nationalstaats* (München: R. Oldenbourg).

Ong, A. (1999), *Flexible Citizenship: The Cultural Logics of Transnationality* (Durham: Duke University Press).

Parreñas, R. S. (2001), *Servants of Globalization: Women, Migration, and Domestic Work* (Stanford: Stanford University Press).

Parsons, T. (ed.), *Social Structure and Personality* (New York: Free Press).

Parsons, T. and White, W. (1964), 'The Link between Character and Society', in Parsons, T. (ed.), 183-235.

Shachar, A. (2003), 'Children of a Lesser State: Sustaining Global Inequality Through Citizenship Laws', *Jean Monnet Working Paper* No. 20 (New York: New York University School of Law).

Soysal, Y. N. (1994), *The Limits of Citizenship* (Chicago: University of Chicago Press).

Stasiulis, D. K. and Bakan, A. B. (2003), *Negotiating Citizenship: Migrant Women in Canada and the Global System* (London: Palgrave Macmillan).

Index